WITHDRAWN

CONTEMPORARY EVANGELICAL THOUGHT

JESUS OF NAZARETH: SAVIOUR AND LORD

CONTEMPORARY EVANGELICAL THOUGHT

JESUS OF NAZARETH: SAVIOUR AND LORD

PAUL ALTHAUS

F. F. BRUCE

GORDON H. CLARK

BIRGER GERHARDSSON

R. LAIRD HARRIS

EVERETT F. HARRISON

CARL F. H. HENRY

KENNETH S. KANTZER

ADOLF KÖBERLE

JAMES P. MARTIN

RALPH P. MARTIN

JOHN W. MONTGOMERY

LEON MORRIS

CLARK H. PINNOCK

MERRILL C. TENNEY

BASTIAAN VAN ELDEREN

Edited by

CARL F. H. HENRY

WILLIAM B. EERDMANS PUBLISHING COMPANY
GRAND RAPIDS, MICHIGAN

CONTENTS

FOREWORD

THE VOLUME *Jesus of Nazareth: Saviour and Lord* is the fifth in the series initiated with the title *Contemporary Evangelical Thought* (1957). Subsequent volumes were *Revelation and the Bible* (1959), *Basic Christian Doctrines* (1962), and *Christian Faith and Modern Theology* (1964).

Evangelical scholars in England, Germany, Sweden and the United States share in this latest symposium. Although they hold membership in more than a dozen denominations, they all address the contemporary theological scene from the perspective of historic Christian faith. Amid the hesitancies of the current theological debate they emphasize evangelical concerns and convictions.

This volume is aimed more directly than its predecessors at the moving frontiers of contemporary Protestant speculation. The breakdown of Barthian and Bultmannian perspectives calls for a fresh investigation of revelation and history and of revelation and truth. The strength of the evangelical alternative to the liberal, dialectical, and existential options of our century is increasingly apparent alongside the frustrations of theological frontiersmen who seek an escape from the present turmoil and confusion in current religious thought.

As in the earlier volumes it has been my distinct pleasure to assist evangelical scholars in correlating their efforts into a symposium of great relevance and theological power. I am grateful for their ready cooperation in lightening my editorial labors in this evangelical cause. I wish also to express their thanks and mine to Mrs. Elmer Bisbee, whose generous interest in this publication helped to make it a reality.

The essay "Fact and Faith in the Kerygma" is excerpted from David Cairns' translation of Professor Althaus's *Fact and Faith in the Kerygma of Today* (Philadelphia: Muhlenberg Press, 1959), and is used by permission of Fortress Press. Professor Bruce's essay, "History and the Gospel," is a shortened and revised version of an article of the same title which appeared in *Faith and Thought*, Vol. 93 (1963-64), pp. 121-45. It is used by permission of the Victoria Institute.

CARL F. H. HENRY
Editor, *Christianity Today*

CROSS-CURRENTS IN CONTEMPORARY THEOLOGY

Carl F. H. Henry

Carl F. H. Henry is editor of the interdenominational fortnightly Christianity Today. *He has held the chair of Philosophy of Religion at
Northern Baptist Theological Seminary, and of Theology and Christian Philosophy at Fuller Theological Seminary. Among his many
books are* Remaking the Modern Mind, The Drift of Western Thought,
Christian Personal Ethics, *and* Aspects of Christian Social Ethics. *He
is editor of the* Contemporary Evangelical Thought *series, of which
this volume is the fifth. He holds the Th.D. degree from Northern
Baptist Seminary and the Ph.D. from Boston University.*

1. Carl F. H. Henry

CROSS-CURRENTS IN CONTEMPORARY THEOLOGY

A SUDDEN and significant shift in European theological fortunes marks our decade as another time of transition in the realm of Protestant thought. This theological crossroads has come into view almost without warning. As recently as July, 1963, the Montreal Faith and Order Conference of the World Council of Churches carried no hint of such a major turn in contemporary theological destinies. On the continent nobody had spoken publicly of the beginnings of another significant theological transition. Translations of recent dogmatic literature reflected considerable turbulence and mounting theological debate but supplied little if any indication that an hour of agonizing decision once again confronted continental theologians. Not even American evangelicals completing doctoral studies abroad had become aware of the deep dilemma now facing Protestant theology.

All the more remarkably, my European sabbatical in 1963-64 coincided with the sure signs of a new and significant theological development. The crisis of continental Protestantism became increasingly apparent in the course of interviews with some three dozen theologians and New Testament scholars, most of them prominent and influential on the theological scene. It was my special fortune to interview these leaders privately for an hour or so and to probe their personal convictions about the theological situation today. In a highly privileged "seminar in contemporary European theology," I enjoyed the unique opportunity of asking questions of Karl Barth, Emil Brunner, Rudolf

3

Bultmann, Helmut Thielicke, Wolfhardt Pannenberg, Adolf Köberle, Edmund Schlink, Ernst Fuchs, Günther Bornkamm, Gerhard Friedrich,
Otto Michel, Ethelbert Stauffer, and many others.

Something theologically exciting was apparently under way in Europe.
Not only had Bultmann been dethroned as king of the theological
scene but, even more significant, Bultmannian theology itself was now
on the defensive. Although *Time* magazine (May 22, 1964) reported
that Bultmann's disciples ruled the theological situation in Europe
much as the Russians dominate chess (the vocal post-Bultmannians on
the American scene would prefer it that way), it was clear that the
Bultmannians and the post-Bultmannians were both in trouble. Contemporary European theology was in transition and flux; for the third
time in the twentieth century Protestant theology on the continent was
passing through deep waters.

The importance of this development for the American scene cannot
be glossed. The history of the recent past shows that when the theology
of the continent veers in a new direction, that of Britain and the United
States soon swerves with it.

I. THE REVOLT AGAINST RATIONALISTIC LIBERALISM

For the sake of overall perspective it may be well briefly to recall the
main outlines of the theological trend in the recent past. The rationalistic liberalism of Schleiermacher, Ritschl, and Troeltsch was the dominant religious force in the forepart of our century. Classic modernism,
a theology of intensified divine immanence, so neglected God's transcendence in relationship to man and His universe that it left no room
for miracle, special revelation, or special redemption. The Christian
religion was viewed as a variety of religion in general — even if it had
certain unique features, and could in some respects be viewed as "higher"
than the others. Compatible with this basic outlook, Christian religious
experience was viewed as a variety of universal religious experience.
Against this speculative immanentism, Karl Barth reasserted God's
transcendence and special divine initiative, His wrath against man as
sinner, and the reality of miraculous revelation and miraculous redemption. So contagious was this "theology of crisis" that by 1930
most German theologians conceded the death of rationalistic modernism, or classic liberalism, which Barth had deplored as heresy. They
proclaimed the triumph of dialectical theology over immanental philosophy.

Americans who still read their theology in the context only of the
fundamentalist-modernist controversy little sense what this dialectical
overthrow of classic liberal theology meant for the European seminary

world. When I traveled in Germany and Switzerland with Evangelist Billy Graham during his 1960 crusades, it was my privilege to address meetings of ministers in several key cities. The night Dr. Graham's crusade opened in Berne, Switzerland, I had as my dinner guest Dr. Walter Luthie, minister of that great cathedral where the throngs turn out for Sunday service twenty minutes early to be sure of a seat. Dr. Luthie related something of his own theological encounter from the time of his first interest in the ministry. After his conversion experience and a call, he left his Swiss home and farm to prepare for the pulpit. In seminary, he said, "my professors were liberal, and one by one they took from me the beliefs I had prized. Many times I thought I could not go on. Then in my last year of seminary study, one of my professors spoke now and then of a minister who had recently written a book. Every time he referred to this author he described him as 'that fool.' I went out and bought the volume. It was Barth's *Römerbrief,*" he said. "And Barth saved me for the ministry!"

In Europe many ministers in the "regular churches" came to read the theological climate by the index "B. B." and "A. B." — before Barth and after Barth. Before Barth, no prayer meetings in these churches; after Barth, prayer meetings. Before Barth, no Bibles open in the churches; after Barth, young people's meetings and a searching of the Bible to probe its "witness" to God's special revelation in Christ. If one sketches the main outlines of the modern period, this transition from classic modernism to the dialectical theology constituted the first major transition in European theology and its net result was that Barthian theology reigned from 1930 to 1950.

II. THE REVOLT AGAINST DIALECTICAL THEOLOGY

What signaled the erosion of Barth's influence, if one seeks a landmark, was a book of theological essays now translated as *Kerygma and Myth* (edited by Hans Werner Bartsch). This volume contained Rudolf Bultmann's essay on the New Testament and mythology, first prepared in 1941, which had comparatively little impact at its first appearance. But this book attested the momentum of the gathering Bultmannian forces. Barth's *Römerbrief* (1919) had refused to ground Christian faith in objective history and objective knowledge, and his dialectical theology was then wholly compatible with existential emphases and in broad early agreement with Bultmann. Bultmann redirected the dialectical approach and conformed it to his own interests — to *Formgeschichte,* to demythology, to *Existenz. Formgeschichte,* said Bultmann, establishes the New Testament as the viewpoint of the primitive Church, rather than of Jesus of Nazareth. Modern science, said Bultmann, requires a non-miraculous understanding of the New Testament. And Christian faith demands no historical foundation other than the mere "thatness" of Jesus' existence, so that the New Testament is to be understood existentially.

Barth broke with Bultmann between 1927 and 1929, and in the 1932 revision of his *Church Dogmatics* he rejected existentialism. Since that revision Barth has steadily added "objectifying" elements to his theological perspective to forestall any existentialist takeover of his position. Yet Barth's theology hurried over the relationship of faith and history, the relationship of faith and science, and important New Testament exegetical problems. Bultmann concentrated attention on all these areas. He persuaded many young intellectuals in the seminaries that Barth's theology deals only halfheartedly with its underlying dialectical presuppositions, whereas his own existentialism more consistently applies these very same premises. If Barth reigned from 1930 to 1950, Bultmann and his disciples clearly held the theological initiative in Europe between 1950 and 1960. In 1960 when I visited Emil Brunner at his Zurich home, he acknowledged that "Bultmann is now king! But," he added, "not for long, because he thins out the Gospel too much." In Basel Karl Barth likewise conceded, "*Ja, Bultmann ist jetzt König.*" No longer Barth, no longer Brunner, no longer dialectical theology (in its pre-existentialist form), but, as Bishop Hanns Lilje of Hanover characterized it, "a revival of the old liberalism in connection with *Existenz*" ruled the centers of theological learning.

III. THE REVOLT AGAINST EXISTENTIAL THEOLOGY

Today the search is under way for an alternative to Bultmann. That remarkable development signals the third crisis in twentieth-century continental theology. From classic liberalism to dialectical theology; from dialectical pre-existential theology to existentialism; and now, the revolt against existentialism. We can chart this search for an alternative to Bultmann in three steps: first, the revolt of Bultmann's disciples against Bultmann; second, the sharp disagreement among the post-Bultmannians themselves; third, the growing vitality of the anti-Bultmannians.

There is some exaggeration in the comment of Ernst Fuchs at Marburg that Bultmann "no longer has disciples"; but it does indicate that Bultmann has been deposed from theological leadership: "Karl Barth has his aprioris, he has vitality, and he has disciples. But Bultmann has only aprioris. His disciples are at odds with him, and *they* have the vitality." In 1954 Ernst Käsemann read the revolutionary paper which focused attention on the mere "thatness" of Jesus' existence — which was all the historical visibility that Bultmann demanded for Jesus. Käsemann now put the central difficulty in clear focus: to stress the apostolically proclaimed Christ (the kerygmatic Christ) and to say no more about the historical Jesus than "thatness" runs the risk of dissolving Christianity into a Gnostic redeemer myth, and of falling into Docetism, that is, of diluting the historical reality of Jesus' humanity into mere appearance. Since that time the historical Jesus has become an increasing concern of most of the Bultmannian school. Most of Bultmann's disciples now insist, for both theological and historical reasons, that some knowledge of the historical Jesus is indispensable.

If that development reflects the revolt, it marks the occasion also of sharp disagreements in the Bultmannian camp among the professed followers of Bultmann. Some scholars continue to reject all interest in the historical Jesus. The so-called Mainz radicals, Herbert Braun and Manfred Mezger, hold that only interpersonal relationships — that is, relations between persons, and these alone — are significant for encountering God. To add to the confusion, Bultmann has divided his followers by apparently contradictory comments and commendations of certain of their positions. But most Bultmannians now insist on some necessary connection between the historical Jesus and the content of the Christian faith, but they differ widely about the nature and extent of this relationship.

The theological scene is also marked by the emergence of vigorous alternatives to post-Bultmannian positions. In characterizing the current outlook in continental theology one must no longer speak of Bultmann as king, nor even of the aggressive dominance of the post-Bultmannians, for the post-Bultmannians are now but one of a number of schools struggling for supremacy in the present open situation. There are the traditional conservatives, among them such New Testament scholars as Otto Michel of Tübingen, Joachim Jeremias of Göttingen, Walter Künneth of Erlangen, Leonhard Goppelt of Hamburg, Karl Rengsdorf of Münster, Gustav Stählin of Mainz, and others. There are the *Heilsgeschichte* scholars, whose views do not coincide in all respects with those of the old Erlangen *Heilsgeschichte* school at the turn of the century. Whereas conservative scholars champion salvation history, *Heilsgeschichte* scholars are not as such thoroughly conservative. Oscar Cullmann of Basel illustrates the transition from the conservative to the *Heilsgeschichte* school: on the one hand, he declines to be regarded as a traditional conservative; on the other hand, he looks more largely in the conservative direction than do most *Heilsgeschichte* scholars. Cullmann insists that the decisive event of all history has already occurred, and that one cannot really be a Christian without believing that Jesus of Nazareth regarded Himself as Messiah. Werner Kümmel of Marburg and Cullmann are leading spokesmen for the *Heilsgeschichte* movement today in the debate between exponents of historical and existential revelation; Eduard Schweizer of Zürich belongs with this group also. Kümmel, Bultmann's successor at Marburg, has always been a foe of Bultmannianism. Another group is the Pannenberg school, named for a former student of Barth's who is now an influential scholar at Mainz, Wolfhardt Pannenberg. Around his standard a company of vigorous younger scholars has gathered. Finally, one must speak also of independents, who cannot be catalogued under any single label: men like Helmut Thielicke of Hamburg and Ethelbert Stauffer of Erlangen. Thielicke combines liberal, neo-orthodox and conservative elements; he is an ardent critic of Barth, and his modernist tendencies do not fully surface in his popular preaching and publications.

A remark of Herbert Butterfield may perhaps reflect a certain British sensitivity about German scholarship, but it makes its mark nonetheless about the continuing influence of the German scholar on Anglo-Saxon thought. Butterfield says:

> It was often noted in the earlier decades of the present century how greatly it had become the habit of Protestants to hold some German scholar up their sleeves, a different one every few years but always preferably the latest one, and at appropriate moments strike the unwary Philistine on the head with this secret weapon, the German scholar having decided in a final manner whatever point might have been at issue in a controversy. From all of which the charge arose that for the Protestants the unanswerable pope was always some professor — a system more inconvenient than that of Rome, partly because the seat of authority might change overnight and be transferred to a new teacher who had never been heard of before, and partly because if one has to have a pope it is at least better that he should be subject to certain rules and traditions, and be appointed by a properly constituted authority. The tendency was not confined to Protestants, however, for almost a century ago the young Acton was warned not to play this game of waving German professors at his fellow Catholics; though he not only failed to take the advice but added the weight of his influence to a tendency that was making historical scholarship perhaps over-arrogant and certainly too pontifical. When therefore the other week I happened to hear two theologians congratulating one another that the very advanced German professors who had been thrown at our heads in the days of my youth had long been exploded, I had the feeling that we who study the past must be all alike; the new school of thought in the 1950s is evidently as sure of itself as the old one of the 1920s used to be (*Christianity and History* [New York: Scribner, 1949], p. 9).

We may summarize our broad overview of the theological mainstream in this century in terms of the rise and fall of classic liberalism; the rise and fall of neo-orthodoxy; the rise and fall of existentialism. In view of this succession we do well to examine these unstable theological movements with special attention to certain of their controlling ideas. For some factors suggest that we are not really dealing with three eras, but at most only two — that Barth and Bultmann, for all their differences, may really be part of one line of theological development. From a still longer perspective perhaps we should speak not of two lines but only of one line from Schleiermacher to Bultmann, with a spectacular and unsuccessful effort by Karl Barth to rise to a higher plane.

IV. PERSPECTIVE ON CONTROLLING IDEAS

In his *The New Modernism* Cornelius Van Til tried to establish an essential continuity between Schleiermacher and Barth. But since Barth called modernism "heresy," it is a moot question whether this was the happiest assessment, however valuable its insights. While the application of the label of modernism to Barth is debatable, Van Til had the merit of emphasizing the "neo-" rather than the "orthodoxy." G. C. Berkouwer's *The Triumph of Grace* and Gordon H. Clark's *Karl Barth's Theological Method* took a somewhat different tack, giving Barth his due without surrendering a sharp evangelical critique.

Against the old classic liberalism Barth emphasized the transcendence, initiative, and wrath of God; moreover, he reasserted man's sinfulness, and special miraculous redemptive revelation as his only hope of rescue. These theological ingredients appealed to evangelicals in Europe and in the Anglo-Saxon world as well on first hearing of the Barthian thrust. Many evangelicals readily forgave neo-orthodoxy its higher critical and evolutionary concessions because of its lucid critique of the old liberalism. The preoccupation of fundamentalism with the errors of modernism, and neglect of schematic presentations of the evangelical alternative, probably gave neo-orthodoxy its great opportunity in the Anglo-Saxon world. J. Gresham Machen had led the way in a powerful statement of evangelical positions, alongside the exposure of the weaknesses of liberalism, but his untimely death removed him from the theological scene just as neo-orthodoxy was beginning to be a religious contender on the American scene. If evangelical Protestants do not overcome their preoccupation with negative criticism of contemporary theological deviations at the expense of the construction of preferable alternatives to these, they will not be much of a doctrinal force in the decade ahead.

The theology of crisis did more than reassert God's transcendence and initiative and wrath, and man's sinfulness, and the reality of special redemptive revelation and miraculous salvation. Equally significant, it predicated — integrally to its view of radical divine transcendence and its extreme disjunction of eternity and time — the premise that divine revelation is communicated only in personal confrontation and response.

Dialectical theology insisted that divine disclosure is never given objectively in historical events or human concepts and words. On its
view, God's revelation is not expressed in intelligible propositions
and universally valid truths.

Barth and Bultmann both reject the objectivity of God as an object
of rational knowledge. Bultmann, on the one hand, makes this premise
decisive, correlating it with Heidegger's existential philosophy as well as
with anti-miraculous philosophy of science. Since personal confrontation
and internal miracle are the fulcrum of divine revelation, all else can be
demythologized. Barth, on the other hand, with a surer instinct for
biblical theology, insists on objectifying elements. The problem faced
by Barth and his gifted student Emil Brunner was this: having rejected
the objectivity of God as rationally knowable, how can one escape the
subjectivity of Bultmann's existentialism? For both Barth and Brunner,
existentialism implies a denial of God's reality, since it accords God
no assured existence outside of one's own experience.

It will be well at this point to recall some difficulties that ran through
the formulations of the case for Christianity by Brunner and Barth on
dialectical terrain. In the original German version of *The Mediator*
(1926), Brunner depicted the atonement not as an event in A.D. 30,
but as a present divine revelatory act. By 1942 (well into the post-
Bultmann era, when Bultmann had expropriated dialectical theology in
an existential direction at the expense of its historical elements) Brunner stressed in *Revelation and Reason* that the cross, the death of Jesus
Christ, is the high point of God's revelation. Now, here is the problem.
If divine revelation is not objectively given in historical events, then
the death of Jesus Christ cannot carry revelation. If the crucifixion of
Jesus Christ is an event-carrier of divine revelation, then the dogma
that God nowhere reveals Himself in historical events must be abandoned.
Moreover, if, as saving event, the cross bears divine revelation, then why
does not the whole of salvation history do so? Brunner never worked
these tensions out of his system. Brunner's long-standing insistence
that liberalism means nihilism — the end of everything for Christianity
— echoes his high confidence in the uniqueness of the Judeo-Christian
heritage. His emphasis on general revelation, moreover, tends to undergird his stress on special revelation alongside insistence on the supreme
revelation value of the cross. Yet Brunner's halting correlation of revelation and reason and his ready surrender of the historicity of the virgin
birth, for example, leave his theology vulnerable to additional demythologizing and to existential expropriation. In his most recent revision of
The Divine Human Encounter, he does indeed stress the need for
Christian philosophy over against Barth, whose view of philosophy is
wholly negative. Yet Brunner does not really revise his doctrine of reve-

lation to effect its closer correlation with reason, nor does he admit divine revelation of universally valid truths. Like Barth, Brunner has added objectifying reinforcements against existential alternatives, but he has not repudiated his underlying dialectical thesis so highly serviceable to existential theology. But when it suits his purposes, Brunner is also hospitable to demythology; he views acceptance or rejection of the virgin birth as a decisive test case as to whether Christianity stands with myth or with history. "And this is myth," he insists.

For the dialectical theologians, who seem to play legerdemain with history, the unsolved problem remains how to reconcile historical revelation in the cross-event with the overall dialectical denial of historical revelation? In the first edition of his *Church Dogmatics* (I/1, p. 188) Barth describes "the rabbi of Nazareth" as "One whose activity is a little commonplace alongside more than one other founder of a religion." In his earliest writings, moreover, he locates the atonement and the resurrection of Christ outside ordinary historical and calendar time. When I visited the late Karl Heim in Tübingen, he said, "Barth has told us that the resurrection took place on the rim of history. And ever since that pronouncement, the European theologians have been trying to find this rim, but nobody has been able to locate it."

When Barth came to Washington three years ago he attended a luncheon in his honor at George..Washington University with the understanding that there would be no address but there would be a question period. When the question period began, I asked about the factualness, the historicity of the resurrection. "Over at that table are newspaper reporters," I noted, "the religion editor of United Press International, the Religious News Service correspondent, and religion editors of the Washington papers. If they had these present responsibilities in the first century, was the event of the resurrection of Jesus Christ of such a nature that covering it would have fallen into the area of their reportorial responsibility? That is, was it *news* and *history* in the sense in which the man in the street understands news and history?" Barth became angry. Since I had identified myself as editor of *Christianity Today*, he retorted, "Did you say *Christianity Today* or Christianity yesterday?" Rather taken aback, I replied only by quoting the Scripture text "yesterday, today, and forever," certainly a hurried misappropriation. Barth then responded to the question obliquely: "The resurrection had significance for the *disciples* of Jesus Christ! It was to the disciples that He appeared!" But this wasn't in question at all. On the way out, the United Press correspondent remarked to me, "We got his answer. His answer was no."

Nowhere is the objectivity in Barth's theology accessible to historical research. Whenever the dialectical and existential schools run into

trouble with history or science, they shift the emphasis to the confrontation of God. This dialectical reliance on divine confrontation, unan-
chored to objective history and to objective knowledge, was vulnerable
to Bultmann's existentialism. Try as Barth did to reinforce the objectifying features of his theology, he did not really transcend or reject the
principial repudiation of historical revelation that inheres in dialectical
theology. Even when the post-Bultmannians defected from Bultmann
by reviving interest in the historical Jesus, Barth deplored this development; in 1960 he wrote disparagingly of New Testament scholars "who
to my amazement have armed themselves with swords and staves and
once again undertaken the search for the historical Jesus, a search in
which I now as before prefer not to participate."

But the disconnection of revelation and history was not the only ob-
stacle facing dialectical theology; there was also the problem of revelation and reason. The notion that divine revelation occurs only as a
miracle of personal grace, exclusive of objectively given concepts and
words — that is, of universally valid propositions — clashed head on
with the scriptural representation of divine disclosure. What is one to
do with the claim of biblical writers to communicate the very Word
of God, indeed God's revealed truths and words? What of the repeated
Old Testament use — some 1200 times — of the formula, "Thus saith
the Lord"? In *Revelation and Reason,* Brunner swept aside the New
Testament doctrine of verbal inspiration as based on a "post-apostolic"
misunderstanding, and he brushed aside the Old Testament as exhibiting
a "lower level of revelation" than that given in Jesus Christ. But the
question in debate, of course, is not whether Jesus Christ is the supreme
manifestation of God; that truth is not disputed. The issue is whether
prophetic concepts and words (call this a "lower" level if you wish)
are genuinely divine *revelation.* If these statements truly are divine
revelation, as the prophets represent them to be, then one must repudiate the dialectical premise that revelation is not given in human concepts and words.

In his exposition of the knowledge of God, Barth's dialectical dogma
that divine revelation is not conceptually given falls into similar difficulty. His *Römerbrief* in 1919 scorned all efforts at knowledge of God-
in-Himself. Barth deplored such claims to knowledge as speculative,
and he bluntly disowned propositions and concepts as media of divine
revelation. But later, over against the one-sided liberal emphasis on
faith as trust, he increasingly stressed that faith is a call to cognitive
understanding. In his work on Anselm in 1931, and his revision of his
Church Dogmatics, Barth reflects this reorientation. So noticeably
does he strengthen the historical and rational elements in his *Dogmatics,*
in fact, that Gerhard Friedrich of Erlangen, who edited the revision of

Kittel's *Wörterbuch,* has remarked facetiously that "Barth has almost become a Protestant scholastic again." Barth now holds that the believer's concepts are adequate to the knowledge of God. But if concepts and propositions are admitted as revelatory of God on any basis whatever, must not the dogma be challenged that divine revelation is never given in concepts, words and events? Barth, however, insists that the adequacy of concepts exists only on the basis of internal miracle, thus still stopping short of viewing revealed knowledge in terms of universally valid propositions.

But truth in the recognized sense — as critics of the dialectical theology are quick to insist — holds its claim for men universally, independently of their subjective decision. The denial of the universal validity of the truth of revelation goes hand in hand with the detachment of revealed truth from historical, scientific, and philosophical truth. Concerned over this severance, anti-dialectical scholars increasingly stress that truth requires a broader base than kerygmatic theology allows. Whether on Barth's basis or on Brunner's, they contend, the dialectical outlook — for all its contrary intention — cannot avoid losing in subjectivity the faith in revelation.

On the dialectical left remain the vocal champions of the old liberalism now revived in association with *Existenz.* Bultmann's ambivalent comments, moreover, left some observers unsure who could be considered his real followers. Ernst Fuchs at Marburg remarks that where Bultmann stands on some issues God alone knows, and not even Bultmann. In one essay Bultmann spoke with special appreciation of Herbert Braun who, with Manfred Mezger, has projected at Mainz a version of existentialism more radical than that espoused by most of Bultmann's disciples. Braun and Mezger together question the possibility of speaking of God as being independent and distinguishable from the world of man. In asserting God's subjectivity, they not only deny the objectivity of God, but seem also to deny His reality. Because of Bultmann's commendation of Braun, uncertainty mounted among some of Bultmann's disciples as to where Bultmann now stands. When Bultmann was asked which disciples he considers "genuine" and which "spurious," he preferred to speak only of genuine disciples: "They are all my disciples, although with disagreements." When the matter of his approval of Braun was mentioned alongside the Mainz scholar's reduction of revelation to inter-personal relations, Bultmann sought to put the record straight: "I repudiate any denial of the reality of God. If Braun and Mezger leave the reality of God in doubt, then I must dissociate myself from this. God always confronts us," he said "when there is revelation." So Bultmann, although rejecting the objectivity of God, nonetheless insists: "I will not dissolve the faith in revelation into subjectivism."

Yet if Bultmann feared that Braun and Mezger, as radical Bultman-nians, are subjectivizing revelation, precisely this same charge is pressed against Bultmann himself by Emil Brunner. Bultmann wants no part in the objectifying elements on which Barth and Brunner insist. They in turn contend that he dissolves the faith in revelation into subjectiv-ism. Brunner asserts that Bultmann endeavors to "make theology" out of Heidegger's atheism.

To escape the subjectivistic alternative, the dialectical theologians in-sist on objectifying elements asserting that the reality of the self-re-vealing God does not hang in mid-air as the existentialists would have it, but must be related to the biblical events, although dialectically. But precisely this dialectical reinterpretation of revelation in relation to history and reason makes the crisis theology vulnerable to existentialism.

V. THE RECOGNITION OF SALVATION HISTORY

That is why a "third force" voices "a plague on both your houses" against the dialectical school and the existential school. New Testament scholars, particularly in Europe, are drifting away from conversations with the dialectical theologians, who increasingly are left "to paddle for themselves," as the quest for the historical Jesus once again gains mo-mentum. The liveliest theological discussion in Europe today, particu-larly among New Testament scholars, is taking place at the frontier of revelation-and-history concerns. That development, in turn, establish-es a possible point of conversation and connection with the traditional conservative scholars. While conservative scholarship on the continent makes more concessions to higher criticism than Anglo-Saxon evangelicals characteristically do, the conservatives have always come down firmly on the side of historical revelation. As a matter of fact, the mounting in-terest in historical revelation represents a conjunction of concerns in-volving the old-line conservatives, the newer *Heilsgeschichte* school and the so-called Pannenberg school.

The kerygmatic theology, whether simply dialectical or existential as well, emphasizes the Christ of faith to the neglect of the historical Jesus. It refuses to find a ground of faith in the life, teaching, and work of the historical Jesus, and shifts the center of revelation and redemption to present experiential relationships. As disciples who re-main most representatively loyal to his own point of view, Bultmann singles out Hans Conzelmann of Göttingen and Erich Dinkler of Heidel-berg. They most consistently veer away from any emphasis on the rele-vance of the historical Jesus, and they insist with Bultmann that Christ-tian faith demands only the "thatness" of Jesus' historical existence. While most post-Bultmannians attach somewhat larger significance to the historical Jesus, they are not on that account "anti-Bultmannian," since they do not really make the historical Jesus decisive for faith. They seek to establish some continuity of the historical Jesus with the preached Christ, but they do not reinstate the historical Jesus as a center of revelation and as a ground of faith. So the post-Bultmannians too, influenced by dialectical prejudices they hold in common with Bultmann and Barth, engage in legerdemain with the historical hinterlands of revelation.

The *Heilsgeschichte* school emerges, significantly, as a formidable foe of this one-sided kerygmatic emphasis. Although it does not coincide in all respects with positions of the old *Heilsgeschichte* school of Erlangen at the turn of the century, it coincides fully in at least one important respect, its emphasis on historical revelation, on revelation in history. Longstanding evangelical positions are reasserted, among them the concrete historical character of divine revelation and the recognition that the saving events of sacred history supply an essential ground and support of Christian faith. In brief, Christian faith is faith not only in the kerygmatic Christ but in the historical Jesus.

This remarkable development signals the breakdown of three basic Bultmannian positions. First, whereas Bultmann held that Jesus was only a Jewish prophet whose life and message were not of fundamental importance to Paul, the historical Jesus is now regarded as decisively significant for New Testament studies. The relevance of works such as J. Gresham Machen's *The Origin of Paul's Religion* again comes into view, and the efforts to update sections of this monumental work, such as Longenecker's recent *Paul: Apostle of Liberty,* are timely.

Second, whereas Bultmann viewed the Gospel of John and other New Testament writings as decisively influenced by Gnostic emphases, the Dead Sea Scrolls are now seen as establishing the Palestinian and Judaic character of this literature. One recalls William F. Albright's comment: "The Dead Sea Scrolls have utterly demolished Bultmann's critical analysis of John" (*History, Archaeology and Christian Humanism* [New York: McGraw Hill, 1964], p. 27). Influenced by his own aprioris, Bultmann remains uninfluenced by the Scrolls; he is at work on a commentary on John's epistles in which he proposes to show that Gnostic tendencies decisively color the background of the Johannine epistles as well. But the tide of New Testament scholarship on the continent is passing him by.

Third, whereas for Bultmann the existential understanding of the New Testament is the task of exegesis, the Gospels are again being seen as primarily intending the communication of a new knowledge of God. The tendency is no longer to view the purpose of the Gospels as a dis-

covery of what the New Testament tells about *me* and *my* spiritual relationships.

One result of this expanding interest in historical revelation is the
critical reassessment of *Formgeschichte,* and particularly of its biased
notion that the New Testament does not provide a reliable report or
reflection of the historical Jesus, because it presents the theology of the
early Church. There is mounting emphasis now on the continuity of
the teaching of the primitive Church with that of Jesus, and of the apostolic Christ with Jesus of Nazareth. The work of conservative as well as
of liberal critics of *Formgeschichte* is winning new attention. C. H. Dodd
in Britain had long registered significant protests from the liberal side.
The Swedish New Testament scholars Harald Riesenfeld and Birger
Gerhardsson, respected conservatives, acknowledge that every Gospel
pericope indeed has its life situation, but they emphasize that this fact
reflects a firm historical tradition rather than the notion of sheer creation
of the data. Ethelbert Stauffer of Erlangen wrestles with the problem
of the relationship of Jesus to the primitive Church along other lines.
Since the disciples would be least likely to invent passages in which they
are brought under criticism, he finds the most significant clue to continuity in those passages in which Jesus criticizes rather than approves
His disciples. But Stauffer is apparently operating here on the liberal
premise of a fundamental misunderstanding of the historical Jesus by
His followers, of an essential discontinuity rather than continuity of
Jesus and the Church. For this reason some conservative New Testament
scholars view Stauffer as a twentieth-century Renan; although he is
interested in the historical Jesus, over against exponents of the kerygmatic theology, Stauffer nevertheless pursues his quest on presuppositions akin to nineteenth-century historicism.

The central problem of New Testament studies today is to delineate
Jesus of Nazareth without dissolving Him as the Bultmannians did,
without demeaning Him as many dialectical theologians did, and without
reconstructing Him as nineteenth-century historicism did, so that it
becomes clear why and how He is decisive for Christian faith. In this
theological quest, the *Heilsgeschichte* school reflects important points
of agreement with evangelical positions. First, divine revelation and redemption are acknowledged as objective historical realities. Second, the
sacred events are considered as knowable to historians by the methods
of historical research. Third, the Old Testament is interpreted as the
history of God which was fulfilled in Jesus Christ, and the New Testament is interpreted as the fulfilment of the Old Testament. Fourth, the
meaning of these events is held to be divinely given, not humanly
postulated.

Although Marburg has been known throughout the theological world as a Bultmannian center, primarily through Bultmann's influence on that campus, the successor to Bultmann's New Testament chair, Werner Georg Kümmel, resisted Bultmann's views in the classroom from the first, and has been a leading spokesman for *Heilsgeschichte* positions. But although the tide of New Testament scholarship has been turning in their direction, carried along by common interest in historical revelation, an important area of divergence weakens the *Heilsgeschichte* school. There is agreement that the meaning of saving events is divinely given, not humanly postulated, but *Heilsgeschichte* scholars are divided over how the meaning of sacred history is given to faith.

Is salvation history a process whose inner meaning can be demonstrated? Is subjective experience the focal point of the revelation of its meaning? Is this meaning of sacred history objectively given in an authoritative Scripture, which the Spirit illumines the minds of men to accept and appropriate?

No one answer applies to the *Heilsgeschichte* scholars. Leonhard Goppelt of Hamburg asserts that "the Word is revealed 'in, with, and under' the history," a phrasing which seems to accommodate the Lutheran formula to dialectical patterns of thought. Professor Kümmel holds that the scriptural meaning is divinely given but, if I understand him aright, that its validity is grasped only in personal response. He resists the idea of Scripture as authoritative, propositional information, and maintains the right to criticize the scriptural formulations. Hence he implies a norm that is inconsistent with the Scripture and independent of it. But what is that norm? Nowhere does he tell us. Among many *Heilsgeschichte* scholars there remains a tendency to split divine revelation in two, to divide divine disclosure somehow into deed-revelation in past history and meaning-revelation in present experience. This tendency was characteristic of some liberal Protestants toward the end of the nineteenth century in the old classic liberal tradition, and B. B. Warfield's criticisms of their views in *The Inspiration and Authority of the Bible* retain much value against such recent expositions.

Among *Heilsgeschichte* scholars, Cullmann most nearly approaches traditional conservative terrain. Nobody can possess authentic Christian faith, Cullmann contends, unless he believes the historical fact that Jesus regarded Himself as Messiah. This emphasis, of course, is wholly anathema to the Bultmannians, who associate faith with the kerygmatic Christ and deprive it of any ground or support in the historical Jesus. In his latest book, *Heil als Geschichte,* Cullmann emphasizes numerous points of vital interest in the current discussion of history and kerygma. He notes the meshing of historical fact and interpretation in both the Old and New Testaments, and he recognizes the reality of revelation in both the event as such and in its interpretation. He stresses, for example, that the New Testament relates salvation history to eyewitnesses, thus placing it in a truly historical setting. The New Testament revelation, he notes, not only carries forward and enlarges but reinterprets the earlier scriptural interpretation in connection with this new saving history. In New Testament times the revelation of new events and meanings is compressed into a much shorter time span than in the Old Testament era, and these divine realities now center in one person. The New Testament reinterpretation is linked, in fact, to a dual history of salvation: on the one hand, to the Old Testament kerygma; on the other, to the great central event along with Jesus' own kerygma about it. Furthermore, the meaning of events after Jesus' death was disclosed to the apostles simultaneously with those events, not subsequently or progressively as when they were eyewitnesses of His works. As eye-witnesses they saw and heard and yet lacked full understanding; later, the complete revelation reinterpreted the kerygma so that they *remembered* what Jesus had told them. This along with their eyewitnessing is of greatest importance in designating Jesus Himself as the originator of the reinterpretation of the kerygma. But critics of the *Heilsgeschichte* scholars ask whether the reality of revelation presented in terms of divine act and interpretation does full justice to the biblical representation of the God who both speaks and acts, and who sometimes speaks through chosen prophets and apostles independently of special external deeds and their subsequent interpretation. Beyond authentic interpretation of His actions, does not God also reveal reliable information or ontological propositions about His own nature? Hence the character of revelation, as well as its setting and scope, emerges as a frontier issue.

VI. THE RECOGNITION OF REVELATION AS TRUTH

The problem of the character of revelation as truth has therefore become no less important as a contemporary theological concern than the question of revelation as history. Is the meaning of revelation carried by the biblical interpretation or is it determined in spiritual decision? Is the truth of revelation valid for all men or does it exist only for some persons in and through a miracle of faith? What heightens the importance of this question is the current breakdown of the *Wort-theologie,* the so-called theology of the Word of God. Through the heresy of modernism, continental theology had lost its grip on the specially revealed Word, and Barth promised a recovery of the lost Word of God. But the rise of the Bultmannian theology undermined even Barth's dialectically dimmed assurances about the Word of God. In reaction to this breakdown of the recent theology of the Word of God some contemporary scholars are formulating divine revelation in non-verbal and non-intellectualistic categories, on the gratuitous assumption that any classification of revelation as Word is too narrow. There is larger emphasis today on revelation as divine deed or act. In accordance with this mood, some theologians and New Testament scholars quite readily assign a new role to historical revelation, but hesitate to move again in the direction of a theology of the Word of God in view of the failure of the dialectical theologians in that area. Barth had stressed that man must hear the Word of God anew. Then Bultmann came, dissolving the quasi-objective features that Barth claimed for the Word, and contended that revelation has no semblance of objective form.

Adolf Köberle of Tübingen has premonitions of a judgment upon German Protestantism because of its departure from scripturally based theology. Attacking the dialectical-existential emphasis on revelation, Köberle stresses that "what God has done and what He has said is fully as important as what God is doing and is saying and, in fact, is the presupposition of what He is doing and saying." Edmund Schlink and Peter Brunner of Heidelberg think, on the contrary, that the ecumenical dialogue with Rome and orthodoxy will force Protestantism anew to orient its theological discussion to the great ecumenical creeds. Others note that Faith and Order Conferences thus far supply little encouragement for recovery of a normative biblical theology, since they are predominantly platforms for diverse points of view. In this next generation, thinks Gerhard Friedrich, we shall hear less about the Word of God and more about Jesus as Lord — and revelation, he predicts, will be formulated in association with this thesis of the Lordship of Christ over human life. But if one dissolves the intellectualistic aspect in order to emphasize trust or volitional response as the essential element in revelation, contemporary theology will drift again to the liberalism of Hermann, from which Barth tried to extricate it.

Barth is understandably troubled by the growing emphasis on divine deed in abstraction from divine Word, an emphasis which serves to displace the word-character of revelation. Barth's theology was, after all, in intention a theology of the Word of God, not simply of the deed of God. After his revolt against existentialism, Barth applied theological additives to bolster his own emphasis on revelation as truth. "Any disjunction of deed and word would be nihilistic," he insists. Although in the early years Barth refused to speak of revelation as "information," he now asserts that "revelation is an informative whose *goal* is to be universally recognized." Here we are not yet dealing with information that meets the standard criteria of truth as knowledge which is universally accessible and universally valid. For all his extensive theological revision, Barth still disowns conceptual revelation; his philosophical limitation of the competence of human reason in the realm of metaphysics (not wholly unlike the Kantian restriction) and his suspension of Christian truth upon private response, jeopardize the truth-status of divine disclosure.

Wolfhardt Pannenberg of Mainz, one of Barth's former students, has launched a frontal assault against the vacillation of the dialectical theologians in regard to the truth of revelation. "Their denial of the objectivity of revelation is a threat to the very reality of revelation," says Pannenberg of the dialectical-existential camp. For Pannenberg revelation is objective in the form of historical events but he refuses to acknowledge that it is given in conceptual form. Revelation does take the form of thought, he holds, but not (as Christian theology has traditionally insisted) in divinely inspired inscripturated propositions. He insists that revelation does take the form of truth, and as "the truth of revelation" it must be universally valid. Pannenberg ridicules Barth's "objectifying elements"; what Christian theology really demands is objective revelation, not existential or dialectical revelation, not even if it is bolstered by "objectifying elements." Pannenberg realizes that the specially revealed God not only requires a theology of historical revelation as the *Heilsgeschichte* scholars would have it, but revelation in the form of truth, and as such, universally accessible and universally valid apart from any personal decision for or against it.

Pannenberg joins in the widening attack of European scholars upon the dialectical formulation of transcendence, an exaggerated emphasis inspired more by Plato or Kierkegaard than by the Bible. Anders Nygren of Lund emphasizes that the overseparation of eternity and time inevitably involves difficulty for the whole conception of revelation in relation to nature, history, and conscience. Helmut Thielicke of Hamburg stresses that Barth's notion of the revelation of God as known only in individual response inevitably deprives the world at large of any knowledge of the divine criterion by which God will judge it.

Pannenberg's insistence that the truth of revelation is universally accessible and valid calls attention by contrast to a remarkable assortment of compromises and adjustments among the European theologians of the objectivity of revealed truth.

The dialectical notion is, at bottom, that truth of revelation becomes truth only for individuals in a miracle of grace. Peter Brunner and Edmund Schlink at Heidelberg hold that "Christian revelation has a universal truth claim, wholly apart from subjective decision. But this truth claim is mediated by divine grace." Otto Weber of Göttingen says that revelation is "for all," but no man can know revelation as truth until he becomes a Christian. "Revelation is true for me as a Christian and therefore for all men." Over against this point of view

Nygren insists that "the truth of the Christian message can be understood without personal faith and it is universally valid for all men in all times and in all places."

Whereas for Weber divine revelation is true for me as a Christian and therefore for all men, for Pannenberg, divine revelation is true for all men and therefore true for the Christian and the Church. This important controversy over the relation of revelation and truth attests the fact that Christian theology has not yet extracted itself from the concessions made by the modernists to Kant and by the crisis-theologians to Kierkegaard. It may be well to repeat here what the writer has said elsewhere of this present conflict: "So dawns the end of an era in which Ritschl held that the validity of religious judgments can be known only through an act of the will, in which Troeltsch found himself unable to assert the universality of the Christian religion, and in which both Barth and Bultmann failed to vindicate the universal validity of Christian revelation apart from a miracle of personal grace or an act of subjective decision. But if the deepest truth of God is found in Jesus Christ, if the contention is to be credited that Christianity is a religion for all nations, bringing men everywhere under judgment and offering salvation of import to the whole human race, then it is imperative that the Christian religion reassert its reasoned claim to universality" ("Revelation as Truth," *Christianity Today,* Vol. 9 [January 1, 1965], p. 337).

VII. THE EVANGELICAL OPPORTUNITY

Alongside the wistful longing that ecumenical theology will lift contemporary Protestantism from its subjectivistic theological propensity, despite the fact that ecumenism recognizes no sure norm beyond ecclesiastical consensus, the long-neglected evangelical theology emerges once again as a formidable alternative to recent dogmatic projections. For evangelical theology gathers up the *Heilsgeschichte* emphasis that revelation and salvation are objective historical realities, Pannenberg's emphasis that the truth of revelation is universally valid irrespective of personal decision, and Cullmann's emphasis that the meaning as well as the event belong to the reality of revelation. And it goes beyond the recent modern refusal to honor Scripture as an authoritative canon of divine truth.

How far the contemporary discussion of revelation and truth has drifted from the Christian heritage is apparent from a comment by the Cambridge theologian, the late J. M. Creed:

> Had any Christian of any Church between the end of the second century and the closing decades of the eighteenth been asked a question as to the content of the Christian religion, his answer could scarcely have

failed to be to the general effect that the truths of the Christian religion were contained and conveyed in the inspired books of holy Scripture (*The Divinity of Jesus Christ* [Cambridge University Press, 1938], p. 105).

The failure of the Barthian and Bultmannian theology to return to this evangelical heritage is the primary reason that the much-heralded "springtime in European theology" soon gave way again to a barren wintertime. This bleak season swept by tempestuous crosswinds will emerge into a fruitful theological harvest only if the supernatural resources of the Christian religion are fully recovered.

THE NEW QUEST
OF THE
HISTORICAL JESUS

Ralph P. Martin

Ralph P. Martin is Lecturer in New Testament Studies in the University of Manchester, England. He has been Lecturer in Theology in London Bible College, and served recently as Visiting Professor of New Testament in Bethel College, St. Paul, Minnesota. He has written The Epistle to the Philippians *in the Tyndale Bible Commentaries,* An Early Christian Confession, *and* Worship in the Early Church. *He holds the Ph.D. degree from the University of London.*

THE NEW QUEST
OF THE
HISTORICAL JESUS

O NE OF THE most vigorous currents in mid-twentieth century theology" is a recent description[1] of the New Quest debate, which in 1964 entered its tenth year. The title, "The New Quest of the Historical Jesus," fixes attention upon one of the most heavily documented themes of modern biblical and theological scholarship; and equally it exposes the critical nature of this discussion. For all participants agree that this is no peripheral matter lying far away on the extremities of Christian teaching, and of speculative interest only; but, on the contrary, it concerns the center and substance of the Church's proclamation: *the person of Jesus Christ as the preached Word of God, and His relation to history.*

I. BACKGROUND TO THE DEBATE

To trace back the current debate to its sources is a complex business, for many tributaries flow into the main stream at the point where it rises. Indeed, it is not easy to fix precisely the place at which the

---

1 The present writer owes this quotation — and some valuable guidance as to procedure and bibliographical control — to J. Benjamin Bederbaugh's comprehensive survey, "The First Decade of the New Quest of the Historical Jesus" (*The Lutheran Quarterly*, 16 [Aug. 1964], pp. 239ff.) .

origins of the controversy lie. Perhaps the chief determinants which shaped the rise and development of the new movement are the Deist challenge to the orthodox Christian faith in Europe, the influence of the Ritschlian theology with its ambivalent attitude to Gospel history, the rise of new methods of historical science and enquiry, the relentless probings of biblical criticism which placed question marks against many of the age-old, time-honored assumptions and convictions of the Church; and (as a later factor) the influence of existentialist philosophy upon Christian thinkers.

Subsequent events have confirmed three factors (noted below, pp. 28, 29) to be important as far as twentieth-century biblical studies in the life of Jesus are concerned. Prior to the arrival of these methods which were applied to the Gospel materials, no one seemed in doubt that a portrait of Jesus as a figure of first-century Palestine could be sketched by a careful and sympathetic drawing together of the Gospel data. As it turned out, pious imagination and wishful reconstruction filled in whatever gaps were discerned. This desire to come close to the humanity of Jesus by a study of His inner life, His psychological development, His traits of personality and human emotion and choice — in a word, His "biographical" material — is known as the "Life-of-Jesus Movement." As a species of biblical methodology, it produced a number of "lives" of Jesus which all reflected more or less the theological status and religious devotion of their authors. The main European examples were collected and critically examined by Albert Schweitzer, whose book carried, as its title, the names of the two terminal points of the Life-of-Jesus era: *Von Reimarus* [1694-1768] *zu Wrede* [1901]. Schweitzer's comprehensive chronicle ended with a negative appraisal: "Those who are fond of talking about negative theology can find their account here. There is nothing more negative than the result of the critical study of the Life of Jesus" (*The Quest of the Historical Jesus,* tr. W. Montgomery [New York: Macmillan, 1910], p. 398). His own attempt in a concluding chapter to make good the deficiency and to depict Jesus as an apocalyptic visionary, the deluded victim of a fixed eschatological program which, in the end, crushed Him in despair and failure, did not escape the same verdict.

Schweitzer's book marks the end of an era. Already at the turn of the century the stage was being prepared for some new and dramatic changes. The precursor of the New Testament scholars' revolutionary assessments of the Gospel portrait was Martin Kähler, whose diminutive essays on "the so-called historical Jesus and the historic, Biblical Christ" contained all the seeds of the new approach. Kähler engaged in a warm polemic against the nineteenth-century historicism which produced the vagaries of the Life-of-Jesus portraits. He objected that such a portraiture inevitably led to a false picture, which obscured the transcendental qualities of the biblical Christ. The living Christ is essentially the Christ of apostolic proclamation, accessible to us today in a spiritual encounter and not to be "dug out" of historical documents by an application of psychological enquiries.

Many reasons may be supplied for Kähler's antagonism to the historiographical methods and theological presuppositions of his day. These are carefully noted in Carl E. Braaten's essay "Revelation, History, and Faith in Martin Kähler," prefacing his translation of Kähler's *The So-Called Historical Jesus and the Historic, Biblical Christ* (Philadelphia: Fortress Press, 1964). Of central importance, however, was his conviction that the Gospels do not provide the kind of biographical data which would give us a window of access into the inner life of Jesus. They are "passion narrative with extended introduction," containing the content of early Christian preaching and intended to awaken faith in Christ as Redeemer. The Gospels are, by design, theological documents, written from faith to faith and serving an exclusively religious interest. The Christ they portray is the Christ of faith, the proclaimed Lord whose encounter with His people today is not at the mercy of historical investigation and systematic doubt. Only by insisting on the exact nature of our access to the "historic, Biblical Christ" can we be delivered from the clutches of historical relativism (for which nothing in the past is absolutely certain) and be given an "invulnerable area" (*sturmfreies Gebiet*), unassailed and unassailable by historical enquiry. Braaten's essay provides an invaluable discussion of the philosophical, historiographical, and theological *milieu* of the immediate background to the twentieth-century New Testament problem in regard to the Jesus of history. Our present concern with this issue will permit us to come directly to the theme of New Testament (and, in particular, Gospel) studies as the background of our enquiry.

As far as the study of the Gospels as historical records of Jesus' earthly life is concerned, the development of scholarly attitudes and estimates may be conveniently traced to a point of new departure in H. J. Holtzmann. Recently the history of Synoptic criticism in continental Europe and England has been carefully chronicled by W. R. Farmer in his book *The Synoptic Problem* (New York: Macmillan, 1964). Farmer rightly directs attention to Holtzmann's book, *Die synoptischen Evangelien*, published in Leipzig in 1863, which gave a classic statement of the so-called "Marcan hypothesis," *viz.*, that Mark's Gospel as the foundation-document underlying the other Synoptic Gospels contains a clear, factual, unembellished record of the life and public career of Jesus.

Albert Schweitzer accurately assessed the significance of Holtzmann's work.

> Scarcely ever has a description of the life of Jesus exercised so irresistible an influence as that short outline — it embraces scarcely twenty pages — with which Holtzmann closes his examination of the Synoptic Gospels. This chapter became the creed and catechism of all who handled the subject during the following decades. The treatment of the life of Jesus had to follow the lines here laid down until the Marcan hypothesis was delivered from its bondage to that a priori view of the development of Jesus. Until then anyone might appeal to the Marcan hypothesis, meaning thereby only that general view of the inward and outward course of development in the life of Jesus, and might treat the remainder of the Synoptic material how he chose, combining with it, at his pleasure, material drawn from John. The victory, therefore, belonged, not to the Marcan hypothesis pure and simple, but to the Marcan hypothesis as psychologically interpreted by a liberal theology (op. cit., p. 204).

Farmer sees this penetrating assessment of the Life-of-Jesus school, which was a vigorous reaction against the dominance of the Tübingen school since 1835 (the year of D. F. Strauss's *Leben Jesu* and two literary works of F. C. Baur), as highly significant. For it shows that Holtzmann was motivated by a *theological* concern to defend the liberal estimate of the historical Jesus against the mythical interpretation of Strauss. And Holtzmann's vindication of Mark's priority and historicity held the field until the turn of the century, when three powerful forces were at work which ultimately assailed and destroyed the Holtzmann doctrine as far as German scholarship was involved. These new approaches to Synoptic history may be tabulated.

(A) Wilhelm Wrede's discussion (in 1901) of the messianic secret in the Gospels, chiefly in Mark's Gospel, concluded that Mark is *not* a record of unvarnished history, portraying Jesus "as He actually was," but a dogmatic treatise, in which the doctrine of the messianic secret is imposed upon the historical materials.

(B) K. L. Schmidt considered (in 1919) "The framework of the story of Jesus," and, by an analysis of the sections (*pericopae*) of the Gospel material in a form critical manner, came to a startling verdict:

> As a whole there is no life of Jesus in the sense of a developing biography, no chronological sketch of Jesus' history, but only single stories (*pericopae*), which are put into a framework (*Der Rahmen der Geschichte Jesu*, p. 317).

(C) The doctrine of *Sitz im Leben* (the principle that each section of Gospel teaching and narrative may be suggestively placed in the setting of its historical context, when we have regard to its literary form and theological content) was taken by the early practitioners of the "form critical Method" a stage farther than that of a purely literary exercise. From an analysis of the "types" or "forms" (*Gattungen*) of the literary materials of the Gospels — into such categories as "miracle-stories," "conflict-stories," "biographical *apophthegmata*" or "tales" — some of the form critics moved on to appraisal, and gave a critical judgment on the historical worth of the data. Thus, in a well-known instance, Rudolf Bultmann's skepticism inclined him to treat the narrative of the plucking of the ears of corn (Mark 2:23-28) as derived from the work of "the Community" (that is, the post-Easter Church) which read back the justification for its own Sabbath freedom into the mouth and example of Jesus. By this judgment on the historical value of Synoptic incidents, what the Church has traditionally regarded as authentic, factual, episodic history is evaporated into an idealized reconstruction invented by the later Church of the apostolic era. The *Sitz im Leben Jesu* is transformed into *Sitz im Leben der alten Kirche* by a stroke of the form critic's pen; and Gospel history is subsumed under the ominous category of *Gemeindetheologie*.

The name of Rudolf Bultmann occurs, in this discussion, as the author of a study *Jesus* (1926: an English translation, *Jesus and the Word*, appeared in 1934). This book may be taken as indicative of the effect of a radical form critical approach to the historical data of the Gospels. What emerges from Bultmann's literary analysis of the Gospel material is the negative conclusion that the Jesus there presented is the Christ of the Church's proclamation (kerygma) and the Christ of post-Easter experience. No historical foundation may legitimately be sought in the Gospels. This negative judgment of Bultmann is based on a twofold premise:

(A) *Form critically,* it is impossible, Bultmann avers, to recapture Jesus as He moved in Galilee and to know "precisely what took place" in A.D. 27-30. The Gospels do not give scientific biography; they show no interest in Jesus' personality; they offer no psychological study. There is no fascination with Jesus' charm, no window into His "inner life." In the phrase of Albert Schweitzer's, there is no estimate of "the inward and outward course of development in the life of Jesus" (*loc. cit.*). The Gospels accentuate not Jesus' personality, but His work; and that work is seen through the eyes of the later Church.

(B) *Theologically,* also, a negative verdict must be returned to the question of whether we can know the Jesus of history as a figure of the past. Even if it were possible to learn of the Jesus of history, it is illegitimate so to inquire, for faith can never be at the mercy of historical criticism and suspend its activity while the historians debate the issue. The person in whom Christian faith confides is the risen Christ, living in the Church, having ascended (as it was once facetiously put) into the kerygma and now mediated by the morning sermon of the Lutheran rector in his pulpit!

The Gospels perform the necessary function, not of directing faith to a past figure of whom certain historical values may be predicated, but of certifying that Jesus of Nazareth once embodied the Word of God in His existence in time. About this "Christ-event," that is, the appearance of Jesus as an eschatological prophet of God who announces the imminent reign of God, nothing *of theological significance* need be known except *that* He once lived, taught, and died. The mere "that-ness" (the *Dass*, the fact that He once existed) is sufficient. As to the character of Jesus (the *Wie,* how He acted) and the content of His message (the *Was,* what He said in words which ruffled the air in Palestine long ago), these are beyond recovery and unnecessary to faith anyway. The real importance of the Gospel testimony lies in its endorsement of Jesus' bare factualness about which, to be sure, certain "features" may be predicted. Van A. Harvey and Schubert M. Ogden quote from Bultmann's *Jesus* to show that he was willing in 1926 to accept certain features of Jesus' person and work. In 1960, he summarized his assessment of Jesus' earthly career thus:

> Characteristic for him are exorcisms, the breach of the Sabbath commandment, the abandonment of ritual purifications, polemic against Jewish legalism, fellowship with outcasts such as publicans and harlots, sympathy for women and children; it can also be seen that Jesus was not an ascetic like John the Baptist, but gladly ate and drank a glass of wine. Perhaps we may add that he called disciples and assembled about himself a small company of followers — men and women (quoted by C. E. Braaten and R. A. Harrisville, *The Historical Jesus and the Kerygmatic Christ* [Nashville: Abingdon Press, 1964], pp. 22f.)

Both the early and later Bultmann, then, make much of the distinction between Jesus' *person* (including His existence and certain "features" which belong to His activity and mission as healer and prophetic teacher, announcing an impending in-breaking of the divine rule) and His *personality* (the traits of His character and our knowledge of the inner working of His mind). This distinction may be seen also in Emil Brunner, *The Mediator,* (Eng. tr., 1934), pp. 265ff., 318ff., 345ff.

Bultmann is willing to affirm cautiously the factuality of Jesus' person (although he goes on immediately to deny to it any real theological value *(ibid., pp. 24f.)*, because the Gospels are, by definition, not concerned to supply "objective historicity"). Yet he stoutly denies any hint that Jesus' personality may be seen in the Gospels. Thus he is led to deny that we have any knowledge of Jesus' understanding of His death. Mark 10:45 is a "prophecy after the event," read back into the life of Jesus. It is conceivable that Jesus died in utter bewilderment and abject despair, a frustrated and rejected prophet of God.

Accepting, therefore, J. M. Robinson's revised estimate of Bultmann's skepticism concerning the historical Jesus, we may use his words to summarize the situation which was the immediate background of and precursor to the new quest debate:

> [Bultmann's] form-critical analyses corroborated the view that a Life-of-Jesus research after the style of the nineteenth century is impossible, and his existential interpretation undermined the thesis that such a Life-of-Jesus research was legitimate (*Kerygma und historischer Jesus* [1960], pp. 10f.).

Dr. Robinson adds, providing us with an entree to the debate "Therefore it is not surprising that the critical restudy of his [Bultmann's] position by his pupils should begin here" (*A New Quest of the Historical Jesus* [London: SCM Press, 1959], p. 12).

II. THE COURSE OF THE "NEW QUEST" DEBATE

The situation in 1953/54 may be summed up in the following manner. Under the direct influence of form criticism and Bultmann's kerygmatic-existentialist theology, German left-wing scholarship had made an hiatus between the Jesus of history and the Christ of the Church's proclamation. The historical Jesus was regarded as an eschatological prophet *simpliciter* who announced the imminent arrival of the kingdom in non-messianic categories and called for a radical repentance and "decision" in the light of the kingdom's near realization.

A decade of debate in reaction to this minimal interpretation of the life and ministry of Jesus was set afoot by a series of continental articles, the chief impetus being provided by Ernst Käsemann's address to the "old Marburgers" in October, 1953 (published in *Zeitschrift für Theologie und Kirche*, Vol. 51 [1954], pp. 125-153).

E. Käsemann

Käsemann shares many of Bultmann's presuppositions. Chiefly, his approach to the Gospel records is controlled by the view that biography and the revealing of traits of personality are not to be found therein. Nevertheless, Käsemann exhibits a definite move away from the classic Bultmannian position in three ways:

(A) Although he grants that it is not possible to construct a Life-of-Jesus containing exact chronological data, a detailed *curriculum vitae* with stages of psychological development ("The Problem of the Historical Jesus," in *Essays on New Testament Themes* [London: SCM Press, 1964], p. 45), he is unwilling to admit a "disengagement of interest from the earthly Jesus" (p. 46). In a significant statement, Käsemann proceeds:

> If this were to happen, we should either be failing to grasp the nature of the primitive Christian concern with the identity between the exalted and the humiliated Lord; or else we should be emptying that concern of any real content, as did the docetists. We should also be overlooking the fact that there are still pieces (*Stücke*) of the Synoptic tradition which the historian has to acknowledge as authentic if he wishes to remain an historian at all (*ibid.*).

In this statement Käsemann shows himself sensitive to the danger of Docetism with its denial of interest in the earthly Jesus; and shows a more open regard for the possibility of recovering the historical Jesus whose preaching (he is anxious to show) is in continuity with the Church's proclamation.

(B) It is the preaching of Jesus which Käsemann highlights as the distinctive element in the Gospel data. Two citations will demonstrate this:

> Our investigation has led to the conclusion that we must look for the distinctive element in the earthly Jesus in his preaching and interpret both his other activities and his destiny in the light of this preaching (p. 44).
> My own concern is to show that, out of the obscurity of the life story of Jesus, certain characteristic traits in his preaching stand out in relatively sharp relief, and that primitive Christianity united its own message with these (p. 46).

(C) Here is a decisive break with Bultmann's thesis of a disjunction between the eschatological announcement of a future kingdom which Jesus simply heralded and the Christian proclamation that Jesus is the Messiah and inaugurator of God's reign on earth. To be sure, Käsemann doubts whether Jesus claimed messianic status (*ibid.*, p. 38), but the evidence he adduces shows that this is the only title which properly fits Him. The evidence forms a fivefold pattern: Jesus' authority is seen in His overriding the venerable Mosaic Torah — an assumption of authority in the Sermon on the Mount which no rabbi or Jewish prophet would ever have made; His freedom in dealing with the Sabbath rules and with the prescriptions for ceremonial purity and dietary regulations (e.g., Mark 7) ; His masterful dealing with demoniacs, which thereby destroyed the basis of classical demonology; His immediate apprehension of God's will for human life, evidenced by His possession of the Spirit (Matt. 12:28) and use of such asseverations as

Amen which "signifies an extreme and immediate certainty, such as is conveyed by inspiration" *(ibid.,* p. 42) ; and, most persuasively, Jesus' status *vis-à-vis* John the Baptist. John ushered in the turning point of the ages *(Aeonenwende),* and announced the advent of God's reign in the coming of Jesus. "Evidently, [Jesus is] he who brings with his Gospel the kingdom itself"; and so in Jesus Christ the kingdom arrived, and was not simply announced as proximate.

Käsemann's original propositions were received sympathetically (cf. the literature in Robinson, *A New Quest,* pp. 13f.) , and were carried forward by significant contributions.

Günther Bornkamm

Bornkamm's distinction is a notable one. His *Jesus of Nazareth,* (London: Hodder and Stoughton, 1960) is offered as an appraisal of Jesus' life, ministry, and challenge from within the Bultmannian school. And it takes the debate a stage farther. An assessment of Bornkamm's contribution is provided in the following:

> Käsemann accepts as authentic, evidence concerning the *teaching* of Jesus, and concerning one aspect of his *work,* that of dealing with demoniacs. Bornkamm goes on to other aspects of Jesus' work (especially in his dealings with people) and makes a tentative beginning in regard to the *attitude* of Jesus. He deals with the significance of Jesus' forgiveness of sins and his table-fellowship with publicans and sinners (W. R. Farmer and Norman Perrin, *Religion in Life,* Vol. 29 [1959-60], p. 93) .

A representative statement in Bornkamm's volume bears out this estimate:

> Quite clearly what the Gospels report concerning the message, the deeds, and the history of Jesus is still distinguished by an authenticity, a freshness, and a distinctiveness not in any way effaced by the Church's Easter faith. These features point us directly to the earthly figure of Jesus" *(op. cit.,* p. 24) .

Ernst Fuchs

Fuchs marks the most violent swing-away from the traditional Bultmannian position. For him the outstanding trait of Jesus' ministry was His readiness to consort with tax-collectors and sinners and to share meals with them. This act was no simple illustration of sociability or condescension. It means, rather:

> Jesus forwent the publication of his own private eschatological experiences; rather he determined only to draw the consequences from them and to begin here on earth with the work of God visible only in heaven! This is why he celebrates his meal . . . This conduct *(Verhalten)* is neither that of a prophet nor that of a sage, but rather the conduct of a man who

dares to act in God's stead, by (as must always be added) calling near
to him sinners who apart from him would have to flee from God (Fuchs,
Studies of the Historical Jesus, as quoted by Robinson, *A New Quest,*
pp. 14f.) .

The high peak of Jesus' mission is seen in His teaching (especially
the Parable of the Lost Son) and His conduct towards the wayward
and outcasts. By these means He effectively communicates God's will,
for, as He accepts the repentant sinner in mercy, it is implied that so
God is graciously disposed to men. Jesus, furthermore, envisaged after
the death of John the possibility of His own suffering and death; and
thus read into John's martyrdom a personal significance for His own life
and destiny.

With Fuch's treatment two important novelties within the Bultmann
school are clearly to be seen. First, in his use of John's death as having
a significance for Jesus, Fuchs is adopting a psychologizing method,
which the Bultmann school have hitherto eschewed. Secondly, the
relation between the message Jesus preached (and its ensuing be-
havioral pattern) and the kerygma of the apostolic Church is one of
intimate association. For Jesus' message is the implicit declaration
of His own self-understanding as One who acted *in loco Dei,* which became explicit in the post-Easter proclamation of the Church. There is
no disjunction between the two, as Bultmann had insisted; but rather
a linear continuity. Bultmann, in a later response to his errant disciple, criticizes the "relapse into the historical-psychological interpretation" which Fuchs has adopted, a relapse which is reprehensible, according to Bultmann, because it "describes Jesus' attitude as a phenomenon
perceptible to the objectifying historian" ("The Primitive Christian
Kerygma and the Historical Jesus," in Braaten and Harrisville, *op. cit.,*
pp. 32f.) . In fact, in an earlier response *(Zeitschrift für Theologie und
Kirche,* Vol. 54 [1957], pp. 244-54) . Bultmann had conceded some elements of Fuchs' construction of Jesus' attitude to sinners and consciousness of His mission, but had shied away from any biographical-psycho-
logical interpretation, especially of Jesus' understanding of His death.

James M. Robinson

Robinson, the chronicler of the "new quest" debate, is responsible
for the introduction of this new phase of New Testament science to
the English-speaking world. The position which he adopted in 1959
(in *A New Quest*) was characterized by the statement of three theses:

(A) The quest of the historical Jesus still remaining to be carried
out is a *new* quest. Its "newness" is a double one: first, in relation to
the nineteenth-century attempt to reconstruct the Jesus of history, and

second, in relation to Bultmann's wedge between the Christ of kerygma and Jesus of Galilee. The new quest has an approach which differs from that of the nineteenth-century quest, and it employs a more refined methodology.

As to approach, the old quest treated the Gospels as biographical quarries from which factual, objective and psychologically plausible materials could be dug. When pieced together, these formed a portrait of Jesus as men knew Him "in the days of His flesh." The newer approach sees the Gospels as kerygmatically built, and as representing the confessional deposit of the Church in its preaching, worship, catechetical instruction, apologetics, and self-awareness.

As to methodology, the liberal scholars who espoused the "old quest" were critical in refusing all that did not conform to the liberal idea of what Jesus should be. The Gospels were regarded as a pool into which the critic looked and saw only a pale reflection of his own face. This attitude was motivated by a desire to get behind the Christ of the apostolic kerygma, the pre-existent and heavenly Lord, to the human Jesus, the prophet and teacher of Galilee. Nineteenth-century historiography was a pliable instrument for this task, for history was, at that time, regarded as a descriptive science on a par with the natural sciences (cf. E. Troeltsch in *Hastings Encyclopedia of Religion and Ethics,* Vol. VI, 716ff.) and thereby concerned with "brute facts" and unembellished biographical details.

The newer treatment sees history as an existential undertaking on the part of the historian, who is no detached and impartial observer standing outside the stream of the historical process which he seeks to interpret (Robinson, *op. cit.,* pp. 76f.). Gospel history is not exempted from this attitude of modern historiography; and the scholar engaged in the new quest seeks to show that the kerygmatic portrait of Christ is a faithful representation of the historical Jesus so far as He may be known. The method is clearly stated by Robinson (*ibid.,* p. 90). There are now two ways of access to the person of the Church's Lord: the *via kerygmatica,* by which the proclamation of Christ in the Church presents an understanding of Jesus which it presupposes to be a continuation of His own self-understanding; and the *via historica* which, by using the modern historiography of Dilthey, Collingwood, and Bloch, takes up the non-kerygmatic material of the Gospel to reconstruct the self-understanding of the Jesus of history.

Examination of the Gospels by critical methods and the application of certain criteria lead to the possibility that one can expose a residuum of authentic sayings of Jesus which betray His understanding of His existence. Such an examination excludes all elements in the Gospels which are kerygmatic or confessional, all material which can be paralleled in apocalyptic or rabbinic contemporary Judaism, and all possibly doubtful Aramaic *Logia* which could be considered on other grounds as the inauthentic creation of the early Church in Palestine (for example, the name "Lord" [κύριος, Aramaic *Mar (an)*]). Sayings of Jesus such as those contrasting humiliation and exaltation (e.g., Matt. 23:12; Luke 18:14. See also Anderson, *Jesus and Christian Origins* [New York: Oxford, 1964], pp. 241-306) reveal an authentic understanding of existence on His part. Later these became "mythologized" in the apostolic kerygma as Christ's pre-existence, incarnation, and enthronement (Phil. 2:5-11; I Tim. 3:16; I Pet. 3:18-22). Here, it is claimed, is a direct continuity between pre- and post-Easter situations, an illustration of the claim of the new quest that, by an uncovering of Jesus' understanding of existence, "the historical Jesus confronts us with existential decision, just as the kerygma does" (Robinson, *op. cit.*, p. 77).

Secondly, in relation to Bultmann's disavowal of interest in the Jesus of history and his driving a wedge between the Christ proclaimed in the kerygma and the Jesus of Galilee, the new quest seeks to reopen the lines of communication between history and kerygma.

(B) and (C) Robinson's second and third theses assert that the quest is "possible," "legitimate," and even "necessary," though the grounds of legitimacy and necessity are clearly not the same as those of the nineteenth-century quest.

The grounds for the new quest as stated by the early Robinson are to be sought in what he (apparently erroneously) called Bultmann's "classical position." The latter maintained according to Robinson that nothing can be known about the historical Jesus, and that there is no kind of recognizable continuity between the proclamation of Jesus and the subsequent kerygma of the Church. The statement is summarized by Van A. Harvey and Schubert M. Ogden (quoted by Braaten and Harrisville, *op. cit.*, p. 203). Harvey and Ogden severely criticize this description, drawing attention to Bultmann's early concession that at least *some* knowledge of the historical Jesus is possible, and to his clear affirmation that there are important differences in the forms of expressions used in the kerygma of the Church and Jesus' own proclamation (see Bultmann, *Jesus*, pp. 212ff.). In a recent contribution to the ongoing debate, Bultmann has affirmed the possibility of recovering a cautious outline of biographical detail (cf. p. 30); and he has clarified his understanding of the relation between the historical Jesus and the kerygmatic Christ.

Bultmann affirms a historical continuity between the two, but qualifies this by remarking that continuity is not identity; for the sole function of the Gospel record is to declare the factuality *(Dass)* of Jesus. The continuity is that which binds together the historical Jesus and the early Christian preaching, but he still wishes to place an hiatus between the pre-Easter Jesus and the "mythological Son of God" of early Christian proclamation. Thus, he avers, there is no "essential relationship" *(sachliches Verhältnis)* between Jesus and the apostolic Christ; the first is the proclaimer of the kingdom to come, the second is the proclaimed, heavenly Lord, dressed up in mythological garb, the bearer of the saving Word in the Church's contemporary preaching.

Professor Robinson, responding to this statement in a clear, forthright fashion, sets out the issue between him (representing the post-Bultmannian "wing") and Bultmann himself. In a 1962 article in the *Journal of the Bible and Religion* (Vol. 30 [1962], pp. 198-208), he seeks a justification for positing a closer relation than Bultmann was willing to allow between the Jesus-portrait in the Gospels and the kerygmatic Christ. In effect, his argument turns on a new situation created in the post-Pauline Church. In Paul's historical context, he could simply maintain the factuality of the heavenly Lord as a one-time historical phenomenon, but a dangerous situation, of which hints are seen at Corinth, developed in the later Church, where Jesus was becoming regarded as a divine epiphany, a mythical "heavenly visitant," after the pattern of the "divine men" of Hellenistic religion or (it may be added) like a temporary incarnation of Apollo in Admetus' home (Euripides, *Alcestis*). For the Gospel writers, this danger could be avoided only by an insistence upon the Jesus-tradition, that is, a clothing of the factuality with biographical descriptions of "how" Jesus acted and "what" He said. "This is the *Sitz im Leben*, the *Tendenz*, which accounts for and justifies the practice of the Synoptics, so different from early kerygmatic texts and from Paul, and which also authenticates the Gospels as canonical and, with them, the validity and necessity of the new quest in our situation" *(ibid.,* p. 204).

In a word, whereas Bultmann drives a wedge between Jesus' preaching, which is regarded as simply preparatory for the later kerygma, Robinson argues that already in Jesus' message there is implicit "a structure corresponding to the kerygma's reference to the once-for-all event of cross and resurrection" *(ibid.,* p. 206). Robinson counters the criticism that his view is a reversion to the nineteenth-century quest — "a complete capitulation to the heirs of Schweitzer"[2] — or that it falls into the trap of psychologism (a judgment passed by Bultmann on Fuchs' view). Aware of these pressures, Robinson has modified his earlier view, which based an existential understanding of Jesus' mes-

---

2 Paul W. Meyer, *Novum Testamentum,* Vol. 4 (1960), p. 133. Cf. the critical question of Harvey and Ogden: "Are not both quests seeking the same object — the inner life of Jesus?" *(loc. cit.,* p. 236).

sage upon His selfhood (*Selbstverständnis*). This position was criticized
by Harvey and Ogden:

> Is the new quest for the *existentiell* selfhood of Jesus different from the
> old quest for the "inner life" of Jesus, his "personality"? And if it is
> impossible to recover Jesus' "inner life" — as Robinson claims — is it any
> easier to recover Jesus' *existentiell* selfhood? (*loc. cit.*, pp. 222ff., 234).

Instead of "understanding of self," Robinson now prefers to speak of
"understanding of existence" (*Existenzverständnis*) (*Journal of the
Bible and Religion*, Vol. 30 [1962], p. 208, n. 36).

But he is still faced with the same double embarrassment even with
a change of terminology. R. H. Fuller has set his finger on this. The
new quest still leaves unresolved the uneasy combination of the older
historical-critical method (employed by the older quest in the nineteenth century) and the new "existential" approach to history. This
employment of the critical method of the old quest leads to an equivo-
cation, "a cloudy uncertainty as to whether in their reconstruction the
new questers are giving us history or kerygma. If it is history, then
history is disclosing ultimate theological truth without the resurrection;
and if kerygma, what has happened to the solid core of historical
actuality which the kerygma must contain?" (*Anglican Theological
Review*, Vol. 47 [Jan. 1965], pp. 119f. Cf. *idem*, 41 [1959], pp. 232-35).

Later discussion has faced the issue of this disjunction. As a further indication of the waning of Bultmann's influence, "post-Bultmannians" like Käsemann are moving in the direction of a more positive
attitude to history by an acceptance of a *Heilsgeschichtlich* scheme, that
is, a view that the history which the New Testament records "discloses"
the redemptive purpose and acts of God, which are temporal and
factual, yet invested with an eschatological significance. This respectful attitude to history has long been maintained by Oscar Cullmann,
Joachim Jeremias, W. D. Davies and Alan Richardson, and has received fresh stimulus from the work of such scholars as W. Pannenberg
and G. E. Wright.

At the opposite end of the scale, other scholars are taking a negative
attitude to Gospel history and seeking to ground the Christian claim and
challenge in a more purely philosophical interpretation of the Christ-
event. Schubert M. Ogden (*Christ Without Myth*, New York, Harper,
1961) and Paul van Buren (*The Secular Meaning of the Gospel*, New
York, Macmillan, 1963) are willing apparently to detach the Christian
kerygma from its historical moorings and to equate it with a call to
existential decision.

A singular fact is that no contribution from within the Anglo-
American evangelical section of the Church has striven to wrestle with

this disjunction; and to offer an evangelical perspective from which the inter-relation of history and kerygma may be appraised. The present volume seeks to fill this gap, and to provide such an evangelical perspective.

By way of final summary we shall offer certain criticisms of the principles and program of the new quest; and in this way point out certain basic evangelical *credenda* which may be submitted as important in any satisfactory solution which seeks to resolve the tension between the Gospel picture of Jesus as the proclaimer and the post-Easter proclaimed message of the Lord of the Church.[3]

III. SOME QUESTIONABLE ASSUMPTIONS OF THE NEW QUEST

The Interest of the Evangelists in the Human Jesus

New Testament scholarship in the post World War II period has grown accustomed to the assertion — often stated as an *ipse dixit* of unquestioned certainty — that the early Christians had no interest in biographical details of the earthly Jesus; and that the Evangelists did not write their Gospels as "Lives of Christ" in the sense of modern psychological studies of human personalities.

The absence of the latter intention in the Evangelists' purpose may be freely granted (cf. John 20:30, 31) ; but it may be seriously doubted that there was no interest in the human Jesus. British scholars (like T. W. Manson, Vincent Taylor and A. M. Hunter) have argued that this Christian interest in the details of our Lord's earthly ministry and the high value placed upon His teaching (reflected in Paul's letters) are part and parcel of apostolic Christianity; and it is a priori unlikely that the first generations of Gentile believers were content to commit their lives to a mythological Lord whose "history" was (on the form critical claim) as uncertain and adventitious as that of the cult divinities of the Hellenistic mystery religions. Christian preaching, as Karl Holl showed some decades ago, met with success in conversion and transformation of character because it was a distinctive entity, offering a salvation markedly different from the deliverance proclaimed by rival

---

3 Strangely, what pass for evangelical emphases in this debate are shared by Roman Catholic scholars; in particular, our closing section is indebted to Raymond E. Brown's perceptive critique in "After Bultmann, What? — An Introduction to the Post-Bultmannians" *(Catholic Biblical Quarterly,* 26:1 [Jan. 1964], pp. 1-30; cf. P. J. Cahill's subsequent contribution, "Rudolf Bultmann and Post-Bultmann Tendencies," *ibid.,* 26:2 [Apr. 1964], pp. 153-178) . Worthy of special mention, too, is the Roman Catholic-Protestant symposium *Faith, Reason, and the Gospels,* ed. John J. Heaney, S. J. Westminster, Maryland: Newman Press, 1961) .

cults. And one outstanding element in that distinctiveness, we may affirm, was its announcement that God had been, and still was, decisively present as Redeemer and Lord in Jesus Christ who *had lived a historical life*. This fact leads on to the next point.

The Danger of Docetism

The recent discussion, insofar as it shares the presupposition of Bultmann's radical dealing with Gospel sources, still is bedeviled by the threatened danger of Docetism.

Although Bultmann's writings are often cautiously framed, they have not escaped the criticism that in his final assessment the human Jesus is lost in a welter of speculation and reservation about what may or may not be authentic in the Gospel picture. The fear is widespread, among Bultmann's critics and those who see the new quest as sharing his methodological approach, of so evaporating the Jesus of Galilee and Jerusalem that His place is taken in a theological schema by a cipher, a symbol, a formula, or an idea, dignified as it may be by a title like the "Christ-event" or "metahistorical reality."

E. Lohmeyer finds fault with Bultmann's *Jesus* for this reason:

> It is one of the most characteristic features of Bultmann's book about Jesus that it dispenses not only with all biographical questions but also with all "personal" questions. . . . It is in a sense a Jesus-book without Jesus.[4]

The same criticism has been applied to Bultmann's later writings. N. A. Dahl claims that he runs the risk of a "kerygmatic-theological docetism" (*Kerygma und Dogma* [1955], p. 129). Zahrnt says that "the history of the earthly Jesus threatens to fall apart in his hands" (*op. cit.*, p. 89). He quotes Günther Bornkamm ("Mythos und Evangelium," *Theologische Existenz Heute*, Vol. 26 [1951], p. 18) to the effect that "Jesus Christ has become a mere saving act and ceases to be a person" (*ibid.*, p. 90), thereby indicating an awareness of the danger confronting any approach to the Gospels which is thorough-goingly form critical in the interests of a kerygmatic theology built simply on the *Dass* of Jesus' existence. Giovanni Miegge points out that Christ is reduced on that assumption to a mere *"punctum mathematicum,"* which has position but no magnitude (*Gospel and Myth in the Thought of Rudolf Bultmann* [Eng. tr., Richmond, Va.: John Knox Press, 1960], p. 128). In similar vein Joachim Jeremias finds that it is one of the many "grave dangers" in the keryg-

---

[4] Citation in W. G. Kümmel, *Das neue Testament, Geschichte der Erforschung seiner Probleme* (1958), p. 65, translated in Heinz Zahrnt, *The Historical Jesus* (New York: Harper, 1963), p. 89.

matic theology that we are *ex hypothesi* required to surrender the affirmation "the Word became flesh" and to dissolve "salvation history,"
God's activity in the man Jesus of Nazareth and in His message. "We
are in danger of Docetism, where Christ becomes an idea" (*The Problem of the Historical Jesus* [Philadelphia: Facet Books, Biblical series 13,
Fortress Press, 1964], p. 11).

But this preoccupation with sheer factuality invites us to a Christianity which is no more than a system of abstract ideas and philosophical
notions — in effect, to a gnosticized Christianity which has severed con-
nections with empirical history. Bultmann may protest that this is not
his intention and that his affirmation of Jesus' coming in the flesh and
His crucifixion preserve the kerygmatic-existential theology from the
error of Docetism. But Zahrnt has noted that Bultmann's sole insistence
on the mere *fact* of Jesus is meaningless.

> As though there could be a 'fact' without content! History is never
> made up only of the mere fact of an event, for this fact always includes
> the questions 'who?', 'how?', 'where?', 'when?', and 'what?' (*op. cit.,* p. 93).

A Preoccupation with Existentialism

The historiography of the Bultmannian and post-Bultmannian school
reflects a too one-sided preoccupation with existentialism. There are
two applications of this line of criticism which may be brought forward.

First, the type of human person whom the new questers envisage as
representing "modern man" is one who struggles for the meaning of existence. The image in which modern man is made is that of Augustine's
"existential man," — singling out but one element of Augustine's teaching — caught in the dilemma of discovering his true life over against
an inauthentic existence and torn by inner anxiety and conflict, and
obsessed by *cor inquietum* whose plaintive confession is, "I was at strife
with myself, and rent asunder by myself" (*Confessions,* viii. 10.22).

The New Testament is interpreted as providing the answer to such
an existential predicament. But the question has been raised whether
this interpretation both of man's need and the New Testament answer
does not unduly narrow the latter and force it on to a Procrustean bed
of existential philosophy.

> If it is interpreted as such, are there not many features in the message
> which, because they cannot be interpreted as part of the answer to man's
> existential question, will have to be eliminated? Bultmann repeatedly
> claims that demythologizing aims at interpreting (existentially) the New
> Testament message. May it not be that in practice, and despite this oft-
> repeated intention, he does eliminate those parts of the New Testament
> message which are not susceptible of existential interpretation? (R. H.
> Fuller, *The New Testament in Current Study* [New York: Scribner, 1962],
> p. 21).

If the Bultmannian interpreter adopts a pick-and-choose approach to the New Testament and discriminates between what fits his existential scheme and what does not, it is equally possible that his estimate of man's need is too restricted. Raymond E. Brown has written: "Is not the hypothetical man who encounters the Jesus of the new quest too much a creature of volition and anxiety in search of freedom and love, and too little a rational creature with an insatiable desire to know?" (*Catholic Biblical Quarterly*, Vol. 26 [1964], p. 25). He then goes on to offer a telling quotation from Herbert Butterfield's *Christianity and History* to the effect that there is a case for an academic history which is not all-consumed with providing the meaning of life.

Secondly, an existentialist interpretation of the Gospels falls into the same trap as the earlier quest of the historical Jesus, namely, that of constructing its own image of Jesus. T. W. Manson has pointedly remarked on this consequence of the adopting of an a priori approach to the New Testament:

> It is easy to laugh at those who, a couple of generations ago, saw in Jesus a good nineteenth-century liberal humanist with a simple faith in a paternal deity. It is less easy to see the joke when the Jesus of history is a twentieth-century existentialist, a kind of pre-existent "Heidegger" ("The Life of Jesus," in *The Background of the New Testament and its Eschatology*, ed. W. D. Davies and D. Daube, [Cambridge University Press, 1956], p. 220).

Too Narrow Criteria for Authenticity

Earlier we mentioned some of the criteria by which the post-Bultmannian scholars decide which sayings and incidents in the canonical Gospels may be accepted as genuine (see pp. 35, 36). But one can legitimately protest that these criteria for authenticity are too narrowly conceived. Raymond E. Brown justly objects: "The minimalest rules used to isolate authentic material in the Gospels would be applicable if the Gospels were written to deceive" (*op. cit.*, p. 27).

Besides this general comment on the hyper-skeptical approach adopted by the new questers, further comment may be made on the specific criteria which they have stated to be their working tools for the ascertaining of so-called "authentic material" in the evangelical narratives.

(A) Negatively, we may remark that "since Jesus was proclaiming a message himself, we would expect many of his words to have a kerygmatic ring. Since Jesus was a Jew, we would expect many of his words to have parallels in Jewish literature" (*ibid.*). The question here turns upon responsibility for the burden of proof. James Robinson wishes to place it squarely on the shoulders of those who maintain that we should accept statements attributed to Jesus unless it can be conclusively shown that they are inauthentic. But this skeptical approach to the Gospel data which implies that we are duty-bound to justify every saying of the incarnate Lord must be resisted.

(B) On a positive level, two important observations of Gospel hermeneutic must be registered. The one is that of Brown, who calls attention to the attested phenomenon that some of the *dicta* of characters in the Gospels (in particular, the Fourth Gospel — and of Jesus *par excellence*) contain what may be called the germinant principle. That is, statements made during the ministry of Jesus are presented with a signification appropriate to the ministry, yet also holding a much deeper meaning appropriate to a post-Easter insight. He cites John 1:29 as an example. We may illustrate also by the use of the term "salvation." When Jesus promised "salvation" to His responsive hearers (notably in Luke 19:1-10), obviously the connotation of the term was not equivalent to the post-Easter and Pauline sense; yet there is a continuity of development, so that what was offered in embryo to the contemporary auditors of Jesus' kingdom-preaching is fully grown and realized in the apostolic kerygma, as it is filled out with a new content derived from the passion and triumph of Christ. We should hesitate before concluding that the apostolic keyterm "salvation" is being read back into the earthly ministry on the ground that Jesus could not, in a pre-Easter situation, have made this offer.

T. W. Manson (whose methodology J. M. Robinson particularly berates) presents a second cogent insight.

> We too hastily assume that one of the main creative tasks of the Primitive Church was the putting back of its own ideas and beliefs into the mouth of Jesus; there is one fact worth pondering. We have considerable evidence of a collection of written words of one of the most productive minds of the Apostolic Age, St. Paul. All his letters were probably written before any of the Gospels. They abound in striking sayings, brilliant ideas, and definite expressions of belief — a magnificent quarry for any evangelist — yet how many Pauline sayings have been put into the mouth of Jesus? (*Bulletin of the John Rylands Library,* Vol. 27:2 [1943], pp. 12f. Cf. Manson's article in *Expository Times,* Vol. 53 [May 1942], pp. 248-251).

This paragraph calls our notice to the fact that *logia* of Jesus dealing with crucial issues in the apostolic Church, for example, circumcision and the Jew-Gentile debate, were not read back into Jesus' life and ministry.

The New Quest and the Fourth Gospel

The enigmatic nature of some of Jesus' kerygmatic teaching and the incidents which accompanied and exemplified it is clearly to be seen in John's Gospel. Germane texts are:

John 12:16: "His disciples did not understand this [the triumphal entry into Jerusalem] at first; but when Jesus was glorified, then they remembered that this had been written of him and had been done to him."

John 12:37: "Though he had done so many signs before them, yet they did not believe in him."

John 13:7: "Jesus answered him, 'What I am doing you do not know now, but afterward you will understand.' "

John 16:12, 13, 14: "I have yet many things to say to you, but you cannot bear them now. When the Spirit of Truth comes, he will guide you into all the truth . . . for he will take what is mine and declare it to you."

John 21:22, 23: "Jesus said to him, 'If it is my will that he remain until I come, what is that to you?' " etc. (a *logion* which was apparently misunderstood and needed an interpretative comment) .

The Fourth Gospel contains two further elements in addition to these instances of Jesus' words and actions which took on new significance in the post-Easter period: it professes to contain eyewitness testimony (19:35; 20:30; 21:24, 25) and it records the promise of the Holy Spirit whose function will be to awaken the disciples' memory to what the earthly Jesus said (14:26). It is true that eyewitness testimony in the Gospels has been recently re-evaluated and its value minimized (D. E. Nineham, *Journal of Theological Studies,* Vols. 9-11 [1958-1960]). But to overlook the presence of men and women in the apostolic Church whose personal reminiscences and recollections of what Jesus looked like, said, and did, we may safely presume, is an oversight or denial which must be corrected. The alternative is the assumption that the original disciples and followers of Jesus were spirited away after Pentecost — a possibility too ludicrous to contemplate!

It is also true that John's Gospel is dismissed, in the recent debate, as a piece of dogmatic *Tendenz* which makes no claim to historical veracity. Thus G. Ebeling writes of the Fourth Gospel: "a historical account in the strict sense is not expected of it" (*The Nature of Faith* [Eng. tr., New York: Collins, 1961], p. 50). Oscar Cullmann's discussion on 'L'évangile Johannique et l'historie du Salut' (*NTS,* 11:2, Jan. 1965) is a welcome reaction.

The new questers have as yet shown little appreciation of the so-called "new look" on the Fourth Gospel, as A. M. Hunter (*The Gospel According to John,* 1965), C. H. Dodd (*Historical Tradition in the Fourth Gospel,* 1963), J. A. T. Robinson (in *The Roads Converge* [ed. P. Gardiner-Smith], 1963), and R. E. Brown (*CBQ* 24, 1962, pp. 1-14) have outlined it. Brown comments: "A reintroduction of some of this Johannine material into the new quest would perhaps give body to its sketch of the historical Jesus" (*CBQ,* 26, 1964, p. 29) .

CONCLUSION

There are some slight indications that the men of the "new quest" are moving farther away from Bultmann's historical radicalism and apparent uninterest in the historical Jesus; and this determination not to lose contact with the historicity of Jesus has been applauded by other, non-Bultmannian participants in the debate. At the same time, others (like Conzelmann and Ogden) have advocated a more thorough-going application of the Bultmannian methodology and have disdained the aim of the new quest.

So far the chief contributors are scholars in continental Europe and America. British scholars tend to be more *pre*-Bultmann than either *pro* or *con*. And the witness of one such eminent British New Testament scholar, who wrote before the debate, but whose sympathy, convictions, and advocacy clearly point in one certain direction, may serve to round off this survey:

> The greatest problem of Christianity is not concerned with . . . ecclesiastical questions of orders or belief or ritual, but with the historical question of a person and a life. The supreme task of New Testament scholarship is to make Jesus Christ Crucified a living reality in the *thought* of our time, to bring out all that there is of fact and meaning in these three words: and the supreme task of Christian preaching is but little different . . . to make Jesus Christ Crucified a living reality in the *lives* of men and women in these days, to renew in them the awe and wonder, the faith and courage, which He inspired in men and women who knew Him in the days of His flesh (T. W. Manson in *Church Quarterly Review*, Vol. 11 [1933], p. 12, quoted by H. Anderson, *Jesus and Christian Origins*, p. 88).

THE AUTHENTICITY
AND AUTHORITY OF
REVELATION

Birger Gerhardsson

Birger Gerhardsson is Professor of Biblical Theology in the University of Lund, Sweden. He has been Assistant Professor of New Testament Exegesis in the University of Uppsala, Sweden. He is author of several books, the most recent of which has been translated into English under the title Tradition and Transmission in Early Christianity. *He holds the Th.D. degree from Uppsala.*

3. *Birger Gerhardsson*

THE AUTHENTICITY
AND AUTHORITY OF
REVELATION

T HE GOSPEL must be demythologized!" This demand has been
raised incisively and forcefully in our generation and the intense controversy that has broken out reveals how burning are the issues. What
attitude have members of the serving Church taken to the proposed program of demythologization (I take the liberty of using a summary term
for a phenomenon that has many facets) ? Many have seen in it a pattern
of treachery, retreat and the devastation of the Church's own terrain,
a kind of spiritual scorched-earth policy. It has been said that never before in the Church's history have Christian theologians gone as far as
this to meet doubt and denial. Other churchmen have looked on the
program of demythologization with more favor. They have interpreted
the new theology both as a symptom of the deep spiritual need of our
time and as an honest attempt to find salvation for distressed humanity.
In this connection, however, we may disregard the fact that certain pio-
neers of demythologization are themselves ministers of the Church. For
it is scarcely possible to regard them as *representative* churchmen. No
Church, *qua* Church, has accepted any of the recent proposals for radical
demythologization.

I. THE DIFFICULTIES OF "MODERN MAN"

No one will deny that from the point of view of the traditional church the demythologizers have courageously faced and tried to find a remedy for a very gloomy and perplexing ideological situation. "Modern man" (I recognize that this hackneyed and commonplace yet convenient term does not actually cover more than Western man and those who live in the Western fashion, and hence excludes the majority of the peoples of the modern world) is brought up in an ideological atmosphere which has no metaphysical perspectives. For him there remain no vivid or specific ideas of heavenly things and of the realities which in classical Christian belief exist beyond time and space. A couple of generations ago discussions were still carried on with concreteness and literal objectivity outside the framework of interior worldliness: God was a given factor in judging and planning. But our ideas of such things, once so concrete and vivid, have now faded. In the modern environment divine things appear unreal, and a person who is brought up under such conditions does not have a good foundation for understanding divine intervention or divine revelation.

Political and social developments ever since the Age of Enlightenment, accelerated and rendered more effective by the breakthrough of democracy, have brought about considerable change in our conception and experience of authority. Without casting any aspersions on democratic ideals, it may be noted that in the modern democratic community the individual does not get the kind of practical experience of how absolute authority works which he did in different types of community. The importance of this fact cannot be exaggerated. The need of authority seems to be one of the primitive elements of man's being. Psychological investigations have shown that submission is a characteristic of the human psyche: we need and seek to resort to the right authority. One might add that certain basic authoritative links still operate, at least in an elementary form — for example, the important link between the child and its parents. Yet even with these reservations we can still maintain that in the modern democratic community man does not have the same experience of absolute authority as he had in centuries past.

The Western European of today sucks in rationalism with his mother's milk. A scientific and critical skepsis is a basic constituent of our attitude towards existence from childhood. Reality presents itself to us as an object which our exploring and overestimating *ratio* criticizes and evaluates. Needless to say, this basic attitude does not have the best influence on such functions as belief and obedience, but shapes a psychological background contributory to modern man's difficulties in relation to the Christian message.

II. ATTEMPTS TO DEMYTHOLOGIZE THE
CHRISTIAN MESSAGE

When many modern theologians try to meet modern man halfway
with a demythologized gospel, we get a strong impression that modern
man's need is seen from within themselves and is a subjective experience.
The demythologizers themselves represent modern man and are trying
to find a gospel which is really a gospel *for him*. As we know, their program largely amounts to a demand that the Church abandon the categories of thought in which modern man no longer lives or understands
or finds acceptable, meaningful and right. Their abandonment of the
Church's historic positions is not being undertaken for tactical reasons;
it is not a strategic retreat in order to carry on a more effective struggle
for souls. It is a matter of fighting an honest and courageous battle for
spiritual liberation. It is ultimately the demythologizers' own struggle
for spiritual clarity and freedom that we are witnessing, a struggle that
they are carrying on on behalf of modern man.

The demythologizers' feeling of solidarity with modern man causes
them to go a great distance with him and to accept much of his rejection
of the traditional content of the Christian message. This appears most
clearly in the most radical and consistent representatives of the demythologizing school. Herbert Braun, Bultmann's pupil, contends that we
must now reject even the idea of the existence of God. Modern man,
we are told, cannot conceive of the existence of God. The Christian
message must therefore also rid itself of this little "mythological remnant," which even Bultmann found necessary to retain for practical
purposes in religious life. When the program is thus consistently represented, we clearly see its anthropocentric foundations. For the sake of
modern man the preacher is to rid his message even of the idea of the
existence of God.

If we turn to the new message that these theologians put in place
of the old, it is perhaps not as easy to see a genuine concern for the difficulties of modern man. The content of this new message discloses an
ideological apparatus that modern man can scarcely understand without
extensive study of both in philosophy and theology. What lies behind
all this? Does the new gospel require as its background a "new kind
of Old Testament" — that is, a certain philosophy? Is the Church to lay
an existentialist foundation for the purpose of going on to re-build the
Church with the new gospel?

Similar questions arise if we consider how the demythologizers conceive of the function of the message. In view of their identification with
the perspectives of modern man, we may ask whether it is realistic after
all to expect a radical decision *(Entscheidung)* from modern man. In biblical times a man's decision in relation to the divine Word appeared to be

an absolute and radical decision. This was natural at that time and in that environment; in the biblical documents indifference or differentiated attitudes did not play the same part as in modern society, in which relativism and compromise are important democratic virtues and in which the most common attitude in religious and other questions is want of zeal, oscillation between a few degrees of positiveness and a few degrees of negativeness. If we are now to go as far to meet modern man as the demythologizers are prepared to go, can we in that case require of him something so out of date as a radical decision?

III. THE REACTION IN TRADITIONAL CHURCH QUARTERS

No Church, *qua* Church, has yet acknowledged the new radical signals, for reasons that are easily understandable. A Church that wishes to speak in any way on behalf of *God* to men in all times and in different environments, and not to the isolated man in a certain temporal situation, cannot make an individualistic, anthropocentric and markedly time-bound philosophy the basis of its preaching. The need of the individual man surely holds an importance that must not be belittled in any way. But this need cannot be satisfied outside a framework that shows him wider prospects and that has fairly well settled his relations with his fellow-men, the community, tradition, creation and God. It is hardly likely that the right way in this case would *begin* with the individual and end with God. When in the past the Church has tried to apply theocentric arguments, man has perhaps been left out of account sometimes, but in principle this has not been due to lack of care about man.

How have traditional church quarters — I restrict myself to evangelical Christian Churches — reacted to the demythologizing program? It seems important to me to take note of this reaction. We are living through a phase of human history. The modern demythologized gospel is not being presented in a vacuum, nor on virgin soil. It is being proclaimed in a nominally *Christian* culture and is being proposed as a solution to the problem of the content and form of the *Christian* message in the actual circumstances of the present day. The question of its authenticity is inescapable. Even if — contrary to expectation — it is viewed as only a first step towards a more genuine Christian education, we must test its Christian legitimacy: in this case it will, sooner or later, be correlated with what the Church preaches, teaches, and maintains in other respects.

The first question we must then put is this: why have champions of traditional Christianity, on the whole, demurred so much in the presence of different forms of the demythologizing theology? To this question the demythologizers will presumably reply that tradition, conservatism, and habitual thinking play a great part in Church life. This answer implies, more precisely, that traditional Christianity lacks the support of "modern" men and is an evidence of backwardness: the sophisticated man, aware of modern realities, cannot any longer wholeheartedly share this faith.

This notion must be countered with another question: by what right should we suddenly belittle such important factors in the personal and social life of man as habit, custom, tradition, and so on? Although it has been said, and not without reason, that modern man has no traditions, this statement is a picturesque hyperbole, and not literally true. No man brought up by men and influenced by human cultural products in any form is quite free of tradition. This also applies to the Church as a historical phenomenon. All Churches live by a tradition to which they take slightly different official attitudes. This tradition is regarded in different ways as authoritative and binding. The Lutheran Church places a definite part of the tradition, namely, that which has a place in the Old Testament and the New Testament, in a class by itself, and regards this as the decisive source of revelation and also the critical standard for everything that the Church is to preach. The Church's creed is regarded as a genuine and authentic *summary* of the most essential contents of the biblical revelation.

If, now, a kind of Christian preaching that is new in content and form is to be presented in a culture that has such criteria (maintained and taught by the Church, forming a part, as more or less conscious ideology, of the thinking even of people who are not directly engaged in Church life), the authenticity and legitimacy of the new message must be shown in some way. At any rate, the person who is engaged in the Christian life — whether as layman or minister — must be given acceptable information as to the authenticity of the new message. A whole series of theoretical and practical questions presents itself. On what grounds is the new message described as Christian? What is its relation to the authorized canon and to the creed? What are we to imagine is the relation between the content of the traditional message and the new message? How is the transition to be made? And so on.

In my opinion, the growth of the radical theology of demythologization has been partly due to obscurity on one element in the viewpoint of the Reformed Churches, the restrictive view of tradition, which often regards it as a dubious competitor of the Scriptures. This invites a fateful uncertainty as to what tradition really is, how it functions, and what positive part it plays *de facto* in the Church's life, even in the life of our own Church. It is particularly important that the Protestant world now supplement the intense discussion of the authority and right use of the Bible with some energetic work on the questions of tradition: its essence, its different forms, its functions, its significance and its (relative) authority. Few phenomena have exposed an uncertainty on a definite point in the general Reformed view so revealingly as the modern Protestant theology of demythologization.

IV. THE QUESTION OF AUTHENTICITY

Thus the question before us is how a message is to be apprehended as authentic Christian preaching or, in classical terminology, how it is to be apprehended as authentic revelation. Many evangelical theologians sternly — indeed, indignantly — reject all attempts, in interpreting revelation, to speak of identity, authenticity, legitimacy, and so on. In this connection they are suspicious of attempts by the human spirit to seize upon the divine revelation by violent means, change its character, and counteract its real aims. Revelation is to be self-authenticating. It is to be *das ganz Andere,* which strikes us *senkrecht von oben her* and is as impossible to intercept as lightning. It is to be respected as something which cannot be fitted into human functions and phenomena such as doctrine, precept, tradition and so on, without losing its authenticity. The wind of the Spirit bloweth where it listeth, the prophets of God act in sovereign independence, and the task of man is "not to see and yet to believe."

It is at once clear that arguments of this type are intended to defend extremely important values. But although these arguments ultimately originate in mental constraint dictated by a philosophical schema they are so severely stylized that they permit of very gross abuse. Not every self-authenticating message necessarily comes from the source of all truth. The questions of legitimacy and authenticity are justified questions. They need not be taken as demands for a sign or a desire to base faith on seeing. They may originate either in the distressed person's simple need for the ability to distinguish God's voice from man's or (to speak in another style) in every man's duty to distinguish between the spirits.

Using the customary criteria, one has great difficulty classifying the message presented by the demythologizers as a genuine Christian message. The reform which they recommend is not of the same type as Jesus' institution of a new covenant nor is it like the Reformers' break with the Roman Catholic Church. Neither in early Christian times nor during the Reformation was the reform a matter of denying the realities expressed in the terms of the traditional message or the elements in the factual content of the message. On the other hand, this is what we are faced with in the demythologizing theology of today. God, heaven, life after death, the resurrection, are rejected as non-existent. They are replaced by a self-authenticating message with a quite different factual content than the biblical one: indeed, the truth of the content of the old message is denied.

Formerly, in the biblical and post-biblical Christian tradition, when new revelations were judged against the background of the old revelation, there was a basis for this judgment which was in part psychologically accessible. The new had broken through against the background of the old and was dependent on it, as new shoots are dependent on the old stem. Through this link with the old, the new was identifiable and understandable. The history of biblical revelation is not like a series of isolated gleams of light in a great darkness: rather, it is like a string of pearls, in which each pearl, retaining its own individuality and its specific part, is defined by its connection, deriving its importance from the background of what goes before and will itself in its turn play its part for that which follows after.

What we are concerned with are two simple, basic data: that the religious life is not the private experiences of isolated individuals but has a communal character, and that the individual factor consequently also forms part of a traditional context. It has definite relations to what was previously experienced and transmitted and may itself be a fermenting agent in the tradition, which then goes on to influence what comes later. Thus the transmitted fund of patterns, forms, categories, ideas, concepts, opinions, and terms plays a tremendous part in the life of the Church. To place oneself suddenly outside this is like becoming a branch without a trunk and without soil.

In his recent, very stimulating book, *Has Christianity a Revelation?* Gerald Downing has shown how diffusely Christian theologians use the concept of revelation, and argues that, if these dealings are to be understood in a biblical way, this concept is highly inappropriate as a summary of God's dealings with humanity. Thus Downing reinforces the criticism made by many other theologians of a one-sided intellectual concept of revelation. However, he has gone too far in this respect, due primarily to two factors. He does not pay sufficient attention to the part that tradition has played as a substratum for revelation, nor to the fact that the God of the Bible not only acts but *speaks*. When the Bible relates from time to time that God reveals Himself, that He speaks by the mouth of a prophet, and so forth, this is important partly as a special event and partly as a fermentation of tradition. When a phenomenon like this has been recorded, related again, transmitted as a sacred tradition or sacred writing, read, expounded, and used, it has taken on an importance for the tradition-transmitting people of the covenant which does not immediately appear if we analyze the particular passage. It is, for example, quite a fruitful study to examine how the New Testament regards and uses the Old Testament as God's Word, even to a new age. In my opinion particular importance must also be attached to the part which God's speech and God's words play in the biblical tradition. It is true that in the biblical view the divine Word has the character of an *act,* but this view must not be pushed too far, for the Word has a factual content. An articulated, verbalized revelation is presented in it. This means that we cannot go as far as we choose, in our desire to avoid an intellectual conception of revelation. It is significant that the modern efforts at demythologization are often supported by a denial that the biblical revelation has an apprehensible factual content.

The question of authenticity takes on its special significance when we abandon the comprehensive term "revelation" and concentrate on terms such as "gospel" and "kerygma." Here we have to do with terms which have denoted, ever since the early days of the Church, a message that is in part quite unambiguous and definite in content, an announcement that communicates, on the one hand, purely concrete facts (a man was tormented, executed, buried) and, on the other, an interpretation of these facts that is fixed as regards its essential content. Here our question becomes critical: how can a message which does not agree even in this essential factual minimum with the traditional Christian message — indeed, perhaps simply denies this essential factual content directly — be described as a gospel and be presented and understood as a Christian message? That A must be A is not an out-of-date theological fancy that the situation of modern man can change; it is a requirement of identification, which is both logically and psychologically inescapable.

As soon as we concentrate on the essential part of the New Testament message, we also discover another thing: the question of authenticity is finally connected with the question of truth. I shall not discuss here the complicated question of the relationship between revelation and history. But one thing seems to me to be indisputable: the essential part of the traditional Christian message is connected to a definite part of history (Jesus, His person, speech, acts, and destiny as a whole) and is *dependent* on this historical substratum. The Christian message — in its classical form — purports to be *based* on this substratum. It will therefore be not only unintelligible but also invalid if the essential parts of its historical basis are shown to be unhistorical (cf. I Cor. 15) or if they are interpreted in a completely new way. It is symptomatic that most of the demythologizers reject with a radical aprioristic skepsis both the extraordinary features in the events of

Jesus' life and the possibility of getting at Jesus' own view of Himself and His work with any exactness.

What I have been maintaining here is not that the Christian message must be capable of verification or of being proved. I have argued only that a message which is represented as a Christian message must in some way make a positive appeal to the existing criteria of belief. It must demonstrate its basic agreement with the essential factual content of the biblical message. When this demand for authenticity is presented, it discloses the definitive difference between the modern demythologizing message and the Church's previous attempts to translate its message into new terms and lines of thought. In these attempts at translation the Church desired to preserve the message's factual identity with the original. Since the new theologians dispense with this requirement, the result is not an authentic translation but a radical re-interpretation.

V. QUESTION OF AUTHORITY

To inquire about the authenticity of the new message is also to inquire about its authority. "Authority" is also a term that belongs to the conceptual sphere that many theologians firmly reject. But some profound theological work is both necessary and urgent in this present situation, work devoted to elucidating the essence, the different forms, the ways of functioning, and the legitimacy of *authority* in an evangelical Church.

In this brief essay I shall only set down a few simple reflections. When the Christian Church presents its message, which is in accordance with the Bible and the creed, it claims to speak and act with absolute and divine authority. This idea — that revelation has divine authority and that a correct reproduction of it also has this authority — is not a secondary idea in the Church's history. We see clearly the authority of the revelation itself and the authority of its mediator in the Old Testament tradition and against this background we encounter the same phenomena in the New Testament. The early Christian sources speak of Jesus' *exousia* (a term which corresponds to the Hebrew *reshut*, meaning legitimate authority, competence, powers, might). The apostles also appear with *exousia,* an authority which the early Christians were convinced was bestowed by the risen, divine Lord. The Church has this authority to fall back upon: it calls itself "the Church of Christ, built upon the foundation of the prophets and the apostles." I shall not discuss here the question of the relationship between formal and factual authority, between the authority of the messengers and the authority of the message. I shall only call attention to the fact that the category of authority has been connected with the Christian message from the beginning. When some demythologizers dismiss this category with a reference to such catchwords as secondary legalization, *Frühkatholizismus,* and the like, they seem to me to be again removing revelation from the history of the covenant, the history of salvation, and, indeed, history as a whole. The Church has still to take note of the authority of the divine revelation: in what way is she herself bound by this authority? How is she herself to maintain the authority of revelation, so that her message or, more precisely, the message of her Head retains its power to create faith and give what it is intended to give?

VI. CONCLUSIONS

What has been said above can be summarized as follows. No one should make light of the Church's duty to face modern man's difficulties honestly, courageously, and clearly. No one should make light of the task of bringing the Christian message to modern man in such a form that it will be not only understood but may also be experienced as something living and powerful, coming with real deliverance, guidance and judgment. But the Christian Church cannot regard modern man's problems as the problems of the existence of an isolated individual. She has to bring to men — not an isolated man nor a certain type of man in a certain situation — a message that is partly fixed as regards its content and that cannot today be something *entirely different* from what it was yesterday. If this message is to be presented as Christian, its Christian authenticity and authority must be preserved. Now as formerly, we can in this connection do nothing more than demonstrate that the current message agrees with the decisive revelation in Jesus Christ. This sets definite *limits* to the attempts to "demythologize" the Christian message.

Man's difficulties constitute only one of the poles of the stress-filled world of Christian theology. The other is the God who speaks and acts in Jesus Christ. That the Christian message at the present day shall mediate the given revelation in a genuine way is first and foremost a demand which is inherent in the revelation itself in its character of authentic and authoritative divine self-communication. But it is also a demand that is dictated by the conditions of human existence. Man — traditional Christian or "modern" — is dependent on community and tradition. From these sources he derives — consciously or unconsciously — his religious criteria of identification and categories of interpretation, among other things. One of the criteria which everyone has and must have in relation to a Christian message is that it harmonize in an acceptable manner with the essential passages in the New

Testament, as these passages have been mediated to us by a long tradition, a tradition on which the "Christian" culture of the present century is in fact dependent.

To say this is to say simultaneously that we cannot take the situation and conditions of modern *secularized* man as they are and use them as a principle of elimination when we go to the Bible and the creed. Now as formerly, the Church must try to alter undesirable conditions by instruction and education and by its way of ordering its own existence. Even if a cultural struggle should be necessary, the Church is bound to accept the fact. For a Christian Church has no grounds for helping modern man to manage without God. She must, it is true, seek out the lost sheep, but she must lead it to a shelter that is more secure than the rocky road with its haunts of robbers.

JESUS CHRIST,
THE CENTER OF HISTORY

Adolf Köberle

*Adolf Köberle became Karl Heim's successor on the theological faculty
in the University of Tübingen, Germany, in 1939, having previously
taught systematic theology at Basel. He has written numerous volumes,
among them* Rechtfertigung und Heiligung, *which has been translated
into English as* The Quest for Holiness. *He studied at the Universities
of Munich, Erlangen, and Tübingen.*

JESUS CHRIST, THE CENTER OF HISTORY

U NLIKE THE FLOWERS, which live out their cycles under God's sun with no concept of time, man measures his life in hours. He knows of birth and death, of past, present, and future. Just as surely as man is a historical being and not simply an aspect of nature, he can orient himself to his historical existence in various ways.

Anyone who has studied Indian religious philosophy knows that time is insignificant to the East Asian mind. To know at what point of time one's life emerges and then fades again is of no interest or importance, since, presumably, he can be equally near to God at any and all points of time. Anywhere, any time, in mystical ascent man can break through and unite his tiny being with the Absolute. Goethe expresses the same conviction in *Faust*: "Everything ephemeral is but a symbol." The same attitude confronts us in Fichte, the philosopher, when he says, "Only the metaphysical saves us — not the historical." According to this view, a historical event can illuminate a truth, but it cannot be its basis.

In the biblical witness of the prophets and apostles a totally different view of time and history confronts us. Here time is not seen as a circular sea, anywhere on whose shores man can have equally wonderful visions of God. Time is rather like a stream that constantly pushes forward until through the power of God it has reached its goal in the consummation of all things.

This view allows for times when nothing significant happens. But events may also occur that impel the current of history forward. But whenever such an event has occurred, everything thereafter is different. It is then impossible to ignore the event or to turn back the clock as if this had not happened. The freeing of the children of Israel from Egyptian bondage, the giving of the law by Moses and Aaron, the institution of judges and kings, the destruction of the temple at Jerusalem by Nebuchadnezzar, the Babylonian exile of the defeated people, the return of the Jews to their old homeland — these are all to be seen as stations along the road that have become of crucial significance in the relationship of the chosen people to God.

The same historical consciousness confronts us in the life of Jesus. He says, "My time, my hour, is not yet come." And again that mysterious phrase that can refer both to the cross and to His glorious exaltation at the right hand of God: "And I, *when I* be lifted up, will draw all men unto me" (John 12:32).

Paul gives the historical event of Jesus Christ cataclysmic importance. He says, "But when the fulness of the time was come, God sent forth his Son, made of woman, made under the law, to redeem them that were under the law, that we might receive the adoption of sons" (Gal. 4:4, 5). Because God in the life of Christ intervened mightily in history, the letter to the Romans is able to assert and proclaim the historical juncture — "the night is far spent, the day is at hand." The old world order is shaken in its foundations; God's new eon has dawned and will prove triumphant.

However one may interpret Luke's understanding of the Areopagus address, this message is undoubtedly sustained by the Pauline consciousness of history. He calls to the Athenians, "And the times of this ignorance God winked at; but now commandeth all men everywhere to repent: because he hath appointed a day, in the which he will judge the world in righteousness by that man whom he hath ordained" (Acts 17:30ff.).

We should realize that we must choose between the two views of time that confront us. On the one hand is the approach which claims that it makes no difference in our relationship to God what kind of events have occurred in history. The Indian mind and idealism skim over the whole of time. To them every hour of history is equally immediate, equally near to God. On the other hand is the approach which sees God's acting in history as crucial to our certainty of God and to our fellowship with Him. Unless we orient ourselves according to the great acts that God performed for the salvation of the world, we are left to ourselves and find no access to the eternal Thou.

The struggle between these two fundamentally different views of time will never end. The proud spirit will always maintain that he can grasp the Absolute with equal immediacy at all points of history, and that he is in no way dependent on any particular historical events for the appreciation of truth. But there have always been those who have gratefully acknowledged that if God had not acted in the manger and in the cross, in the resurrection and ascension of Christ, we would be groping in the dark for the knowledge of God and would not know how to free ourselves from the Evil One who ensnares us.

Those living in 1900 may have found access to the biblical understanding of time more difficult than it is for us today. At that time history did not have the contingency, the significance, that it has for our generation. It was much easier then to live without a historical frame of reference, because the events of those days did not pressure or threaten humanity.

How different it is today! We have had to experience and accept historical events that have changed everything, events we cannot repeal. The year 1914 was such a caesura. Since then peace has vanished from the earth. Or recall the battle of Stalingrad. At that time the Russian giant became conscious of its power, and now it will not cease to cause unrest among the nations. But why are men willing to attach significance only to grim and painful historical events, but not to the new beginning that God has provided in Jesus Christ for the salvation of the family of man?

I. SALVATION HISTORY DIFFERS FROM MYTH

The history of salvation that is directly linked to the name of Jesus is fundamentally different from the world of myth. By its very nature myth is without historical context; it describes events of nature that occur and recur in cycles. One cannot ask when Demeter, Isis and Osiris, or Balder lived, or where they lived. As soon as one begins this sort of inquiry, the reported happenings slip through one's fingers. When in mythology a god dies and is resurrected, a historical fact is not being proclaimed; rather a cosmic event is being suggested. How different it is in the gospel! There we find precise data as to time and place. Our attention is directed to Palestine, the land of the Jews, at the time that "there went out a decree from Caesar Augustus, that all the world should be taxed. And this taxing was first made when Cyrenius was governor of Syria."

This is why the name of Pontius Pilate was expressly included in the Apostles' Creed. One might wonder if too much honor was not being done to this Roman administrator, especially since his role in the passion story is a dubious one. But this naming of names is of crucial importance. It indicates that Jesus bled on a real cross and that the occurrence is attested by the records of world history.

II. THE CENTER OF HISTORY

If, as suggested, historical events are indispensable to our life with God, why must it be the life of Jesus in particular that we proclaim as the center of history? After all, we also know when and where Buddha, Moses, and Mohammed lived. Is it not rather arbitrary to single out this historical event above all others?

Sören Kierkegaard writes in his *Training in Christianity* that this must be admitted as *the* stumblingblock — that in the Christian faith the accent of eternity should be placed upon this one point of history. Human reason, which has become so dominant in Western civilization since Lessing, will always take offense at this, especially when we consider that this accent of eternity seems connected with a life that lacks all external signs of glory.

How do we get by this offense? Kierkegaard answers that we must be guided by the two admonitions of Jesus: "Blessed is he that is not offended in me," and "Follow me." Jesus Himself had anticipated the possibility that men would be offended by His claim to the throne, His claim to be the bearer and bringer of God's truth, peace, and life. Jesus knows that this offense can be conquered only by way of discipleship, by way of the practical test. One must surrender one's life to the life in Christ. One must set foot on this bridge joining time and eternity in order to find out that the bridge will bear his weight. John's witness to Christ expresses this relationship in the words: "If any man will do his will, he shall know of the doctrine, whether it be of God, or whether I speak of myself" (7:17).

If one looks at the life of Jesus only as an observer, unwilling to explore it personally, he will see nothing but a devout Israelite who bled to death in his struggle with the religious officialdom. The early Protestant fathers rightly taught that man needs the testimony of the Holy Spirit, the *testimonium spiritus sancti in cordibus,* in order to recognize in Mary's child, in the teacher of the Sermon on the Mount and of the parables, in the form of the crucified one, Him whom God made unto us "wisdom and righteousness and sanctification and redemption."

III. THE SIGNIFICANCE OF CHRIST'S COMING

Under the impress of the works of Jesus, the apostles and their followers testified to three things that occurred through the entrance of this life into time, and which, as a consequence, must be proclaimed and spread abroad.

The early Christian message concentrated on this proclamation: the eternal God whom no man has seen or can see, who lives in a light that no man can approach, has unveiled Himself and, in a manifestation of grace, has become audible, visible, tangible. In Colossians Christ is called "the image of the invisible God" (1:15). In Hebrews He bears the seal of majesty — "the brightness of his glory" (1:3). In Matthew Jesus' witness to Himself confronts us — "neither knoweth any man the Father, save the Son, and he to whomsoever the Son will reveal him" (11:27), and in John, "he that hath seen me hath seen the Father" (14:9). In contrast to Gnostic syncretism, it is said of Christ, "For it pleased the Father that in him should all fulness dwell" (Col. 1:19). In Jesus Christ it was not simply a ray of the light of the glory of God that penetrated time. God turned Himself fully toward man in this life that was full of grace; thus it seems devious and superfluous to look elsewhere for the fulness of the knowledge of God.

There is a kind of pantheism of nature and history that is pervaded by the proud conviction that God can be preceived always and anywhere — in every heartbeat of life, in every event that echoes throughout history. So long as a man cherishes this patently world-bound piety, he will be unable to realize what has really been given us in Christ. But whoever has once been terrified by the abysmal depths of nature — a nature that is indifferent to our personal suffering, whoever shudders before the countless unsolved riddles that history asks but never answers, learns to be grateful that in the vast darkness of this world a light shines in the dark so that we may become children of light.

To the message of God's incarnation in the Logos become flesh, the New Testament adds the word of reconciliation. Jesus was the Saviour of the lost, those gone astray, the fallen. He did not separate Himself from them; He associated with them and broke bread with them. In order to make possible this forgiveness, and for the sake of this alone, Jesus had to go the way of the cross. If He had demanded more asceticism than the late-Judaic merit-system religion as in the case of the desert monastic community of Qumran, no one would have taken Him to court. But He who called the weary and heavy-laden unto Himself, who rebuked the pious in Israel because they could not be happy when the door of the father's house opened to welcome the prodigal son — He had to die, if the whole religious merit and wage system was to be kept from tottering. To His last breath, Jesus loved people with this divine love that sought sinners. On the cross He still prayed for His *enemies,* He received the lost thief into His fellowship and wrested his life from hell.

Man may never presume to say on his own: God won't be too meticulous about our guilt and shame (*Pardonner, c'est son metier* — forgiveness is His business — as Frederick the Great, borrowing from

Voltaire, mockingly remarked). To fall into the hands of the living God is a fearful thing. It is only through the word and work of Christ that we receive the assurance that if our heart condemn us, God is greater than our heart.

The cross as symbol is of ancient and profoundly meaningful tradition. Its ascending line is interrupted, severed, by a crossbeam. The cross as symbol tells us that life does not come close to fulfilling all our wishes, that much of what we desire will not be granted us. But the cross as symbol will not help us when the terrors of conscience overtake us in the hour of death. Nothing can comfort us then but the look at Him who on a cross of history bore the burden of the world's guilt.

The Swedish theologian Gustaf Wingren has rightly pointed out, in numerous publications taking vigorous issue with Karl Barth, that the human predicament is not only that we have removed ourselves from God and hence no longer know who and what God is. The greatest need of our existence is due to the fact that we are imprisoned under the despotic rule of a power that is against God and that will not release us. Thus we have not fully understood the implications of the coming of Jesus into history if we glorify Him only as the revealer of the Father. Above and beyond this, Jesus must be recognized and proclaimed as the Redeemer who has appeared to destroy the works of the devil.

The whole life of Jesus was a dramatic conflict with God's adversary. Jesus exults in His spirit when He can free bound men from their bondage. He thus sees Satan falling from his throne. But He also knows that the enemy will persecute Him and follow Him into the night of death. The early Christians, at any rate, saw the death of Christ as the decisive battle that was fought and won against all the powers and forces of the underworld, and in His resurrection they saw the divine confirmation of this triumph.

It is of course true, as Romans 6 states, that Jesus' suffering, dying, burial, and resurrection are to be realized and appropriated in the Christian life. But the prerequisite to this consummation-after-the-event is always that the world-shaking historical events actually took place. If Jesus did not live, if He did not die on Golgotha, if the crucified one was not resurrected, then all existential appropriation of these things is left hanging in air. How is it possible, therefore, to disparage the "facts of salvation," to totally compress the objective occurrence into its subjective consummation in the life of the believer, when everything depends upon the fact that faith has firm ground beneath it because God has acted in Christ as the Saviour?

IV. CHRIST AND THE FUTURE

When by faith we comprehend the life of Jesus as the sovereign God of history breaking into time, this point in time not only takes on the character of the absolute, but also from this midpoint gleams of comprehension must fall on and illuminate other points of time in both directions. The Christ-event becomes the center of history, which has its beginnings in time, and strives toward the final attainment of its goal.

In the light of Christ, the Old Testament becomes the "dawn of world redemption." It began when Abraham was taken out of a heathen environment, out of a world of polytheism and astrology, that he might heed a God who justifies the guilty and raises the dead. Like Abraham in his time, the nation born of his seed is, through judgment and grace, brought by God into a holy discipline. It is taught by command and rite, it is prepared by prophetic preaching for the day of days, when the dayspring from on high will appear to all people for salvation. But when Christ came to His own, to those who were waiting for Him, they did not receive Him. They cast Him out of the camp and made a cross for Him.

Since then (another temporal designation!) the secret burden of the unrecognized Messiah troubles the soul of the Jewish people. If Jesus as the center of history is left out of the picture, the history and destiny of this people remain an insoluble riddle. Why are the Jews still here when all the other peoples of their original surroundings have long been carried away by the currents of time? Why was this particular people privileged to give to humanity, through Moses and the prophets, a set of lofty moral principles that are without precedent? Does it not have something to do with the fact that a divine mystery hangs over this people — a mystery that can be illuminated only by the gospel?

But the light by which we may interpret history falls on the future, as well as on the past, when we contemplate the hour that has become the starting point for the Christian reckoning of time. Jesus always saw His entrance into time as a mighty, God-wrought beginning that will and must go on until God is all in all. He can say, "I am come to send fire on the earth; and what will I, if it be already kindled?" In Ephesians, Christ is called the cornerstone that God has laid with the immovable significance of eternity in the swaying foundations of this world. On this foundation stone rest the testimonies of the prophets and apostles like mighty hewn rocks. And now we too are challenged to let ourselves be incorporated as living stones in this temple, upheld by others and, in turn, upholding still others, until the whole is built up to perfection; in this Christ is not only the foundation and cornerstone, bearing the whole weight, but also the keystone, joining and crowning the whole.

Whoever opens his eyes to this future horizon becomes a man of hope. Of course the New Testament knows the vertical look as well: Lift up your hearts! John's Gospel is especially rich in statements that, in fullness of faith, anticipate the *eschaton*. "Verily, verily, I say unto you, He that heareth my word, and believeth on him that sent me, hath everlasting life, and shall not come into condemnation; but is passed from death unto life" (5:24). Yet in the present anticipation of ultimate salvation we must not forget how much is still pending, how much creation still groans under the stress of the ephemeral, how far away we are, in this world of conflict and war, from the new heaven and the new earth in which righteousness dwells, and where death will be no more, nor suffering, nor crying, nor pain.

For this reason it is necessary to overcome the nonhistorical trend of thought which, as our present age discloses all too clearly, constantly seeks to dominate not only philosophy but also theology. Today it is popular to say that faith is the historical event *per se*. The idea here is that faith is always expressed and consummated in obedience to the call of concrete historical events. That is certainly true. But it is forgotten that faith is capable of bearing this historical role in the present only when it lives by the power of the divine acts through which Jesus Christ changed history.

THE LAST DAYS
IN THE BIBLE
AND QUMRAN

R. Laird Harris

R. Laird Harris is Associate Dean of the Faculty and Professor of Old
Testament in Covenant Theological Seminary, St. Louis, Missouri.
He has also served Trinity Evangelical Divinity School in Deerfield,
Illinois, as visiting lecturer. He holds the Ph.D. from Dropsie College.

5. *R. Laird Harris*

THE LAST DAYS
IN THE BIBLE
AND QUMRAN

THE PHRASE "last days" or a near equivalent is used half a dozen times in the New Testament. The present age of Christ's ministry is called the "last days" in Hebrews 1:1. Pentecost is recognized as a phenomenon of the "last days" in Acts 2:17. The scoffers who deny Christ's second coming are recognized as typical of the "last days" in II Peter 3:3. From such verses it would appear that the early Church considered that it was living in the "last days."

Two conclusions have been drawn from this circumstance. First, many have thought that the early Church was in error. Regard for the Lord became so great after the experiences in which men thought they saw the risen Saviour that — so it is asserted — they attached to Jesus the expectations of apocalyptic Jewish thought. They felt that Christ would appear very soon and therefore that this present world would soon come to an end. They were living in the last days. It might be debated whether their apocalyptic expectation was derived directly from Christ, from alleged resurrection appearances, from mystery religions, from Jewish apocalypticism or some other source. But in any event, their error at long last became obvious and the later generations — though not until the third century — spiritualized these teachings and turned to the humdrum business of canon, creed, and details of church organization.

A more conservative point of view accepts the thesis that the early Church held itself to be living in the last days in the sense that there are no times between this era and the time of Christ's return. This was the view of Calvin, and many others have followed him. We are still in the "last days." We just do not know how long the last days will continue. It is not necessary to hold that the early Church lived in a constant fever of messianic expectation. Certain verses of the New Testament can be cited (the Parable of the Talents) to show that the present interval was to be some length of time. But the attitude of sober expectancy is nonetheless enjoined. Paul at Thessalonica rebuked a fanatic apocalypticism that led to neglect of daily duties. But no one could charge Paul with a denial of the doctrine of the second coming of Christ.

The present author is not satisfied with either of these conclusions. There is much truth in the second one, it is grantèd. The early Church did expect the second coming of Christ. It did not set any dates. Indeed, Jesus Himself forbade that (Mark 13:32; Acts 1:7). Nor did it teach an immediacy that it later had to retract. Peter, for instance, must first die and the aged John might well have to finish his course likewise (John 21:19-23). But to call this whole period which might stretch to 1900 years (and possibly many more) the "last days" seems to empty the term "last" of normal significance. Are these the "last days?" Is another interpretation of this phrase not more accurate?

There is another and deeper question. Was the New Testament Church just another apocalyptic Jewish sect that, having a more worthy founder and better ideals, succeeded where others had failed? What is the relation of this apocalyptic expectation to that of the Dead Sea community of Qumran? If they also thought themselves to be living in the last days we should possibly want to strip off this apocalypticism from our faith and call it a part of the early Jewish world view which we can well do without. We must examine the usage of the phrase "last days" in the Qumran material and in other intertestamental works.

Inasmuch as both the New Testament and the intertestamental literature are heavily dependent on the Old Testament, it will be helpful for us to note briefly the usage of these phrases in the Hebrew and their rendition in the Greek translation.

I. THE OLD TESTAMENT USAGE OF THE "LAST DAYS"

The major Hebrew equivalent of our phrase seems literally to mean "the end of the days" (*'aḥᵉrîṯ hayyāmîm*). The meaning of the Greek phrase is very similar. A standard Hebrew lexicon remarks that it is "a prophetic phrase denoting the final period of history so far as the speaker's perspective reaches; the sense thus varies with the context, but it often equals the ideal or Messianic future" (Brown, Driver, and Briggs, *Hebrew and English Lexicon* [New York: Mifflin, 1907], p. 31).

This comment is still a rather good summary of the picture, as we may see from various examples. Note that the meaning depends considerably upon the horizon of the speaker. The days spoken of are really "latter days" in comparison to the present. And the translation is much more commonly given as "latter days" in the King James Version than "last days."

To give examples: In Genesis 49:1 Jacob predicts events in the "last days." The tenth verse doubtless predicts the Davidic dynasty and even in Qumran it was given a messianic interpretation (J. M. Allegro, "Further Messianic References in Qumran Literature," *Journal of Biblical Literature,* Vol. 75 [1956], p. 175). But at the most it need only refer to the first coming of Christ. And much of the chapter merely refers to the settling of the Israelite tribes. The Revised Standard Version is probably correct in the translation "in days to come."

In Deuteronomy 4:30; 8:16; 31:29; 32:20, 29, the references are all general and simply refer to future experiences which Israel should expect. Apostasy brings judgment, but repentance results in renewed blessing. The translations of both the King James and Revised Standard Versions recognize that the meaning is the indefinite "future."

Even in Daniel 10:14 the phrase "latter days" (AV and RSV) is not exclusively eschatological. The prophecy runs on through the historical portion of chapter 11 to the events of tribulation and resurrection of chapter 12. But the prophecy includes three kings of Persia, Alexander and his successors, their various struggles and then the "vile person" of 11:21 who may indeed be eschatological. It would seem that the words "future days" would be an adequate translation. In Daniel 2:28, 29, 45, the translation of an equivalent Aramaic phrase by "hereafter" or a similar expression is surely correct.

There are several passages where the classical interpretation assigns the phrase "last days" to the glorious messianic age. They are Isaiah 2:2; Micah 4:1; Ezekiel 38:8, 16 and Hosea 3:5.

There are other passages where there is room for difference of interpretation. Jeremiah 48:47 and 49:39 need mean no more than that in some day future to Jeremiah Moab and Elam would be re-established. Note that the same thing is said of Ammon in Jeremiah 49:6 using the expression "afterward." Also, Jeremiah 23:20-30:24 may include a reference to messianic days or it may be restricted to the near future when the optimistic predictions quoted from the false prophets shall have been shown to be cruelly false.

We may summarize by saying that these Old Testament phrases are not to be taken too technically. Sometimes they refer to the near future of the nation. Sometimes they apparently refer to the glorious messianic era. Sometimes (as in Prov. 5:4) they merely refer to the future results of sin in the life of an individual. The phrase seems to mean "the future." All eschatology of course is future. But all of the prophets' future was not eschatology. We should therefore be slow to allege an active apocalypticism based on such phraseology.

It should be noted, in passing, that this phraseology is not limited to any one book or type of literature. It is used once in the visions of Daniel, but also appears scattered through the prophecies of Jeremiah and Isaiah as well as in the exhortations of Deuteronomy and the counsels of Proverbs. The phrases supply no ground for distinguishing between the attitudes of prophecy and apocalyptic. Apocalyptic had its visions and symbols, but so did Joseph and Balaam, Amos and Ezekiel. The claim to predict the future is characteristic of Old Testament prophecy as well as of apocalyptic.

II. THE NEW TESTAMENT AND THE "LAST DAYS"

Several New Testament passages have already been alluded to. In Hebrews 1:2 the phrase "in the last days" is not used in an eschatological context. The former days of the Old Testament prophets are mentioned. These present days of Christ's revelation are merely the latter days in comparison to those. There is no hint that "these last days" will soon end.

Likewise James 5:3 concerns the "speaker's perspective," as was said above. The rich men were heaping up treasure for retirement, and the warning reminds us of the references in Proverbs to the end of the unprepared man.

Speaking of a salvation prepared for disclosure "in the last time" I Peter 1:5 uses the singular. It is probable that we have here the common usage: our full salvation waits for the day of Christ's return. I Peter 1:20, on the other hand, speaks of the current period, the time of Christ's present manifestation, as the "last days" (plural). Here, as in Hebrews 1:2, a contrast appears between the former times and the present. Christ in His pre-existence was foreordained, but in these "latter days" is made manifest. The second coming and judgment are not in the immediate context. The term the "last" days, therefore, need not denote the whole church age as many commentators allege.

It is often said that II Timothy 3:1 implies that the perilous times then upon the Church were a sign of the end — or that the perilous times of today are such a sign. But does the context refer at all to eschatology? Rather, according to Matthew 24:6-13 perilous times may be taken as a sign that the end is not yet! Perilous times in this world are all too common. Is not this rather a prediction by Paul of what the Church could expect in future times? The same thing can be said of a

similar phrase in I Timothy 4:1. Paul here was not speaking apoca-
lyptically, but very practically. The "last days" here do not betray any
active expectation of a global end, but a sober facing of the future prospects of the Christian Church.

Even in II Peter 3:3 and the verse in Jude 18 which depends on it,
the presence of scoffers of the "last days" does not imply that the last
days were soon to come or were already here. Peter predicted that the
scoffers would be present. But the promise of Christ's coming is said to
be sure even though long delayed. In Jude the phrase is not even linked
to eschatology. In Peter there is almost the reverse of apocalyptic: a fiery
judgment is sure even though it may be long delayed.

The passage in Acts 2:17 has been mentioned already. Pentecost
fulfills Joel's prophecy of the "last days." But curiously, the phrase "last
days" is not found in Joel either in the Hebrew or in the Septuagint.
Joel simply prophesies what will come "afterward." The phrase "last
days" in Acts is an interpretive variant given by Peter. It could mean
that Peter understood Pentecost to be an event near to Christ's return.
But since he says nothing else in the chapter about Christ's return, it is
perhaps more natural to hold that Peter merely designated these New
Testament days as latter days in contrast to the earlier revelation of
Joel. We might favor the translation of the Joel quotation: "It shall
come to pass in a future time, saith God. . . ."

The above passages are all distinct from a series of verses in the
Gospel of John. Here, and only here, the singular is used, "the last day."
John 6:39, 40, 44, and 54 clearly speak of the last day, the final day when
Christ will raise the dead to everlasting life. The context is devoid of
the extensive symbolism thought to characterize apocalyptic. It is simply
a straightforward assertion of the coming day of resurrection. There is
no claim that the day is near at hand, unless the presence of Jesus on
that day were thought to limit it to His lifetime. That would seem to be
an unnecessary limitation in view of His claims in the adjacent verses
33, 38, 46, 50, and elsewhere. John 11:24 repeats the teaching of the resurrection at the "last day," and John 12:48 speaks of the judgment day
in the same words.

Interesting light is thrown on this Johannine usage by John 7:37
which mentions the last day of the feast of tabernacles. The phrase, using
the singular, refers to the last day in the context of the discourse. In
speaking of the feast, it refers to the seventh and final day.

The one New Testament verse which does not fit the above pattern
is I John 2:18: "Little children, it is the last hour." We are reminded of
a section in the Gospels, John 5:21-29, with its references to a present
"hour" or resurrection (v. 25) and to a future "hour" (v. 28). Meyer
gives extensive arguments along with citations from the older commen-

tators to show that the present resurrection is spiritual and is illustrative
of that future hour of literal resurrection of those who are in the graves.
He does remark that the present "hour" extends throughout this whole
church period during which men are spiritually being raised to life.
That may not be necessitated by the text, for the expression "the hour
is coming and now is" could refer only to the commencement of that
period.

"Hour" in the general sense of time usually implies a short time.
For this reason Huther (in the Meyer Commentary) argues strongly
that I John 2:18 is plainly mistaken in its expectation that the second
coming would be very soon. Other verses such as Matthew 16:28 and
24:34 are also now confidently alleged as indicating this same error. It
is beyond our scope to deal with these verses. We remark only that the
phrase "shall not taste of death" in Matthew 16:28 may as well be interpreted of a spiritual immortality as in John 8:52. And Matthew 24:
34 can certainly be held to teach that the Jewish race will not pass away
until Christ's return.

To return to I John 2:18, it is noteworthy that John uses the singular,
so that no direct comparison is to be made with the phrase "last days"
found elsewhere. May we not simply agree that in his old age, observing
the problems into which the Church had fallen, John was actually expressing his hope of the early coming of Christ. The references to anti-
christs as equivalent to false prophets (I John 4:1, 3) remind us strongly
of the book of Revelation. In Revelation 13:11-18 a beast is described
in terms unmistakably in masquerade of Christ the Lamb of Revelation
14:1-5. This beast is thus pictured as an antichrist, though not so named.
The same beast is called "the false prophet" in Revelation 16:13; 19:20,
and elsewhere. Now the watchword of Revelation is "Behold, I come
quickly." Need we find in I John 2:18 any more explicit teaching than
this? An "hour" is a short time. "It is the last hour" denotes an active
expectation of the coming of Christ.

We are not concerned to deny the hope of the early Church. The
early Christians were expecting the coming of the Lord, as do biblically-
oriented Christians today. No date is given, and many details are unclear. But we are not to deny the blessed hope of the Church.

What we question is the idea that the early Church thought of itself
as this messianic kingdom, this glorious commonwealth which had ir-
rupted into the earth. Rather, the eschatological kingdom for the early
Christians was still future. They hoped indeed that the promised day
was not far distant. We today are bidden to have a lively hope too. But
the early Christians distinguished clearly between the present age of
grace, of salvation, and of missionary effort on one hand, and that future
age of resurrection of the body, judgment of the wicked, and glorious

appearing of Christ. That age was to come in future manifestation in history. The prospect of its coming was their comfort (I Thess. 4:13-5-11, and elsewhere). The early Church was not living in the "last days" in the sense that they thought that eschatology is now. There was indeed a present spiritual resurrection often alluded to in the New Testament. Certainly there was a consciousness of Christ's presence now with His Church. There was an understanding that many Old Testament prophecies had been fulfilled in Christ's first coming. But the end, the eschaton, was awaited when the "dead" (in Christ) shall be raised incorruptible and we (living Christians) shall be changed" (I Cor. 15:52). The present time was a new age *vis-à-vis* the former age, but eschatology is not now. The last day of physical resurrection was yet to come.

III. THE "LAST DAYS" IN THE QUMRAN LITERATURE

How was it with the Essenes of Qumran? What did they believe as to their own situation, and what was their expectation? Since their literature was not in Greek, we must search out parallels to the Old Testament expressions already studied. Were they conscious of a new day different from the Old Testament times or did they find themselves partakers of the Old Testament promises of the future days? What was their attitude toward the messianic hope? Was a Messiah present with them, or beyond them, or were they an eschatological community fulfilling all expectations?

To begin with, the phrase "the last days" is not very common in Qumran. "*'Aḥ'rît hayyāmîm*" is only used fourteen times. Two of the occurrences are in the Habakkuk Commentary (2, 5 and 9, 6) in connection with Habakkuk 1:5 and 2:8. The main thrust of the commentary is indeed to apply to the Qumran Community the phrases of Habakkuk. Some scholars have therefore drawn a parallel with certain New Testament quotations. There are some differences, however. Habakkuk predicts the Babylonian invasions of Judah in 605-586 b.c. Repeatedly the commentary interprets these invaders as the "Kittaeans" (Romans?) of its own day. It may really be questioned whether the commentary is here citing a prediction fulfilled, or just making an application as is done, for example, in Matthew 2:18. Matthew's formula in citation "then was fulfilled," sometimes cites a prediction accomplished and evidently sometimes merely cites an interesting parallel, much as is done in James 2:23. In any case the Habakkuk Commentary objects to "traitors of the last days" who will not believe the priestly interpretations of these things. T. H. Gaster translates this phrase "future traitors" (*The Dead Sea Scriptures* [Garden City: Doubleday Anchor Books, rev. ed. 1964], p. 244). They do not believe all that is to come upon the "final age" (*ibid.*). The phrase is identical to that in Psalm 48:13 where it is translated "the generation following." Cross translates it without discussion "the last generation" and thereby finds more apocalypticism than the text requires (F. M. Cross, *Ancient Library of Qumran* [Garden City: Doubleday Anchor Books, rev. ed., 1961], p. 113).

Further, in a comment on Habakkuk 2:8, there is a reference to the "final priests" whose ill-gotten gain will "ultimately" be seized by the Kittaeans (Gaster, *op. cit.*, p. 249). The meaning "future" or "later" is, however, as legitimate as "final." The translation "ultimately" represents the phrase "last days" and recognizes that in the commentary these words do not have eschatological meaning but refer to wars with a heathen foe who would be God's scourge on those Jews who oppressed the Qumran sect. The commentary mentions no messiah or heavenly intervention. It is not apocalyptic in expression or literary style. The phrase "last days" seems merely to refer to time future to the matter discussed. Actually, there is a declaration in connection with Habakkuk 2:3 that the "final moment may be protracted beyond anything which the prophets have foretold" (*ibid.*, p. 248). The word is literally "the latter end." The conclusion of Habakkuk mentions the judgment day. We may naturally infer that the "latter end" is this judgment day. But in any case it was a future event and possibly an event in the distant future.

The Zadokite Document, found in fragments in Qumran and more extensively in the Genizah of the Cairo Synagogue, is a kind of monastic rule for the order, and certainly has no eschatological or apocalyptic in tone. There is, of course, the claim that the covenanters of the sect are the true people of God. In 4, 4 the Document speaks of the true priests, the sons of Zadok (cf. Ezek. 44:15), who are the elect of Israel who shall "go on functioning in the last days" (Gaster, *op. cit.*, p. 75). Rabin translates: "who shall arise in the end of days" (C. Rabin, *The Zadokite Documents* [Oxford: 1954], p. 14). The translation "in future days" is equally probable. The same considerations apply to 6, 11 which complains of apostasy during the current "epoch of wickedness" in which people will not "grasp instruction until there shall arise he who teaches righteousness in *the end of days*," the same phrase (*ibid.*, p. 22). We must note that this "true Expositor" (Gaster, *op. cit.*, p. 78) is not the Teacher of Righteousness referred to elsewhere, nor is he this Teacher of Righteousness resurrected. The phrase may refer to an expected messiah (cf. John 4:25) of which we must speak shortly. In any case the translation "end of days" is too specific. The meaning "future days" fits just as well; and, actually, the community did not at this point consider itself to be in those end days anyway. Both references apparently predict future days when the teacher-messiah will come.

Another usage of our term is found in the *Rule of the Congregation* which begins: "This is the rule for the whole body of Israel when in the future [*i.e.*, the "last days"] they lead their lives in the manner of the sons of Zadok" (Gaster, *op. cit.*, p. 327). The piece is short and very much like the longer *Manual of Discipline*. It provides for the training of children, judicial hearings, military service, and the like, ending with a description of a meal often called a messianic banquet. But the messiah is apparently an anointed king or the anointed king distinctly secondary in rank to the priest who is head of the community. Certainly the *Rule* does not speak as if the last days had come in any eschatological sense. It speaks of the indefinite future of the community.

Several more commentaries use the words "last days" but are difficult to interpret because they are fragmentary. Thus we must pass over the commentaries on Hosea and Micah. Several fragments of a commentary on Isaiah can be noted. At Isaiah 10:32 there is a broken reference to the "last days." Fragments following refer to the war of the Kittim mentioned in the Habakkuk Commentary, and then a comment in Isaiah 11:1 says "[Its interpretation concerns the Shoot of] David who will arise at the en[d of days]." The following lines ascribe him a throne of glory, a rule over Gentiles, and the function of judge as mentioned in Isaiah 11:3 (J. M. Allegro, *op. cit.*, pp. 178-180).

Here we have an interpretation of a Scion of David passage as of a glorious messiah of the "last days." This is doubtless eschatological, but not with reference to the times then present. The "last days" mentioned here were not contemporary, but future. And the future is indefinite.

Further Isaiah Commentary fragments (J. M. Allegro, "More Isaiah Commentaries," *Journal of Biblical Literature*, Vol. 77 [1958], pp. 216-219) show two usages of the phrase "last days" which are not specifically messianic, but connected with the wickedness mentioned in Isaiah 5:11f. and 30:15f. These verses, referring to sinners of Isaiah's day are applied to the enemies of the community, the "men of scoffing" and the "seekers-after-smooth-things" in Jerusalem. There is not enough context to say much more than this. There is no clear indication that these days would be the "last" ones, but only that they were future to the prophet. As noted above, all eschatology is future, but all future is not eschatology.

A last document is the so-called Florilegium of Messianic Testimonies (J. M. Allegro, "Fragments of a Qumran Scroll," *ibid.*, pp. 350-354). Quotations are given from II Samuel 7, Amos 9:11, Isaiah 8:11, Psalm 2:1, Jeremiah 23:5 (the Branch of David) and elsewhere. Four times the phrase "last days" is used, and every time it refers to the Scion of David who is to come. In fine, we are told that he is to arise with the "Interpreter of the Law" who is also a figure of the future (cf. *Zad-*

okite Document 6, 11, discussed above). Much of interest lies in these fragmentary passages, but our purpose is served when we note that the community clearly looked forward to the coming of the promised Branch of David. In this there is a certain similarity to the New Testament Church which also treasured these same passages. But whereas the community looked forward to such a Branch of David, the Church declared on the basis of these texts and its knowledge of the Jesus of history that the Branch of David had come. In this the men of Qumran were like the Old Testament prophets who looked forward to the great David's greater Son. The New Testament differs from both Qumran and the Old Testament in citing the fulfillments. True, the New Testament looks for His return, but these passages are not usually applied to that event. In a real sense, therefore, future time, or the "last days" of the Qumran messianic expectation were the past days of the New Testament fulfillment. The New Testament horizons differ greatly.

IV. THE "LAST DAYS" IN ENOCH

There appear to be no occurrences of the expression "last days" in the Apocryphal books, which, after all, are not apocalyptic in style or notably eschatological. In the book of Enoch there is more, but the study of Enoch is complicated by questions of its unity. F. M. Cross and others hold that since the Similitudes of Enoch (chapters 37-71) are not found at Qumran they may well be post-Christian (*op. cit.,* p. 202n.). We shall therefore pass over this section.

Actually, the phrase "last days" (using only the English translation of the Ethiopic Enoch and the Greek fragments) occurs just twice in the whole book. In Enoch 27, 3 the phrase refers to the day of judgment of the wicked. In Enoch 108, 1 which is counted as a later appendix, the words refer to those who will come after Methuselah and "keep the law in the last days." Further sentences seem to identify those last days as a time of judgment for transgressors and heavenly rewards for the righteous. These "last days" are thus eschatological, not time present to the author.

V. CONCLUSION

At the outset we asked the question, what was the relation of New Testament eschatological thought to that of Qumran? It has been seen that the study of the phrase "last days" does not bear too directly on that question. Did the Church believe that it was living in the "last days"? Not exactly, for that translation does not precisely give the meaning of the phrase. The Church of course was living in "later" days, that is, in days later than those of the Old Testament prophets. Comparison with Old Testament usage shows that the phrase may well mean no more than that. And the Church lived in expectation of the return of Christ who would accomplish the resurrection and judgment at the "last day." The Church expected the eschatological finale, but it did not believe that this finale was now, or necessarily very soon. It was to "come quickly" and would include heavenly signs that would be recognized when they came. In the meantime the people were "not to be shaken in mind" (II Thess. 2:2).

But the Church was sure that many of the Old Testament prophecies had been fulfilled. The great bulk of these citations find a fulfillment in Christ's first coming and work. Matthew, for instance, has about twenty quotations of prophecy, all referring to Jesus' first coming or to John the Baptist, His forerunner. The second coming of Christ was affirmed by the Church not so much on Old Testament prediction as on Christ's own promises. True, some Old Testament statements are applied to the church situation in developments such as the calling of the Gentiles and the unbelief of Israel. But the conclusion should not be drawn that the New Testament community is the final work of God. Rather, it looks toward a future when the Lord of the Church will come again. Even such a passage as Hebrews 9:26, which speaks of Christ's first coming in the "consummation of the ages," goes on to promise His second coming to those who look for Him.

With this in mind we cannot say that the New Testament Church was apocalyptic in the sense often described. Cross quotes Elliger's summary of the apocalyptic outlook, " (1) prophecy is eschatology, and (2) the present is the end time" (*op. cit.,* p. 112). These principles need modification for the bulk of the New Testament. In the specifically apocalyptic book of Revelation, Old Testament prophecies are seldom explicitly cited. Furthermore, whether Revelation was intended to apply primarily to the days of John is in any case in dispute. The plagues are not pictured as having yet begun.

The Old Testament prophets give all their predictions in an indefinite future with very little differences in perspective. For instance, Isaiah foretold the overthrow of Sennacherib's army in closest connection with the birth of Jesse's Rod (Isa. 10:34-11:1). He hoped that the Prince of Peace would soon appear. Not until Daniel's prophecy of the seventy sevens was there a closer indication. But we need not think therefore that Isaiah was wrong and predicted the early coming of Immanuel; his present hope was a dateless expectation. He did not claim to be in the very last days, but he did have a hope of wonderful things in future days. And that hope which centered in the Scion of David persisted throughout generations of prophets. It appears first in the Davidic covenant, then as the Child wonderful of Isaiah, the Bethlehem ruler of Micah, the Davidic tabernacle of Amos, the Branch of David in Jeremiah, the Davidic shepherd of Ezekiel, and the servant Branch of Zechariah. It persists into the literature of Qumran when no Davidic king had ruled for centuries. This was not a hope limited to one horizon. It was a conviction based on the word to David in early days. The prophets as well as apocalyptists interpreted history in terms of teleology. They lacked perspective, but they foretold the "sufferings of Christ and the glory that should follow." Ladd has rightly emphasized the unity of prophecy and apocalyptic thought (George E. Ladd, "Why Not Prophecy and Apocalyptic?" *Journal of Biblical Literature,* Vol. 76 [1957], pp. 192-200). Both Daniel and the other prophets looked forward to a supernatural deliverer and a golden age. We need not think that the apocalyptists came exclusively after the prophets and presented a different view of history. Indeed, dare we assume that historical events either happy or tragic are always interpreted the same way by people of any age? The prophets surely have apocalyptic elements — and these cannot all be neatly excised and dated in a late age.

As to the Qumran material, it is questionable if it should be so largely classed as apocalyptic. It is said that the community felt it was living in the last days and in this shares an apocalypticism with the New Testament (cf. Cross, *op. cit.,* p. 200). But surely the Dead Sea Scrolls can hardly be said to belong to the literary genre of apocalypticism. The only pieces with extensive visions and symbolism are Daniel — which is canonical and cannot be proved to be peculiar to Qumran — and Enoch, which likewise may have originated in a broader stream of Jewish thought. Both of these books are datable at least as early as the times of Judas Macabbaeus, 165 B.C., whereas the Qumran settlement was founded after 145 B.C. (*ibid.,* p. 59). The major works of the *Manual of Discipline,* the *Zadokite Documents, the Genesis Apocryphon,* and the commentaries are sober if often curious pieces. The Qumran Community indeed had an eschatological hope. Some of that is of a piece with the Old Testament — the Scion of David motif. Here there is a sharp difference with the New Testament. They did apply to their own situation much Old Testament historical material, and some of those Old Testament short-range prophecies against the Gentiles. The New Testament does this to only a limited extent. For instance, Acts 13:41 quotes Habakkuk 1:5 with a warning against unbelief such as characterized Habakkuk's day. The Scrolls interpret Habakkuk 1:6ff. and claim that the Chaldaean invasion is the Kittaeans (Romans?) of their day. There is a large difference in the two methods. An exception would doubtless be alleged for the book of Revelation.

But even here, the interpretation of Old Testament prophecies is obviously much different from that of the Qumran commentaries.

Aside from Enoch and Daniel, the *War Scroll* comes closest to being an apocalyptic piece. But it is totally unlike the New Testament in its eschatology. There is no series of visions as in Revelation or an exhortation to watch for the event and there is little emphasis on imminency. God's help is assured in the battle against Satanic hosts, but in no supernatural way. There is no messianic leader, no glorious consequence, or kingly reign of a Davidic Messiah, no judgment day — although we must remember that the last part of the scroll is missing.

In general we may conclude that the men of Qumran obviously considered themselves to be the faithful remnant of Israel. They applied to themselves the Old Testament blessings for the faithful and expected to inherit the promised land after their wilderness exile was over. They apparently expected two Messiahs, a priestly and a kingly one, and probably a prophet as well. This messianic picture greatly differs from that of the New Testament except that the name Messiah is used (which is rare in the Old Testament as a designation of the coming one). They link their kingly Messiah with the house of David as does the Old Testament and also the New. But he had not yet come. The Qumran Community really lived in the Old Testament hope, not in the New Testament period between the coming of the prophesied King and His return.

HISTORY AND THE GOSPEL

F. F. Bruce

F. F. Bruce is successor to the late T. W. Manson as Rylands Professor of Biblical Criticism and Exegesis in the University of Manchester, England. He is editor of the Evangelical Quarterly and the Palestine Exploration Quarterly, general editor of two book series, The New International Commentary on the New Testament and Advance of Christianity through the Centuries, and author of many volumes, including a commentary on the Greek text of Acts, commentaries on Acts, Romans, Colossians and Hebrews, The Spreading Flame, Israel and the Nations, History of the English Bible. His most recent volume is The Letters of Paul, a new translation. He received the M.A. degree with first class honors in classics at Aberdeen and Cambridge, and was awarded the D.D. by Aberdeen.

6. F. F. Bruce

HISTORY AND THE GOSPEL

W E ARE frequently told today that the task of extracting historical data from the four Gospels is impossible, and in any case illegitimate.
But the people who tell us that are for the most part theologians, not
historians. Whether the task of extracting historical data from the Gospels is impossible or not is for the historian to discover, not for the
theologian to tell him; and one thing that no self-respecting historian
will allow himself to be told is that his quest is illegitimate.

The quest has often been called the quest of the historical Jesus.
The old quest of the historical Jesus is reckoned to have reached its termi-
nus with the appearance of Albert Schweitzer's work which bears that
title in its English translation; nowadays there is talk of a new quest
of the historical Jesus, but there is considerable doubt whether the figure
recovered by this quest is one which can properly be called the *historical*
Jesus. The Jesus of the primitive apostolic preaching — yes; but there
are some who hold up an arresting hand and forbid us to cross the boun-
dary which lies between Jesus of the early preaching and the Jesus of
history as the historian understands history.

There are other historical characters for whom our source material
is scanty and problematical — even more so than the source material
for the life of Jesus. But in these cases no scholar holds up his hand
like a traffic policeman and says: The materials for reconstructing the
historical career of this or that figure do not exist, and it is illegitimate
to try to reconstruct them; that is not the purpose for which the available literature was composed. And if anyone were so foolish as to say
so, we should simply reply: We know that is not the purpose for which
the available literature was composed, but nevertheless that literature

is available for the historian to use, with all proper critical safeguards, as source material for his work.

I. THE GOSPELS AS SOURCES

We must look, then, at our primary sources for the historic mission of Jesus — and that, in the first instance, means the four Gospels. (An earlier source is provided by the letters of Paul which, however, were addressed to people who had already been taught the story of Jesus, so that he did not need to tell them what they knew. Yet it is surprising how much of an outline of the story and teaching of Jesus can be reconstructed from incidental references in Paul's letters.) If we wish to establish what, as a matter of history, Jesus actually said and did, we cannot ignore the evidence of the Gospels. We know that the Evangelists did not set out to be historiographers or even biographers. But they did set out to bear witness — or to preserve the witness of others — to what they believed actually to have happened; and their writings provide the historian of early Christianity with the raw material of his craft.

On the source criticism of the Gospels it is not necessary to say much here. So far as the three Synoptic Gospels are concerned, it is easy to distinguish the Marcan material in all three, the non-Marcan material common to Matthew and Luke (conveniently labelled Q), the special material of Luke (L) and the special material of Matthew (M). These four bodies of material are not generally conceived today as four separate documents on which the Synoptic Evangelists variously drew, but that two of them represent distinct documents is fairly certain. Mark, of course, we know; and the arguments for treating his record as prior to those of Matthew and Luke are in my eyes as valid as ever. Nor am I disposed to follow the current fashion of "dispensing with Q" (or rather with the hypothesis of a document from which the first and third Evangelists drew their Q material) ; attempts to account for the non-Marcan material common to Matthew and Luke apart from the Q hypothesis strike me as much more unconvincing than anything in the hypothesis itself. I envisage, perhaps in the early fifties of the first century, the appearance of a compilation based on the model of the Old Testament prophetic books — "The Book of the Prophet Jesus," we might call it — in which, after an account of the inauguration of the Prophet's public ministry, His "oracles" were arranged in a brief narrative framework, but which did not record the Prophet's death (precisely as no Old Testament prophet's death is recorded in the book which bears his name). T. W. Manson suggested that in this work the sayings of Jesus were arranged under four topics: (1) "Jesus and John the Baptist"; (2) "Jesus and His Disciples"; (3) "Jesus and His Opponents"; (4) "Jesus and the Future" (*The Sayings of Jesus* [1949], pp. 39ff.) .

The four bodies of material which have been mentioned as underlying our Synoptic accounts could no doubt be further subdivided; for example, the nativity narratives of Matthew and Luke do not appear to be homogeneous with the rest of the special material in these two Gospels. But when we reach this point, we have left source criticism behind; we have already pressed our quest back to a stage where form criticism promises to help us much more than source criticism ever could.

German scholars have sometimes remarked that outside Germany, and especially in Britain, the form-critical method is either rejected or else limited to a means of formally classifying the traditional material. It is denied, they say (and, from their point of view, denied wrongly) , that it can lead to conclusions about the historical genuineness or otherwise of the material on which it works.

No one, I suppose, has expressed this non-German skepticism about the value of form criticism in more characteristically down-to-earth language than my predecessor T. W. Manson, in a 1949 address, "The Quest of the Historical Jesus — Continued," published posthumously in *Studies in the Gospels and Epistles* (Manchester: University Press, 1962) , pp. 3ff. "Strictly," he said, "the term 'form-criticism' should be reserved for the study of the various units of narrative and teaching, which go to make up the Gospels, in respect of their form alone. . . . But a paragraph of Mark is not a penny the better or the worse for being labelled, 'Apothegm' or 'Pronouncement Story' or 'Paradigm.' In fact if form criticism had stuck to its proper business, it would not have made any real stir. We should have taken it as we take the forms of Hebrew poetry or the forms of musical composition."

How then has form criticism not stuck to its proper business? Because, said Manson, it got mixed up with two other things. One was K. L. Schmidt's theory that the narrative of Mark, for the greater part, consisted of disconnected units joined together by "editorial cement" devoid of any historical value of its own; the other was the doctrine of the *Sitz im Leben,* the "life-setting." In saying this, Manson was defining form criticism a good deal more narrowly than is commonly done. Usually such a study as K. L. Schmidt's and the endeavor to establish the life-setting of the component elements in the Gospel tradition would be regarded as coming within the province of form criticism. Schmidt aimed at determining the character or form of the tradition as it came into Mark's hands, while a study of the life-setting can throw light on the form which an incident or saying originally took, or on the form in which it was transmitted in the believing community.

In its more extreme formulations, however, the doctrine of the life-
setting lays it down that if a saying or action ascribed to Christ in the
Gospels reflects the faith of the Church after the resurrection, it must be
regarded as a creation of the Church rather than an authentic saying or
action of Jesus. If a parallel saying or action is elsewhere attributed to
some rabbi, it must be regarded as a Jewish tradition which has come
to be ascribed erroneously to Jesus. It would follow that only sayings
or actions unparalleled in the early Church or in Jewish tradition could
with any confidence be accepted as authentic. But this involves the two
utterly improbable assumptions: that there was no continuity between
the post-resurrection faith of the Church and the ministry of Jesus and
that the teaching of Jesus and of the rabbis never overlapped at any point.

The study of the forms in which the various units of Gospel tradition
were preserved and transmitted has been handicapped, not promoted,
by excessive skepticism of this a priori kind. Form criticism which has
been unhampered by such skepticism has led to conclusions of considerable positive value for Gospel study, as some work by C. H. Dodd, William Manson, and Joachim Jeremias shows. The value is perhaps greatest when what was originally one and the same unit of teaching or narrative can be shown to have been handed down along two separate lines
in two different "forms"; we are thus enabled to envisage the material of
the unit as it was before it began to be transmitted.

There is a third thing (in addition to the two mentioned by Manson)
with which form criticism has been mixed up, and that is the excessively
skeptical evaluation of the Gospel history which marks the work of Professor Rudolf Bultmann. Since Bultmann was a pioneer in the form
criticism of the Gospels, it is no doubt inevitable that his form criticism
and his historical skepticism should be mixed up together, although logically the two are distinct. To quote Manson again,

> Professor Bultmann's *History of the Synoptic Tradition* is an account,
> not of how the life of Jesus produced the tradition, but of how the tradi-
> tion produced the life of Jesus. And when the work of the tradition has
> been undone, there is very little of Jesus left. I may remark in passing
> that the disseminated incredulity of Bultmann's *Geschichte der synopti-
> schen Tradition* [Eng. tr.: *The History of the Synoptic Tradition* (New
> York: Harper, 1963)] has its nemesis thirty years later in his *Theologie des
> Neuen Testaments* [Eng. tr., *Theology of the New Testament*, 1952-55], in
> which a perfunctory thirty pages or so is devoted to the theology of Jesus
> himself, while a hundred or more are occupied with an imaginary account
> of the theology of the anonymous and otherwise unknown "Hellenistic
> Communities" (*Studies in the Gospels and Epistles*, pp. 6f.).

Professor Manson reasonably concludes his examination of this phase
of Gospel criticism with a plea for "a return to the study of the Gospels

as historical documents concerning Jesus of Nazareth, rather than as psychological case-material concerning the early Christians" (*ibid.,* p. 8).

One of the most interesting of recent developments in Gospel study has been a fresh appraisal of the historical value of the Fourth Gospel. In some quarters this has been influenced by the discovery and study of the Qumran literature; in others it has been the result of further study of this Gospel itself in its New Testament context.

At the "Four Gospels Congress" held in Oxford in 1957, for example, two important papers on the Fourth Gospel were read. Professor W. C. van Unnik of Utrecht read a paper on "The Purpose of St. John's Gospel" (*Studia Evangelica, TU,* Vol. 73 [1959], pp. 382ff.), and the Bishop of Woolwich discussed "The New Look on the Fourth Gospel" (*ibid.,* pp. 338ff.). Professor van Unnik argues that this Gospel was basically a missionary document designed to lead Jewish readers to faith in Christ. One of his arguments is the occurrence of the title "Christ" or "Messiah" in the Evangelist's own statement of his purpose: "these are written that you may believe that Jesus is the Christ . . ." (John 20:31). Agreed, but one could go further. John's purpose is to lead Jewish *and Gentile* readers of the Hellenistic world towards the end of the first century to faith in Jesus: for Jewish readers this will mean faith in Jesus as the Christ, but for the Gentile readers to whom a call to believe in Him as the Christ would not be immediately relevant he adds: ". . . believe that Jesus is the Christ, *the Son of God.*" His desire is that both classes of readers, so believing in Jesus, might have "life in his name."

Bishop Robinson in his paper takes issue with "five generally agreed presuppositions" on which current critical orthodoxy regarding this Gospel has been accustomed to rest.

> These are: (1) That the fourth Evangelist is dependent on sources, including (normally) one or more of the Synoptic Gospels. (2) That his own background is other than that of the events and teaching he is purporting to record. (3) That he is not to be regarded, seriously, as a witness to the Jesus of history, but simply to the Christ of faith. (4) That he represents the end-term of theological development in first-century Christianity. (5) That he is not himself the Apostle John nor a direct eyewitness.

His conclusion is that the crucial question is whether the distinctive tradition of the ministry of Jesus preserved in this Gospel came "out of the blue" around A.D. 100. "Or is there a real continuity not merely in the memory of one old man, but in the life of an on-going community, with the earliest days of Christianity? What, I think, fundamentally distinguishes the 'new look' on the Fourth Gospel is that it answers that question in the affirmative."

Professor C. H. Dodd, whose contributions to the study of the Fourth

Gospel, crowned by his *Historical Tradition in the Fourth Gospel* (Cambridge, 1963), have made him easily chief among contemporary Johannine students, has pointed out how, beneath the diversity of dialogue form as between the Synoptic Gospels and John's there is at times a community of theme which suggests that the Synoptic and Johannine traditions alike go back to an earlier "unformed" tradition. Not only so, but he envisages the probability that more of this "unformed" tradition of Jesus' teaching lies behind dialogues in the Fourth Gospel which have no parallel in the Synoptic tradition, although they can be integrated with it. The recognition of such material must call for very delicate judgment, but the quest, as Professor Dodd sees it, is far from hopeless.

Not only in its discourses and dialogues, but in its narratives, the Johannine account is worthy of at least as much respect as the Synoptic accounts. This is so, for example, with its tradition of an earlier phase of our Lord's ministry in the south of Palestine, simultaneous with the later phase of John the Baptist's activity, and also with its presentation of the events of Holy Week, the chronology of which has been illuminated by the study of calendrical texts from Qumran.

The upshot of all this is that our task is made in a sense more difficult rather than easier. At one time those who believed that the evidence of the Fourth Gospel could be largely ignored in any attempt to reconstruct the course of our Lord's ministry felt themselves able to reconstruct it in the terms of the Synoptic — that is, substantially, the Marcan — framework. Now, let me say that despite all that has been urged to the contrary I still consider that the Marcan framework suggests a sequence and development in the story of the ministry which is too spontaneous to be artificial and too logical to be accidental. But it is no longer feasible to treat the material fitted into this framework in such a way as to distinguish (say) between the optimism of Jesus' hope of the kingdom of God in the earlier period of His ministry and His gloomier forebodings from Caesarea Philippi onwards. Nor is it feasible to treat the Marcan outline as being so watertight that anything in the Johannine narrative which cannot be readily fitted into it (the raising of Lazarus, for example) must for that simple reason be set aside as historically suspect.

If, however, the Johannine tradition claims to be regarded as equally primitive with the Marcan — and Professor Dodd pointed out many years ago that the Second and the Fourth Gospels are the two which preserve the essential kerygmatic outline most faithfully (*The Apostolic Preaching and Its Developments* [1936], p. 165) — the historian's problem is the more complicated. Neither the Johannine nor the Marcan framework can be made the norm to which the other must be accommodated.

On the other hand, the difficulties must not be exaggerated. If the Marcan and Johannine traditions are independent, the greater weight attaches to those features in which they concur, since these may be properly recognized as belonging to the most primitive stratum of the Christian story. In addition to their agreement in associating the beginning of Jesus' public life with the ministry of John the Baptist, and in the main outlines of the passion story at the end of His public life, special attention should be directed to the way in which both Mark and John treat the feeding of the multitude and Peter's confession which followed it as a turning point in the ministry of Jesus. The more this coincidence is examined, the greater importance it assumes.

II. HISTORICAL SKEPTICISM

The historical skepticism of Professer Bultmann and his school, which is paralleled in some parts of the English-speaking world of New Testament scholarship, is unlike the skepticism of earlier generations. Whereas the older skepticism endeavored by the removal of the outer theological layers in the Gospels to get back to a historical Jesus who could still be a moral and religious guide to the undogmatic heirs of the enlightenment, the new skepticism has recognized that the Gospel material is theological through and through, so that when the last layer has been peeled off we are left with little more than the residual affirmation: "crucified under Pontius Pilate." Professor Dodd might point out a quarter of a century ago that, no matter how we classify the Gospel materials, all parts of the record agree in emphasizing the messianic significance of all that Jesus said and did: "we can find no alternative tradition, excavate as we will in the successive strata of the gospels" (*History and the Gospel* [London: Nisbet, 1938], p. 103). The modern skepticism agrees with his findings, but dissents from his conclusions, which were that this messianic portrayal of Jesus has strong claims to be accepted as the authentic portrayal of the historical Jesus. It holds rather that since the material is theological through and through, the history eludes us almost completely; and it bids us come to terms with this state of affairs and be thankful for the theology, since we cannot have the history.

The new skepticism is thus much more radical than the older skepticism, so far as the Jesus of history is concerned. At the turn of the century P. W. Schmiedel isolated nine passages in the Synoptic Gospels which, he said, "might be called the foundation-pillars for a truly scientific life of Jesus" ("Gospels," *Encyclopaedia Biblica,* Vol. ii [1901], cols. 1881-1883). Some shrewd observers at the time recognized that Schmiedel was conceding more than he knew since, for all his belief that these passages ran so counter to later tendencies that they were not likely to be inventions of the church, some of them implied quite a high Christology. But now we find Professor Hans Conzelmann saying of one of these "pillar" passages (Jesus' cry of dereliction on the cross) : "The objection that this saying would not have been put into his mouth, if he had not actually uttered it, fails to recognize the character of the narrative. This saying was taken up in order to portray his death as fulfilment, and thereby to overcome the 'scandal' of the cross. The saying therefore should not be evaluated psychologically, in order to reconstruct the feelings of the dying Jesus" ("Jesus Christus," *Religion in Geschichte und Gegenwart,* 3rd ed. [1959], III, cols. 646f.). With the last sentence we may be disposed to agree; but as for the rest of the statement, my reaction to it — as to so many other statements which I find in the writings of this school — is to reflect that assertion is not proof.

That the Gospel narrative, and especially the passion narrative, should be recorded in the language of Old Testament fulfilment is not surprising when we remember Jesus' insistence that in His ministry and supremely in His passion the Scriptures must be and in fact were being fulfilled. I know it will be said that this is an example of the reading back into His own life and teaching of a theme that was developed for apologetic and other purposes in the early Church. That the theme of fulfilment was developed in the early Church is clear, but the manner in which it was developed can best be explained if Jesus first laid down for His disciples the guiding lines of Old Testament interpretation — that He did for them in one way what the Qumran Teacher of Righteousness did for his community in another way. I have tried to show elsewhere, with reference to one group of Old Testament *testimonia* which play a substantial part in the passion narrative (those drawn from Zech. 9-14), that Jesus led the way in speaking of His passion to His disciples in terms of these oracles (especially the oracle of the smitten shepherd in Zech. 13:7) ; the Evangelists, more particularly the later ones, dotted the i's and crossed the t's of this pattern of prediction and fulfilment, but the initial impetus was given by Jesus Himself. The oracles were not used to create but to explain the recorded events ("The Book of Zechariah and the Passion Narrative," *Bulletin of the John Rylands Library,* Vol. 43 [1960-61], pp. 336ff.) .

Even the geographical data, the sacred sites and ways, which we might have thought were objective enough, have been interpreted as theologoumena. For example: Luke, says one writer, can locate John the Baptist neither in Galilee nor in Judea, for these were both areas of Jesus' activity; John is therefore given a marginal location, in the wilderness and the Jordan valley. (But did not John preach and baptize there, as a matter of history?) In order to be baptized by John, of course, Jesus must come to Jordan, but since the Jordan is John's territory, Jesus has nothing more to do with the Jordan or its neighborhood. But does not Luke bring Jesus to Jericho later in his Gospel (18:35ff.)? Yes, but it is questionable whether Luke knew that Jericho is near the Jordan! (H. Conzelmann, *Die Mitte Der Zeit* [Eng. tr., *The Theology of St. Luke.* New York: Harper, 1960], p. 19). Even if Luke was personally unacquainted with that district of Palestine, he had presumably read Joshua and II Kings, where Jericho's proximity to the Jordan is made plain.

As for Mark's Gospel, its chronological and geographical outline, the same writer assures us, "is not ancient tradition, but literary redaction. . . . The geographical framework of our oldest Gospel is an editorial construction following the schema 'action in Galilee, passion in Jerusalem' (with Mark 10 as the transition between the two; cf. Lohmeyer)." However, we need not take too much account of this: behind the schema "of course, lies historical information" (*RGG,*[3] cols. 622, 627). Of course it does: Galilee *was* the main region of Jesus' public ministry, and Jerusalem *was* the place where He was crucified; if members of the early Church theologized these data (and I am not persuaded that they did, at least to anything like the extent postulated by E. Lohmeyer and R. H. Lightfoot), at any rate the data were historical data before theological significance was read into them.

But it is extremely interesting right now to mark the developments within the influential Bultmann school, to which Professor Conzelmann belongs.

If one looks, for example, at Günther Bornkamm's *Jesus of Nazareth* (Eng. tr., London: Hodder and Stoughton, 1960), it will be seen that this distinguished disciple of Bultmann, while skeptical by the British standards of (say) C. H. Dodd and Vincent Taylor, is more optimistic than his teacher about the possibility of extracting from our records a picture of Jesus' person and career. Nor does he find such an hiatus as Bultmann does between the ministry of Jesus and the message of the primitive Church. Whereas Bultmann places the shift from the old age to the new between Jesus and Paul, Bornkamm places it between John the Baptist and Jesus — a judgment which may be accepted the more readily because, according to the Evangelists, that is where Jesus placed it.

Other members of the Bultmann school, such as Ernst Käsemann and Ernst Fuchs, have also reacted against Bultmann's teaching, but not all in the same direction. Käsemann, for instance, has recently come to view all four Gospels as arising out of the apocalyptic understanding of history in the earliest Christianity; Fuchs has remarked that whereas "we formerly endeavored to interpret the historical Jesus with the help of the primitive Christian kerygma, today we endeavor rather to interpret this kerygma with the help of the historical Jesus — the two lines of investigation are mutually complementary" (*Zur Frage nach dem histor-ischen Jesus* [1960], preface).

In such a situation as this there is every encouragement for the historian of Christian origins to press straight forward as the road opens up before him. There is no need to listen to those who tell him that his task is vain and improper. He knows that the Evangelists were not objective and dispassionate researchers, producing Ph.D. theses — not even Luke, for all his care to "trace the course of all things accurately from the first" (Luke 1:3). Of course not; they were Christians, deeply committed men. They viewed the ministry of Jesus in the light of His resurrection (or, as some prefer to say, in the light of the Easter event). Their aim was to commend the Saviour to others. All four of them, like John, were concerned in one way or another so to write that their readers should believe in Jesus as Messiah and Son of God, and by so believing have life in His name.

The historian of Christian origins knows, moreover, that "if the nineteenth-century view of history found its meaningful expression in 'the historical Jesus,' the twentieth century has found its approach already anticipated in the *kerygma*" (J. M. Robinson, *A New Quest of the Historical Jesus* [London: SCM Press, 1959], p. 39). But what was this kerygma, this proclamation of God's good news in Christ? It was, for the first thirty years or so, substantially the witness of the disciples of Christ to what they had seen and heard. If one of the principal heralds of the kerygma, Paul, had not himself seen and heard the works and words of Jesus, he was careful to acquire the necessary information from eyewitnesses so that he could deliver to others what he himself had first received. It is noteworthy that, in his catalogue of resurrection appearances in I Cor. 15:5ff., he mentions appearances to two individuals, "Cephas" and James — the only two members of the apostolic company whom he met when he visited Jerusalem in the third year after his conversion to have an interview with the former (Gal. 1:18). Dr. Vincent Taylor found it expedient a quarter of a century ago to remind certain leading form critics that the apostles and other original followers of Jesus were not translated to heaven immediately after His resurrection, as one would almost be forced to suppose if some of their theories were true. We do have eyewitness testimony in the Gospels — more of it than is commonly recognized today. Luke knew about what he was about when he assured Theophilus that, although he himself had not been present at most of the events described in his twofold history, he had access to information handed down by "those who from the beginning were eyewitnesses and ministers of the word" (Luke 1:3). Eyewitness testimony was highly regarded in his day, for many ordinary purposes and especially in Roman law. There was a time, too, when eyewitness testimony was highly regarded by historical researchers. It was an important feature of Thucydides' history, for example, that he himself played a leading part in the earlier stages of the Peloponnesian War which he records. Nowadays, however, we hear doubts expressed about the value of such testimony.

In an article in the *Journal of Theological Studies* for October 1960 (N.S. 11, pp. 253ff.) on "Eye-witness Testimony and the Gospel Tradition," Professor D. E. Nineham speaks of the task of today's historian of Christian origins as being "to wring truth relevant to the history of Jesus from the increasing stock of remains of the Judaism of his time." This is true, since our primary sources, the New Testament records, have been so thoroughly sifted and resifted. But in relation to these records themselves, or at least to the element of eyewitness evidence which they claim to contain, he shows himself unduly influenced by some unqualified remarks of R. G. Collingwood, whom he quotes as follows:

> If anyone else, no matter who, even a very learned historian, or an eyewitness, or a person in the confidence of the man who did the thing he is inquiring into, or even the man who did it himself, hands him [the student of history] on a plate a ready-made answer to his question, all he can do is to reject it: not because he thinks his informant is trying to deceive him, or is himself deceived, but because if he accepts it he is giving up his autonomy as an historian and allowing someone else to do for him what, if he is a scientific thinker, he can only do for himself.[1]

But surely, if the historian is handed "on a plate" a ready-made answer by someone who was involved in the situation which he is reconstructing, he will not reject it out of hand. He will not treat it as a ready-made answer, but he will welcome it as a material piece of evidence. Everyone experienced in law-court procedure knows that the testimony of eyewitnesses, not least the testimony of honest eyewitnesses, must be subjected to cross-examination in order to ascertain what really happened; but nothing can take the place of the direct

---

1 The quotation comes from Collingwood's posthumously published *The Idea of History* (Oxford, 1946), p. 256. In this section of the work — a section, incidentally, which his editor, Sir Malcolm Knox, included "with some misgivings" (*ibid.,* p. vi.) — Collingwood pushes to extremes what, as elsewhere set forth by him, is a very sound case in vindication of the historian's right to be a true historian, free to exercise his historical judgment on all the material that comes his way. But one may question whether his work represents such a "Copernican revolution" in historical study as he himself held (*ibid.,* pp. 236, 240); cf. Professor Nineham's remarks on "the 'Collingwoodian' revolution in historical studies" which he sums up by saying that "the modern historian is no longer willing to set the seal of the word 'historical' on events, simply because an authority or authorities exist which allege that they happened" (*The Church's Use of the Bible Past and Present* [London: S.P.C.K., 1963], p. 156). But did any historian worthy of the name — that is, a scientific historian as distinct from a chronicler — ever take his material on trust just like that?

testimony of someone who was on the spot when it happened, and kept his eyes and ears open. Collingwood indeed admits this earlier: "the historian puts his authorities in the witness-box, and by cross-questioning extorts from them information which in their original statements they have withheld, either because they did not wish to give it or because they did not possess it" (*The Idea of History*, p. 237). The distinction which he draws later (p. 268) between the juror and the historian is accidental rather than substantial.

Since Paul has been mentioned in connection with eyewitness testimony, it may be relevant here to point out that Paul does not, as is sometimes alleged, disparage the eyewitness testimony of those who were companions of Jesus during His ministry when he speaks about no longer knowing Christ "after the flesh" (II Cor. 5:16). These words do not disown or deprecate any interest in the earthly life of Christ as has been maintained, e.g., by E. Brunner (*The Word and the World* [1931], pp. 87f.) and R. Bultmann (*Glauben und Verstehen*, I [1961], p. 208), nor do they suggest that the others apostles' earlier companionship with Him was now irrelevant, and of no spiritual advantage. The contrast which Paul is making is between his own present estimate of Christ and that which he had before his conversion, as is brought out very well in the New English Bible: "With us therefore worldly standards have ceased to count in our estimate of any man; even if they counted in our understanding of Christ, they do so now no longer. When anyone is united to Christ, there is a new world; the old order has gone, and a new order has already begun." Whatever Peter and Paul may have talked about during the fortnight that they spent together in Jerusalem in the third year after Paul's conversion, we may be sure that Paul did not write off the story that Peter told him as so much knowledge of Christ "after the flesh."

III. JESUS IN HIS HISTORICAL CONTEXT

When Professor Nineham says that we have to "wring truth relevant to the history of Jesus from the increasing stock of remains of the Judaism of his time," we may perhaps say much the same thing with regard to the Gentile environment too; the history of Jesus can best be understood in the total historical context of His life.

Mark sums up Jesus' early Galilean preaching in the words: "The appointed time is fulfilled, and the kingdom of God has drawn near; repent, and believe in the good news" (Mark 1:15). What would such words have meant in the setting in which they were spoken? This important question has sometimes been overlooked, even where we might most have expected it to receive attention. T. R. Glover, for instance, in *The Jesus of History,* "does less than justice to the central theme of Christ's preaching, 'Repent, for the Kingdom of Heaven is at hand,' and . . . does not sufficiently relate the mission of Jesus to the crisis in Israel's history which incorporation in the Roman Empire involved." That was the judgment of his friend H. G. Wood (*Jesus in the Twentieth Century* [London: Lutterworth Press, 1960], p. 123).

The Roman occupation of Judea from 63 B.C. onwards did in fact lead more than one Jewish group to the conviction that the indestructible kingdom which (according to the book of Daniel) the God of heaven would one day set up was on the very eve of appearance. In particular, we know how this hope was stimulated among the Zealots, in the near-Essene community of Qumran, as well as in other pious groups in Israel, including (it appears) the families into which John the Baptist and Jesus were born. We do well to ask what relation the hope of the coming kingdom as cherished by some of these groups bore to the hope of the kingdom as proclaimed by Jesus.

In the first decade of the present century Dr. Albert Schweitzer could write:

> The apocalyptic movement in the time of Jesus is not connected with any historical event. It cannot be said, as Bruno Bauer rightly perceived, that we know anything about the Messianic expectations of the Jewish people at that time. . . . What is really remarkable about this wave of apocalyptic enthusiasm is the fact that it was called forth not by external events, but solely by the appearance of two great personalities, and subsides with their disappearance, without leaving among the people any trace, except a feeling of hatred towards the new sect.
> The Baptist and Jesus are not, therefore, borne upon the current of a general eschatological movement. The period offers no events calculated to give an impulse to eschatological enthusiasm. They themselves set the times in motion by acting, by creating eschatological facts. It is this mighty creative force which constitutes the difficulty in grasping historically the eschatology of Jesus and the Baptist (*The Quest of the Historical Jesus* [Eng. tr., 1910], p. 368).

Today, while the prophetic and creative activity of both John and Jesus can be acknowledged as heartily as ever, we can no longer say that, eschatologically speaking, there was "silence all around" when they appeared. The Qumran discoveries, to mention no others, have provided us with that "general eschatological movement" of the closing decades B.C. and early decades A.D. which Dr. Schweitzer could not find.

The community which had its headquarters at Qumran, northwest of the Dead Sea, for the greater part of the two centuries preceding A.D. 70, seems to have been an Essene or near-Essene group. There were some Essenes, associate members of the order, so to speak, who lived

102

in the towns and villages of Judea, while others withdrew from public life to embrace a cenobitic life in the wilderness of Judea. Qumran may well have been the headquarters of the principal group of these "separated" Essenes; we are assured by archaeologists that there is no other site which could answer to the description of the Essene settlement between Jericho and Engedi given by Pliny the Elder (*Hist. Nat.* v. 17.4). But Professor Matthew Black has given reasons for thinking that the Essenes themselves were part of a wider movement of nonconformist Judaism which, he suggests, was divided into a northern and a southern group (*The Scrolls and Christian Origins* [1961], New York: Scribner, pp. 18ff. *et passim*). The southern group was the milieu in which John the Baptist was born; the northern group was the milieu in which Jesus grew up. Not that either of them can be accounted for simply in terms of his milieu; both of them, in different ways, took a line which deviated sharply from that of their respective environments. But we do have a background — an eschatologically-minded background at that — against which we can view their ministries with greater understanding than before.

There is a further point: this strain of nonconformist Judaism appears to have had close affinities with Samaritan theology (apart from the more sectarian features of Samaritanism, such as the insistence on Gerizim as Israel's true central sanctuary). John the Baptist discharged part of his baptismal ministry in Samaritan territory, "at Aenon near Salim" (John 3:23); Jesus, not long afterwards, spent two very fruitful days in the same area (John 4:35-43); Philip the Hellenist, a few years later, conducted a very successful evangelistic campaign among the Samaritans, an unintended by-product of which was the emergence of a remarkable brand of *Christian* nonconformity, the Gnostic movement led by Simon Magus (Acts 8:5-25). In the light of all this we may understand better why some of our Lord's hearers in the temple court at Jerusalem, according to John 8:48, charged Him with being a Samaritan. The word was not a mere term of abuse; it had a theological significance. Although He was as far from being a Samaritan in theology as He was by descent, there was something in His teaching which reminded them of the Samaritan way of putting things.

Many of the nonconformists took the view that it was better to await God's time for the redemption of His people, but that when He gave the signal it would be their duty to cooperate with His purpose and play the leading part, under God and His holy angels, in the establishment and administration of the kingdom. But there were .others, pre-eminently the Zealots, who saw it as their duty to offer armed resistance to the Romans at every fitting opportunity, to give no countenance to their claims to imperial sovereignty over Israel, and to hasten the advent of the coming kingdom by violence — thorough-paced "Fifth Monarchy Men."

Attempts have been made to associate Jesus rather closely with the Zealots, but they cannot be called successful. For one thing, they involve an excessively skeptical attitude to the Gospel tradition, as though the apologetic motives of the Evangelists and their predecessors had distorted the original pattern of Jesus' words and deeds almost beyond recognition. Only here and there, it must be concluded, have a few hints of the real state of affairs been allowed inadvertently to be preserved; for the rest, the original picture has been painted over with a new picture of Jesus as one who taught His followers to take the opposite line to the Zealots, to offer no resistance to evil, to turn the other cheek, to volunteer to go a second mile when their services had been conscripted by the military for one mile, to pay Caesar the tribute he demanded (the chief offense of all in the Zealots' eyes). Because the land, and especially the capital, disregarded the way of peace which He showed, and preferred the way of rebellion against the occupying power, destruction would fall on the nation as surely as it fell on the rioting Galileans who were cut down by Pilate's troops in the temple court. That this picture should be a fabricated substitution for the original picture of a Zealot sympathizer is as probable as that today an attempt should be made, with any hope of success, to persuade us that the EOKA leaders of the Greek-Cypriot struggle against the British domination of their island in the later 1950's were pacifists who inculcated in their followers an attitude of sweetness and light towards the occupying power.

That Jesus' death on the cross by the sentence of a Roman court did call for a strong and sustained apologetic is writ large throughout the New Testament. The New Testament apologetic is familiar enough to us, and it certainly was amazingly successful. Could that not have been because it had the advantage of being a true defense? The idea that Jesus' followers, who drew their inspiration from Him, made such headway in the first century with a message which deviated in essential respects from the teaching of the Master in whose name they spoke and acted, is so antecedently unlikely that it should not be accepted without strong and unambiguous evidence to support it — and such evidence we do not have.

That one of the apostles was a Zealot we know; we also know that one was a tax-collector. Simon Zelotes must have been as much an ex-Zealot as Matthew was an ex-tax-collector if the two could coexist peacefully in the same company.

The incident of the two swords at the Last Supper (Luke 22:35ff.) does not even begin to indicate that the Twelve had some of the qualities of a Zealot band. When one of the disciples a few hours later used one of these swords in his Master's defense, he was ordered immediately to sheathe it. A Zealot band would not have been content with two swords; R. Eisler's interpretation (*The Messiah Jesus and John the Baptist* [1931], pp. 369f.), according to which each of them had two swords concealed in his garments, like the *sicarii,* reads into the text what is not there. If a parallel in contemporary life is sought, we have it in Josephus's statement about the Essenes (to which Eisler makes reference in the same place), that since they can always rely on the generous hospitality of fellow-Essenes wherever they go; "they do not carry anything with them when they go on a journey, except that they take arms on account of robbers" (*BJ,* ii.125). But no interpretation of this incident in Luke's narrative is adequate which fails to reckon seriously with Jesus' quotation of Isaiah 53:12 ("he was numbered with the transgressors" and with the peremptory "Enough, enough!" with which He put an end to a conversation which had revealed all too clearly the disciples' failure to comprehend the sorrowful irony of His remark which started it.

The cleansing of the temple, which has also been appealed to in this connection, was not a Zealot action. It was not undertaken against the Romans, and in so far as it was a protest against the chief priests, it was not a protest against them for collaborating with the Romans but for permitting a misuse of the temple precincts. This action was completely in the prophetic tradition, except that where Jeremiah's protest was delivered by word of mouth "in the gate of the Lord's house" (Jer. 7:2), Jesus expressed His protest by deed as well as by word. It was not by accident that, as Matthew tells us, some of His contemporaries called Him Jeremiah (Matt. 16:14). A further reason for comparing Him to Jeremiah was that He urged His hearers to show the same submissive attitude to the Romans as Jeremiah urged upon his fellow-Jerusalemites with regard to the Babylonians.

It is clear that Jesus did have the opportunity, had He so wished, to put Himself at the head of a strong insurgent force. T. W. Manson's interpretation of His compassion because the multitude in the wilderness were "like sheep without a shepherd" (Mark 6:34) is probably correct: He saw them as an army without a captain, and He knew that if they found the wrong kind of captain they could be led to disaster (*The Servant-Messiah* [1953], pp. 70f.). And the kind of captain they would have liked to find is shown by the Johannine narrative of the feeding of the multitude; for, after Jesus had fed them in the wilderness, they tried to compel Him to be their king (John 6:14). He would not be the kind of king they wanted, and they refused to have the only kind of king He was prepared to be; therefore, as John says, many of His followers left Him from then on. Had He been a near-Zealot, albeit an unsuccessful one, His reputation in Jewish tradition would have been different from what it became.

Even before this incident, we can well believe that His closest disciples, in their rather unintelligent zeal, had gone beyond the terms of their Master's commission when He sent them two by two throughout Galilee, and had compromised Him in that part of Herod Antipas's tetrarchy to a point where He found it wise to cross the lake with them until Antipas's interest in Him had cooled off somewhat.

The plain and consistent testimony of the Gospels is that Jesus regarded the policy of the Zealots and those who shared their general attitude as tragically mistaken, and bound to involve them and their fellow-Jews in ruin. Their ideals were noble; their chosen way of realizing them was disastrous. The spirit that hailed Barabbas as a popular hero was the spirit that would one day lay Jerusalem level with the ground.

IV. JESUS' MESSAGE OF THE KINGDOM

What, then, was Jesus' message of the kingdom?

He proclaimed it as a new order in which God's rule was to be established in the hearts of men and in the world of mankind. He did not proclaim it as something to be set up beyond space or time, but as something to be realized here on earth, wherever men and women yield ready and glad obedience to God, that His will may be accomplished in and through their lives. He proclaimed this message not only in His teaching but in all the activities of His ministry, in His own attitude to God and men, and supremely in His acceptance of suffering and death so that His Father's will might be fully done. As a sequel to His suffering and death, indeed, the kingdom of God, already in one sense present in His ministry (cf. Luke 11:20), would come "with power" (Mark 9:1; cf. Luke 12:50). Not the way of violence but the way of love would unleash the powers of the coming age on earth: this is emphasized throughout the ministry of Jesus, spoken and acted alike. And the passion and triumph of the Son of man — that is to say, His triumph through passion — is all of a piece with the preceding ministry; it crowns His historic mission; it reveals and liberates the kingdom of God to make its victorious way in the world. Since the kingdom of God is received where His will is obeyed, nowhere is it more effectively manifested than in Him who said "nevertheless, not as I will but as Thou wilt" — and acted accordingly. In Jesus, to use Origen's great word, we hail the *autobasileia,* the kingdom in person.

In the vision of Daniel 7, which lies behind so much of our Lord's language about the kingdom, the coming kingdom is received by "one like a son of man," who is closely associated, if not absolutely identified, with "the saints of the Most High" (Dan. 8:13f., 18). Indeed, when Jesus proclaimed that "the appointed time is fulfilled, and the kingdom of God has drawn near" (Mark 1:15), we may catch an echo of Dan. 7:22: "the appointed time came and the saints received the kingdom." Manson argued that in the earlier phase of Jesus' ministry He maintained the corporate interpretation of the "one like a son of man," and called His disciples that they, with Him, might be fellow-members of the Son of man (*The Teachings of Jesus* [Cambridge, 1935], pp. 211ff.). Whether this was precisely His intention at that stage is a debatable question. What is not debatable is that, in the event, He fulfilled single-handed all that was written concerning the Son of man, "that he should suffer many things and be treated with contempt" (Mark 9:12).

When we study those passages in which Jesus speaks of the predestined sufferings of the Son of man, it is difficult to avoid the conclusion that He accepted and accomplished His mission as the Son of man in terms of the Isaianic servant of the Lord. This servant, in his humble and faithful obedience to God, endures undeserved suffering and death at the hands of men, but his suffering and death are the very meaning by which he brings his mission to a triumphant conclusion. For in that suffering and death he presents his life to God as a sin-offering on behalf of others, and by so bearing their sins he wins for "the many" a favorable verdict from God and a righteous status before Him. Thus, while Daniel portrays the "one like a son of man" as receiving authority to execute judgment on men, Jesus declares that "the Son of man has authority on earth to *forgive* sins" (Mark 2:10).

As the representative man Jesus thus accomplishes for others what they were unable to accomplish for themselves, taking His people's sins in death upon Himself and by that very act taking them away. But as the representative man He is also, through His passion, the founder of a new humanity, whose members bear the marks of the Son of man, drinking His cup and sharing His baptism, giving service rather than receiving it, forgiving and not condemning, living for others and not for self.

That the bringing into being of such a new humanity was part of the historic mission of Jesus is clear enough in the New Testament record. The very number of the Twelve implies that they were envisaged as the nucleus of the new people of God (cf. Luke 22:30). They, together with Jesus' other disciples who continued with Him in His trials, were the "little flock" to which the Father was pleased to give the kingdom (Luke 12:32). After His death and resurrection their numbers rapidly increased, to the point where they could no longer be described as a *little* flock. But while their numbers might increase, their character must not change, if they were to remain true to their commission to carry forward the ministry of the Servant-Messiah, with the assurance of His abiding presence and power made real to them by His Spirit. They recognized this themselves. The Servant of the Lord was to be "a light to the nations" as well as the restorer of Israel (Isa. 49:6). When Paul and Barnabas at Pisidian Antioch announced their intention of concentrating on the evangelization of Gentiles, they claimed to be fulfilling the servant's role (Acts 13:47): "For so the Lord has commanded us, saying,

'I have set you to be a light for the Gentiles,
that you may bring salvation to the uttermost parts of the earth.' "

The ministry of Jesus is thus the first phase of the mission of the Church; or, to put it more biblically, the mission of the Church is the continuation of the ministry of Jesus.

"Councils, we admit, and Creeds, cannot go behind, but must wholly rest upon the history of our Lord Jesus Christ." These words of R. C. Moberly, in his essay on "The Incarnation as the Basis of Dogma" (*Lux Mundi*, p. 243), have lost none of their validity since they were written in 1889; we repeat them not as an admission but as an affirmation. However authoritative the council, however ancient the creed, it can provide no secure foundation for faith apart from the historical Jesus of flesh and blood who lived in Palestine in the early decades of the first century A.D., who proclaimed the kingdom of God and healed the sick, who suffered and triumphed under Pontius Pilate. Not even the kerygma can supply a sure footing unless it rests upon the history of our Lord Jesus Christ. The history may be difficult to ascertain, but that is no reason for giving up the quest and seeking some other foundation. The very difficulty should challenge us to pursue the quest with redoubled vigor and zest, not that we may remain satisfied to know Christ after the flesh, but that we may, through confrontation with the historical Jesus, see in this same Jesus the image of the invisible God.

THE TEACHING OF JESUS
AND THE
GOSPEL RECORDS

Bastiaan Van Elderen

*Bastiaan Van Elderen is Professor of New Testament in Calvin Theo-
logical Seminary, Grand Rapids, Michigan. He holds the M.A. degree
from the University of California, and the Th.D. from the Pacific
School of Religion. He has been an annual professor at the Near
East School of Archaeology in Jerusalem, Jordan, in 1962 and 1964,
and has also participated in archaeological work in Jordan and Turkey.*

7. *Bastiaan Van Elderen*

THE TEACHING OF JESUS
AND THE
GOSPEL RECORDS

T O DISCOVER the teachings of Jesus, one turns inevitably to the four Gospels as the primary source. Extra-biblical sources are very limited in number, and are often of dubious value because of heretical tendencies (for example, the Gospel of Thomas). Other portions of the New Testament provide some data regarding the teachings of Jesus; however, one would hardly identify these as primary sources. But even the attempt to identify the Gospels as primary sources has been challenged often in recent decades. Bultmann argues that the Gospels contain very little authentic material concerning the life and teaching of Jesus and are for the most part the fabrications of the early Church. Traditional Christianity, on the other hand, has defended the authenticity of every line in the Gospels.

The reader encounters an interesting and varied body of material in the four Gospels. He is confronted by narratives reported two or more times which differ in details. Sayings of Jesus in one Gospel do not agree verbally with those in another Gospel. Pertinent and central details in one Gospel are ignored or omitted in another. Events are recorded in one Gospel in a totally different sequence from that found in another. These facts hardly contribute to a feeling of confidence regarding the reliability and authenticity of the Gospel records.

These seeming discrepancies should not drive the reader to despair and skepticism, however. Rather, a proper understanding of and approach to the Gospels can illuminate their authenticity and reliability. One must fully understand the nature and purpose of the individual

Gospels in order to appreciate them as sources for the teachings and life of Jesus. Each Gospel writer selected and arranged the data according to his specific purpose and intention. Viewed in this perspective, the Gospels must not be harmonized, but rather recognized as four individual witnesses to the life and ministry of Jesus (a fuller statement of this can be found in *Christian Faith and Modern Theology* [New York: Channel Press, 1964], pp. 256-258).

The Synoptic Problem, the problem of differences and similarities in the Gospels, has been extensively discussed in terms of sources. Did one Gospel use another as a source? Did two or more Gospels use a common noncanonical source? What part did oral tradition have in the fixing of units of narrative and teaching? Various documentary hypotheses have been proposed, some defending the priority of Mark, others the priority of Matthew. Some scholars posit the existence of a Q document (*Quelle*) as the source used by Matthew and Luke; others deny that such an hypothesis is necessary.

This essay does not intend to evaluate the Gospels from the standpoint of their sources; volumes have been written concerning that problem, and no convincing solution has yet been found. But in view of the fact that these Gospels are the source of the teaching and life of Jesus of Nazareth, one must recognize and reckon with their differences and similarities in order to discover their full import and message. To achieve this, a method of interpretation is being presented and applied here which will do justice to both the unity and diversity of the Gospel records.

I. THE METHOD

A term that has been used rather extensively in biblical studies is *Sitz im Leben* ("situation in life"). Students of the Bible have carefully studied various pericopes in order to ascertain the specific circumstances under which the pericope occurred and/or was recorded. This type of research is very important for the study of the Gospels. However, in the case of the Gospels, two distinct *Sitze im Leben* should be recognized, the *Sitz im Leben Jesu* ("situation in the life of Jesus") and the *Sitz im Leben des Verfassers* ("situation in the life of the author"). Every event recorded in the Gospels occurred under a given set of circumstances in the life of Jesus. On the basis of belief that the Bible is the Word of God, it is assumed that every event recorded had a *Sitz im Leben Jesu*. The historicity of the events and sayings in the life of Christ are accepted as part of one's total commitment to Jesus Christ and His revelation. Admittedly, this is circular reasoning, but every approach to Scripture proceeds with a presupposition, whether it be a faith commitment to Jesus or an "objective" denial of all supernaturalism.

To recover the *Sitz im Leben Jesu* is greatly facilitated when a given event is recorded in the double tradition, triple tradition, or quadruple tradition. A comparative study of the two, three, or four accounts will reveal modifications that an individual Evangelist has made in his account. By recognizing these modifications and noting the general tendency and intent of the individual Evangelist, the reader can recover some idea of what the original setting of the event was. This is not an attempt to harmonize the various accounts of a given event by reconciling and integrating details which are in themselves disparate and dissimilar. It is a frank recognition of such features, but not a denial of the historicity of the event or the authenticity of the saying.

It is more difficult to recover the *Sitz im Leben Jesu* of an event recorded by only one Gospel. Continued study of events in double, triple, or quadruple traditions will reveal certain procedures and tendencies of a given author, and these can be applied to accounts of events and sayings preserved in a single tradition only. The *Sitz im Leben Jesu* of such an account can never be wholly recovered, but some tentative formulation can certainly aid the interpreter in his understanding of the passage.

Of greater significance to the interpreter is the *Sitz im Leben des Verfassers.* This is the setting and situation in which the present account comes to the reader. It is readily apparent that the author's stance and circumstance had a bearing upon the account when one observes the variations in detail, sequence, and emphasis in the double, triple, and quadruple traditions. The significance and consequence of the *Sitz im Leben des Verfassers* is demonstrated by the futility and frustration encountered when attempts at harmonization founder and miscarry. Failure to recognize the individuality of the Evangelists — their specific intentions, the needs and problems of their readers, their ecclesiastical and cultural environments — has led to two responses to this problem. Some scholars despair, and take a very skeptical attitude toward the historicity and authenticity of the Gospel records. Others engage in forced harmonizations and circuitous reasoning to reconcile discrepancies and eliminate difficulties in the accounts. These two unsatisfactory responses highlight the need to recognize the *Sitz im Leben des Verfassers.*

Evidence points to the fact that the earliest Gospel was written about thirty years after the resurrection and ascension of Jesus. During these thirty years the Church expanded in all directions, especially westward, and by the time of the death of the apostle Paul, the small band of 120 mentioned in Acts 1 had multiplied numerous times. This tremendous increase in numbers was also accompanied by the addition of non-Jewish people from all strata of society. It is in this general background of an expanded and expanding Church that the Evangelists set about to prepare their accounts of the ministry and teaching of Jesus.

Each Evangelist addressed himself to a segment of the Church or group of individuals who faced a certain set of problems as believers or inquirers. A study of the Gospels will give some idea of the character of the recipients. It is very evident that the recipients of the First Gospel, for example, were Jews, because of its apologetic emphasis. The stress upon the miraculous power of Jesus in Mark and upon the loving and kind disposition of Jesus in Luke also reveals some of the characteristics of the recipients of these Gospels. These aspects constitute part of the *Sitz im Leben des Verfassers*.

Of central importance in the *Sitz im Leben des Verfassers* is the purpose that the Evangelist is seeking to accomplish by his writing. To what specific need or problem is he addressing himself? This will determine the emphasis that he will give to a certain event or saying and influence the selection of events and sayings that he will include to advance his argument. Even the sequence in which he presents these will be affected by such considerations as the development of his argument and the unity of the discussion. When these factors are kept in mind, the variations in the Gospel accounts will not present stumbling blocks or occasions for skepticism regarding the reliability of the Gospels.

Another major contribution of the *Sitz im Leben Jesu* and the *Sitz im Leben des Verfassers* is the light they throw upon the account itself. In this way the interpreter sees the passage in its own historical and contextual setting. Too often these factors have been ignored, and grave injustice has been done to the meaning and intention of the author by wrenching a pericope or saying from its context. In terms of the study of the Gospels, this method necessitates a comprehensive understanding of the culture, society, and life of first-century Palestine. This is a significant part of the *Sitz im Leben Jesu* and will elucidate many of the social customs, religious practices, political trends, and environmental influences that are part of the warp and woof of the accounts. For instance, a knowledge of the political situation in first-century Palestine explains many of the tensions and concerns in messianism at that time. Similarly, the Parable of the Sower mentions some practices which are strange for one who is unacquainted with Palestinian agriculture and topography. In this area biblical archaeology has made and will continue to make significant contributions to the interpretation and understanding of Scripture.

However, the *Sitz im Leben Jesu* is only a part of the total picture and, as noted above, in some cases very difficult to recover. In actual fact, the *Sitz im Leben* in the Gospels is that of the Evangelist, and it is in that perspective that the Gospels should be interpreted. The *Sitz im Leben Jesu* can elucidate details, but the interpreter must always realize that he is seeing the event or saying through the eyes of the Evangelist — in the *Sitz im Leben des Verfassers.* The Gospels are not journal accounts nor diary records of the life of Jesus, but they are the witnesses of individuals who wrote about events which had taken place thirty or more years earlier. They are written to interpret certain events and sayings of Jesus of Nazareth, to meet certain needs in the Church, to defend the message of Jesus against certain errors, to correct certain misconceptions, and to advance the Christian Church in her enlarged environment with its concomitant problems. A concern for the *Sitz im Leben des Verfassers* will preclude the submerging of the emphasis of one Gospel in favor of another in order to harmonize them. Each account stands in its own right as a legitimate emphasis and interpretation. Such a concern will prevent the interpreter from ignoring the historical and environmental context, for it will compel him to reckon with these factors which provide important keys to the understanding of the passage. Thus the fragmentation of a given Gospel will be avoided, and the unity of the work will be highlighted as presenting a certain portrait of the life and ministry of Jesus.

II. THE APPLICATION

To demonstrate the application of the method described above, a few examples will be analyzed briefly to suggest the possibilities of this procedure.

A problem that often vexes the student of the Gospels is the matter of sequence of events. It is rather naive to suggest that events which are recorded in different sequences in different Gospels occurred more than once in the life of Jesus, and one Evangelist records the first occurrence, another the second. Although this possibility exists, the number of such examples and the similarity of their basic details makes the universal application of this approach highly improbable. A more realistic answer can often be acquired in the light of the structure and emphasis of the individual Gospels.

A good illustration of this problem is found in the sequence and time of three pericopes recorded in the first three Gospels. These are the stilling of the tempest, the healing of the demoniac(s) in Gerasa, and the raising of Jairus' daughter. Mark and Luke agree by placing these three in the above order in the same phase of the ministry of Jesus, between His teaching by parables and the feeding of the five thousand. Matthew places them much earlier in the Galilean ministry (Matt. 8 and

9; the parables are found in chapter 13). Matthew's change of sequence was occasioned by his desire to group together a number of miracle narratives as his introduction to the second major discourse (chaps. 9 and 10). In view of the basic structure of Matthew's Gospel, which uses five major discourses around which the life of Jesus is built, such a rearrangement of events is understandable and meaningful. In such cases he has actually violated the *Sitz im Leben Jesu* in order to meet the needs of his own *Sitz im Leben* and the structure of his document.

Verbal variations in the sayings of Jesus recorded in two or more Gospels present a more challenging problem. A possible explanation can once again be found in the *Sitze im Leben* of the writers. A good illustration can be found in the accounts recorded by Matthew and Luke in which Jesus discusses the answer to prayer. These accounts are found in Matthew 7:7-11 and Luke 11:9-13. Luke's account is found in the central section of his Gospel (9:51-18:14), often referred to as the great insertion or travel narrative, in which he has grouped together a number of items found in different sequence and contexts in the other Gospels. The Matthean and Lukan accounts of the pericope under discussion are so similar verbally that it appears that these are two accounts of the same event. However, there is one very significant variation: Matthew concludes the discussion by the words " 'how much more will your Father who is in heaven give good things to those who ask him?' " whereas Luke's conclusion uses the phrasing " 'how much more will the heavenly Father give the Holy Spirit to those who ask him?' " Luke has identified the "good things" of Matthew's account as the "Holy Spirit." It appears that Luke has adapted this saying of Jesus to substantiate an emphasis on the Holy Spirit that pervades his Gospel and the Acts of the Apostles.

Another phase of Luke's *Sitz im Leben* can be seen in his references to prayer in the life of Jesus in events which are also recorded by other Gospel writers without reference to or stress upon prayer. Luke is the only Evangelist to report that Jesus was praying at the time of the baptism (3:21), after the cleansing of the leper (5:16), during the night before the call of the Twelve (6:12), at the time of Peter's confession at Caesarea Philippi (9:18), on the mountain of transfiguration (9:28), at the time he taught the Lord's Prayer (11:1), and on the cross (23: 34). Three parables on prayer are peculiar to Luke: the Friend at Midnight (11:5-8), the Unjust Judge (18:1-8), and the Pharisee and the Publican (18:9-14).

Obviously Luke felt a need to stress the place and importance of prayer in his Gospel. This is part of the *Sitz im Leben des Verfassers* of the Third Gospel. A study and awareness of this *Sitz im Leben* will not only account for the differences and variations in the Gospel accounts, but will also greatly enrich the meaning and significance of each individual Gospel.

Another illustration of the bearing of the *Sitz im Leben des Verfassers* on the way that a given Evangelist records his material is in the interpretation of the Parable of the Sower (Matt. 13:18-23; Mark 4:13-20; Luke 8:11-15). Not only are there differences of details here (some of these can be traced back to the presentations of the parable itself in the three Gospels), but there is a distinct difference of emphasis in the interpretations. Some of the verbal differences may be accounted for by the fact that these records present in Greek what was undoubtedly said in Aramaic by Jesus. But there are other variations which can best be explained as arising out of the difference in *Sitz im Leben des Verfassers*.

Matthew's reference to the "kingdom" in 13:19 reflects his and his readers' interest in this concept. Luke's introduction of the idea of faith in 8:12, 13 reflects his emphasis on this concept. The variations in the identification of the thorns likewise reflect the different emphases of the writers. Matthew ("care of the world and delight in riches" — 13:22) and Mark ("cares of the world, and the delight in riches, and the desire for other things" — 4:19) do not differ greatly, but Luke's identification ("cares and riches and pleasures of life" — 8:14) seems to be an adaptation and interpretation of the original saying of Jesus. His negative attitude to riches and the rich is found elsewhere in his Gospel (cf. 6: 24; 11:41; 12:15, 33; 14:33; 16:9), and it is interesting to note that his interpretation refers to "riches," whereas that of Matthew and Mark speaks of "delight in riches." Matthew and Mark identify the "cares" as being "of the world" or "of this age" (αἰῶνος). Luke's omission of this modifier is part of his stress on faithfulness and endurance in the present life. In connection with the "rocky ground," both Matthew and Mark refer to "tribulation" and "persecution," whereas Luke refers to "the time of temptation" (8:13). Both Matthew and Mark designate the amount of the yield, but Luke omits such a designation.

How are these and other variations to be explained? Luke's presentation has given an emphasis to this parable that differs from that of Matthew and Mark. Matthew and Mark have an eschatological emphasis, stressing fruit-bearing and yielding, the end perspective of the Christian life. They accentuate the evils of "this age," which is characterized by tribulation and persecution. These are external attacks upon the seed ("the word") and make it unfruitful. Luke's presentation places the emphasis upon the present life. He wants to exhort his readers to endurance and perseverance. When Matthew (13:22) and Mark (4:19) speak of unfruitfulness, Luke speaks of immaturity (8:14). In regard to the good soil, Luke writes: "they are those who, hearing the word, hold it fast in an honest and good heart, and bring forth fruit with patience" (8:15). Matthew and Mark do not have "hold it fast in an honest and good heart" or "with patience." Here Luke, along with the omission of any reference to variation in yield, is placing the emphasis upon faithfulness and patience in the present life. This is also seen in his reference to temptation (8:13) where Matthew (13:21) and Mark (4:17) refer to tribulation and persecution. The former arises out of the individual whereas the latter two attack the individual from outside. Luke's reference to believing in 8:12, 13 undoubtedly was occasioned by examples of temporary faith. In sum, Luke is stressing the present life; Matthew and Mark, the parousia. A tendency to stress the parousia at the expense of the present life, as happened at Thessalonica, undoubtedly motivated Luke to adjust and adapt the original interpretation given by Jesus. This Lukan emphasis on the present reality of the kingdom, suggesting a delay of the parousia, is also found in the Parable of the Pounds, which was told to correct an expectation of an immediate appearance of the kingdom (Luke 19:11). Luke often omits or softens some of the Marcan passages regarding the imminence of the kingdom. Apparently, part of the *Sitz im Leben* of Luke was a misconception prevalent in the Church regarding the nature and time of the kingdom of God.

III. CONCLUDING OBSERVATIONS

The above examples and discussions point out the relevance and importance of the *Sitz im Leben des Verfassers* in the interpretation of the Gospels. It will provide an adequate explanation for the variations in the Gospel accounts without doubting or denying the historicity of the events or authenticity of the sayings recorded in them.

Can the Gospels still be described as inspired writings? Most assuredly so. These were written under and through the inspiration of the Holy Spirit. In other words, the Spirit of Jesus through the Evangelists is interpreting the ministry and sayings of Jesus to meet the peculiar needs that had arisen in the Church some thirty years after the resurrection. Hence, these are authoritative and trustworthy accounts and interpretations. In some cases it will be impossible to recover the *ipsissima verba* of Jesus, since at times these have been adapted and interpreted to meet the needs of the *Sitz im Leben des Verfassers*. However, it is more honest and respectful to Scripture to recognize this than to engage in dubious harmonizations which the genre of New Testament literature scarcely allows.

A hermeneutics of the Gospels which stresses the *Sitz im Leben des Verfassers* provides a way of interpretation which does full justice to each individual Gospel. Each stands in its own right with its own unique message. And that unique message must be proclaimed — not a forced and watered-down harmonization. In some cases where an event is recorded in the triple tradition, three distinct, although related, interpretations are possible. The homilete must choose that interpretation which meets the needs of his audience, just as the Gospel writer interpreted the event to meet the needs of his readers. Or the preacher may use all three interpretations in successive messages to unfold the riches of the multiple Gospel tradition the Church has received.

In conclusion, it is possible to speak with confidence regarding the Gospel records. They contain the teaching of Jesus, although it is interpreted and modified. Nevertheless, the basic message is one, and a presupposition of the above method is in every case a *Sitz im Leben Jesu* for each pericope in the Gospel records. This presupposition is both the obvious assumption of the Gospel records and the validation of their authority and trustworthiness. Delineating the *Sitz im Leben des Verfassers* and the *Sitz im Leben Jesu* should bring into proper perspective the true nature and purpose of the Gospels. It is hoped that the above presentation will enhance the readers' confidence in the Gospel record, increase his appreciation for the riches of God's Word, and unfold to him the power and dynamic of the Gospel.

THE FOURTH GOSPEL
AND HISTORY

Leon Morris

*Leon Morris is Principal of Ridley College, Melbourne, Australia.
Formerly he was Warden at Tyndale House, Cambridge, England. He
is author of many volumes, among them* The Apostolic Preaching of
the Cross, The Biblical Doctrine of Judgment, The Dead Sea Scrolls
and St. John's Gospel, *and commentaries on I, II Thessalonians in the
Tyndale Bible Commentaries and in The New International Commentary on the New Testament. His most recent work is* The Cross
in the New Testament. *He holds the Ph.D. degree from University
of Cambridge.*

THE FOURTH GOSPEL
AND HISTORY

NO ONE can prove by the accepted canons of historical research that Jesus is the Christ, the Son of God, nor that those who believe in Him have eternal life.[1] But it is this kind of thing, and not the writing of a biography, that clearly matters to John. What is not so clear is how this affects his attitude to facts. In plain language the question is, Does John allow his theological interests to warp his view of the facts? Or does he exercise care to see that nothing is narrated as having happened without good reason? Most scholars these days assume unhesitatingly that there is more interpretation than fact in John, and many feel that this Gospel cannot be relied upon for anything other than the barest minimum of historical fact. Günther Bornkamm's statement is typical:

> The Gospel according to John has so different a character in comparison with the other three, and is to such a degree the product of a developed theological reflection, that we can only treat it as a secondary source (*Jesus of Nazareth* [London: Hodder and Stoughton, 1960], p. 14).

I. FACT AND INTERPRETATION

There is not the slightest doubt that John has a theological purpose. He makes no attempt at all to conceal this, but tells us plainly, "these are written that you may believe that Jesus is the Christ, the Son of

---

1 Thus T. A. Roberts points out that Christianity's claim about the act of God in Jesus "cannot be proved or disproved by the historian, using the techniques of historical criticism, for the claim goes beyond the bounds of what is within the historian's power to assert to be either true or false" (*History and Christian Apologetic* [London, 1960], p. 164).

God, and that believing you may have life in his name" (20:31). He is trying to persuade, not to record facts for facts' sake. He is no objective historian and we completely miss his stated purpose if we assess his work along narrowly historical lines. As he writes about Jesus of Nazareth he writes about "the Christ, the Son of God." He sees significance in the words and deeds of Jesus and his Gospel brings this out.

But this may well be the path of true history, not its negation. C. H. Dodd has pointed out that there are some events "which can take their true place in an historical record only as they are interpreted" (*History and the Gospel* [London: Nisbet, 1938], p. 104) and he gives as examples the beginning of the Reformation at Wittenberg, the fall of the Bastille, and the abdication of King Edward VIII. Unless we include interpretation we will certainly give a false impression, for example, of the events which took place at the Bastille on that July day in 1789. Simply to content ourselves with a "factual" account of what took place that day is to miss the path and to fail as historians. Fact and interpretation are inextricably interwoven and neither may be neglected. We should bear in mind Nietzsche's often quoted dictum, "Not facts, but only interpretations exist." E. C. Rust writes:

> It is an open issue whether we can even speak of a bare historical event. All the data of the historian is a composite of fact and evaluation. Contemporary eyes and records have added a subjective element to what reaches us. We may try to sift the evidence, but we have to make our own judgment of significance. The historian's evidence for a period may be limited, but he still has the task of estimating the relations between the facts which he can delineate and of answering satisfactorily, in the particular mode he chooses, the question "Why?" The past matters insofar as it comes alive to us through an intelligible form. A mere chronicle of the past is dead and meaningless (*Towards a Theological Understanding of History* [New York; Oxford, 1963], p. 5). Cf. also R. G. Collingwood, *The Idea of History* [Oxford, 1963], pp. 131-33.

This is true also of those events in Galilee and Jerusalem of which John writes. Pilate and Caiaphas were intimately concerned in some of them, but nothing is more sure than that these men did not realize what was really happening. They did not understand the significance of the events in which they were taking leading parts. They would have been quite capable of giving "factual" accounts of what "happened" when Jesus of Nazareth came before them. But simply to chronicle the events as they knew them would be to give a distorted and untrue account. For an account which is not misleading something of the significance of those events must be brought out. It is important to be clear on this. An element of interpretation is not only permissible here, it is imperative. If John then introduces interpretation in his

Gospel that does not rule it out as *history*. Of course, it is also possible that his interpretation may be completely inadmissible. At this point all that I am saying is that the nature of the events he is describing is such that in order for justice to be done to them there must be interpretation. We must proceed to examine what kind of interpretation John has in fact given.

II. SOME JOHANNINE ACCURACIES

Attention has often enough been drawn to those facets of the Fourth Gospel which make it difficult for critical scholars to hold it to be a factual record — the differences from the Synoptic record,[2] the advanced Christology, elements which are claimed to be Hellenistic, and so on. These are real, but they need to be balanced by certain other facts. One is that on a number of points John appears to be remarkably accurate. Consider, for example, his topography. John has many references to places, and quite often it is apparent that he knew what he was writing about and has described it accurately. R. D. Potter has concluded from a survey of the topographical references in this Gospel that, as far as our present information goes, John's references indicate that he must have known Palestine.[3]

Another feature of John's work is the frequent notes of time he employs. Again and again he tells us that such and such a thing happened on such and such a day, or at a given hour of the day, or the like. These details often appear to have no significance as regards the flow of the narrative. Thus in John 1:39 there does not seem to be any importance attaching to the fact that it was at about the tenth

---

2 These differences should not be overlooked, but neither should they be magnified. H. Cunliffe-Jones, while rejecting the possibility of a formal harmony between the Gospels, yet sees what he calls "four synoptic Gospels," i.e. four Gospels which give us essentially the same Lord (*Studia Evangelica,* ed. K. Aland *et al.* [Berlin, 1959], p. 24; hereafter this volume is referred to as *SE;* the two subsequent volumes, edited by F. L. Cross and published in Berlin in 1964 are referred to as *SE,* II and *SE,* III). It is also worth bearing in mind that, whereas recent scholars have been impressed with the differences between John and the Synoptics, the Church through the centuries has been impressed by the resemblances. The Church has not worshipped two Christs, but one. It has not felt compelled to choose between the Synoptic and Johannine presentation, but has valued both.

3 "Topography and Archaeology in the Fourth Gospel," *SE,* pp. 329-337. *Inter alia* he says, "Time and again, it will be found that those who have lived long in Palestine are struck by the impression that our author did so. He knew the Palestine that they have learned to know" (*ibid.,* p. 335). He concludes that "we have in this gospel not only the Word of God, but also the narrative of a reliable witness, a Palestinian Jew" (*ibid.,* p. 337). W. F. Albright also stresses the accuracy of the topographical references in this Gospel. See *The Archaeology of Palestine* [Pelican Books, 1949], pp. 244-48; *The Background of the New Testament and its Eschatology,* ed. W. D. Davies & D. Daube [Cambridge, 1956], pp. 158-60.

hour when Jesus invited two disciples of John the Baptist to come and
see where He was staying. Repeated instances of this drive us to the
conclusion that he includes this kind of thing only because he had
information which enabled him to fix the time when certain events
took place. It is impossible to find a dogmatic motive for the inclusion
of these notes of time.

It is all of a piece with this that John has many references to the
feasts of the Jewish year, far more than we find in the other Gospels.
This raises the question of why John did this, and what significance
he sees in the feasts. But the way he uses the Jewish calendar has
convinced many that he knew what he was talking about. He refers
to the Passover, for example, in chapter 6 because the events in question took place at Passover time. E. Stauffer is insistent that John is
the only Evangelist who enables us to fix a chronology of Jesus' life,
and he sees this done through the various references of this kind scattered through John's Gospel.[4]

Very illuminating is this Evangelist's handling of John the Baptist.
He tells us in his first reference to him that this man came "for testimony, to bear witness to the light" (1:7). He sees John in no other
light. Always he depicts him as a witness, bearing his witness to
Jesus so that men might believe in Him. We hear nothing of the
Baptist's ethical teaching. For that we must turn to Luke. We hear
nothing of his denunciation of the "brood of vipers" (Luke 3:7). We
hear nothing from John of the eschatological judgment, the wrath
to come. We do not even read that John baptized Jesus, though there
can be little doubt but that this Gospel refers to the occasion when this
took place. From first to last the Baptist is depicted as a witness, and
nothing more. The writer allows nothing to distract us from seeing
him in this role.

Since this is so clear we might anticipate that the picture of the
Baptist in this Gospel would be woefully inaccurate, perhaps even
distorted to get the effect. Indeed, some have thought that our author
knew little of the real John the Baptist. P. Gardner-Smith, for instance,
asserts:

> What is not so often recognized is that there is little evidence that
> he knew more of the John of history than what he might have learned
> from the vague traditions of the churches before these traditions became

---

4 Cf. the following statements: "The fourth evangelist, John, has cleared up the
chronology of Jesus' story" (*Jesus and His Story* [London, SCM, 1960], p. 15); "It
is clearly impossible to fit the chronological structure of John's gospel into the narrow
frame of the synoptic presentation. *But it is easily possible to insert the synoptic
frame into the Johannine construction.* This is one argument, beside very many
others, for the correctness of the Johannine chronology" (*ibid.*, p. 17).

crystallized in the Synoptic Gospels" (*Saint John and the Synoptic Gospels* [Cambridge, 1938], p. 4).

But in recent times the discovery of the Qumran Scrolls has altered all that. These show us that the portrait of John the Baptist is remarkably accurate. At point after point there are resemblances, and so many are the points of contact that some have thought that John must have been a member at one time of the Qumran Community. Sometimes the points of contact are in set terms like "the spirit of truth" which are unusual enough to demand a link of some sort. Sometimes they refer to ideas like the modified dualism that is such a prominent feature of both the Scrolls and the Fourth Gospel. It seems to me too much to affirm, with some scholars, that John the Baptist must have been at one time a member of the Qumran Community. But we are told that he was in the desert until the time that he was manifested to Israel (Luke 1:80), and there is nothing improbable in the suggestion that during this period he developed an acquaintance with the teaching of Qumran or of a sect somewhat resembling it.

It must be stressed that the contacts with Qumran teaching are not occasional. Here I am stressing the fact that the Scrolls have links with the teaching of John the Baptist. But it is worth noting that they have more points of contact with the Fourth Gospel than with any other book of the New Testament. I have tried to bring out the significance of this in my Campbell Morgan Lecture, *The Dead Sea Scrolls and St. John's Gospel* (London, 1960).

W. H. Brownlee maintains that almost every point in the teaching of John the Baptist, in the Fourth Gospel as in the Synoptics, has its contact with the teaching of the Scrolls. He says, "The most astonishing result of all is the validation of the Fourth Gospel as an authentic source concerning the Baptist" (*The Scrolls and the New Testament,* ed. K. Stendahl [London: SCM, 1958], p. 52). With this we should take the verdict of J. A. T. Robinson, no friend of conservative opinions:

> One of the most remarkable effects of the Scrolls has been the surprising vindication they appear to offer of ideas and categories attributed to John by the fourth Evangelist which recent criticism would never have allowed as remotely historical. Indeed, nothing, I prophesy, is likely to undergo so complete a reversal in the criticism of the Gospel as our estimate of its treatment of the Baptist, and therefore of the whole Judean ministry of Jesus with which it opens. This treatment has almost universally been assumed to spring from purely theological motives of a polemical nature and thus to provide evidence for a very minimum of historical foundation. . . . On the contrary, I believe that the fourth Evangelist is remarkably well informed on the Baptist, because he, or the witness behind that part of his tradition, once belonged to John's movement and, like the nameless disciple of 1,37, "heard him say this, and followed Jesus" (*SE,* p. 345).

All this is most important. There is not the slightest doubt that the Baptist is depicted in a certain way in order to attain a theological end. This is conceded by all and is plainly stated by the Evangelist. But it now appears that when he writes about the Baptist John is accurate. He has been able to effect his aim without distorting the facts. He took what actually happened and recorded it in such a way as to bring out his (and its) meaning. Now if John could do this in one place he could do it elsewhere. If his facts are right while he is painting the portrait of the Baptist why should they not be right also when he is depicting Jesus?

It should further be noted that John does not introduce his theology indiscriminately. While he certainly brings out the theological meaning of some of the things he narrates it is also the case that sometimes he does nothing of the sort. For example, in the trial narrative John relates that at one point the Jews told Pilate that Jesus ought to die because "he has made himself the Son of God (υἱὸν θεοῦ)" (19:7). This is an expression which invites theological treatment. But all that John tells us Pilate did was to ask Jesus "Where are you from?", for he was greatly afraid. That is to say he is taking υἱὸν θεοῦ in the sense "son of a god." He is inquiring whether Jesus is a demigod (in the usual Greek and Roman sense). John does not correct this, or dwell on the true meaning of "Son of God." He does not even make this central to the charge against Jesus. Rather he emphasizes that Jesus was condemned as "King of the Jews," dangerous though this was politically. In other words, John has deliberately passed over an opportunity of bringing in his distinctive view of the Person of Jesus, and that in a place where it would have made things easier for Christians confronted with the Roman might. He could have stressed the religious motif. Instead he has emphasized a politically dangerous thought. I do not see how we can conclude other than that he has chosen to be faithful to the facts. C. H. Dodd draws attention to the words of the Jews, "We have no king but Caesar" (19:15), and comments:

> This might very naturally be read as an admission that Jews were loyal subjects and Christians were not: a damaging admission, surely, in the situation in which Christians found themselves at the time when the gospel was published. If the evangelist set himself to reproduce with essential fidelity the ethos of the actual situation in which Christ was condemned, as it was handed down (however much he may have felt free to dramatize it), the preservation of these challenging traits could be understood; but I should find it difficult to imagine a Christian writer under Domitian (let us say), or even under Nerva or Trajan, going out of his way to introduce them into a relatively harmless account" (*Historical Tradition in the Fourth Gospel* [Cambridge, 1963], p. 115).

III. JOHN AND "THE TRUTH"

One of John's major themes is "the truth." He uses the word ἀλήθεια twenty-five times, compared with once in Matthew and three times each in Mark and Luke. Similarly he uses the adjective ἀληθής fourteen times (once each in Matthew and Mark, not at all in Luke), and ἀληθινὸς nine times (not in Matthew or Mark, once in Luke). The very recital of these statistics shows that John is unusually interested in truth.

He sees truth not only as a quality of words, but also of actions for it is possible to "do" the truth (3:21). This idea is found also in the Old Testament, Gen. 32:10 (Hebrew, 32:11), 47:29 (see the Hebrew text). Moreover, John sees the truth as especially connected with Jesus, who is called "the truth" (14:6). S. Aalen, in a very important article, sees John's concept of truth as central ("'Truth,' a Key Word in St. John's Gospel," in *SE* II, pp. 3-24). It contrasts the true way to God with the false and inadequate ways outlined by other religions. Consequently it constitutes both a rejection of those ways and an invitation to men to walk in the right path.

The fact that truth is one of John's key concepts should not be overlooked. While it is true that he is more concerned to show us the consequences of seeing Jesus as the truth than with any other aspect of truth yet we cannot let the matter rest there. It would be extremely strange if a writer who placed unusual stress on the truth were to play loose with the truth in a book written about Jesus as the truth. This does not mean, of course, that it would be impossible for John to have put down anything that was not strictly true. But it does serve as a warning against seeing him as an incurable theological romancer. He does not see truth as comparatively unimportant, he sees it as critically important. Accordingly, it is unlikely that he will engage in a systematic distortion of the facts. No one could make truth a central concept in a writing like this Gospel if his conscience were not clear that his work expressed the truth as nearly as he could make it.

Along with this we should note John's stress on witness. He uses the noun μαρτυρία fourteen times (not in Matthew, three times in Mark and once in Luke), and the verb μαρτυρεῖν thirty-three times (once each in Matthew and Luke and not in Mark). Obviously this is another of his characteristic concepts. He sees witness as borne by deity, the Father (5:31f.), the Son (8:14, 18), and the Spirit (15:26). Jesus' works bore witness (5:36), as did the inspired Scripture (5:39). There was witness also from a variety of human witnesses, and in this case the witness could of course be verified and interrogated by normal human processes. Among such witnesses are the Samaritan woman (4:

39), the disciples (15:27), John the Baptist (1:7), and even the multitude (12:17).

Witness is a legal term. It signifies the kind of evidence that is allowed in a law court. It would, of course, be idle to pretend that the term was confined to this sort of witness, or that the rules of evidence in first-century Palestine would in all cases commend themselves to us. Nevertheless the term is not without significance, and its constant use in this Gospel shows that the author is confident of his facts. He is telling us that what he writes is well attested. This is incompatible with a romantic theological elaboration of the barest minimum of fact. At the very least John's habitual use of the category of witness shows that he was quite confident that his facts could not be controverted.

IV. THE HISTORIANS

It is worth mentioning that many historians are not as skeptical about the value of the Gospels in general and John in particular as historical sources as are many New Testament scholars. It would be preposterous to suggest that they feel that all is well in the Johannine garden. They are more than a little hesitant, and that at many points. But John has convinced some very hardheaded scholars that he had access to good tradition, and that there are many points in his Gospel which must unhesitatingly be accepted as factual. M. Goguel, for example, has found Johannine teaching of great importance, and there are many points from Johannine material in his *The Life of Jesus.*

Perhaps more important is the thorough examination made by C. H. Dodd in his book, *Historical Tradition in the Fourth Gospel.* In this book Dodd dissents from the view that the religious interests of the Evangelists disqualify them from being seriously considered as historical sources. He reminds us that "it was not for nothing that the early Church repudiated gnosticism, with all its speculative breadth and subtlety and its imaginative mythology" (*op. cit.,* p. 2). Dodd is not arguing for a conservative position, and he freely concedes that theological motives have been at work in the Fourth Gospel, sometimes resulting in distortion. But the main drift of his argument is that behind this Gospel there lies a very early tradition, and one independent of that behind the Synoptic Gospels. This is a serious historical judgment, and is not lightly to be rejected. The work of P. Gardner-Smith already referred to had already convinced many that this Gospel must be thought of as independent. But Dodd's book is much more detailed and thorough. It is difficult to see how the main conclusion can be disputed. But if we accept it then it follows that part, at any rate, of this Gospel must be held to be very reliable.

V. DISCIPLE TEACHING

Probably what looms largest in many minds when they think of the problem of history in John is the difference in tone between this Gospel and the Synoptics. We instinctively feel that if they give an authentic picture, then John can hardly be anything other than erroneous. Yet it is possible to account for this difference. The Church traditionally has not thought of the problem as insuperable, for it has accepted this Gospel as well as the other three.

Recently H. Riesenfeld has made an interesting contribution to the discussion ("The Gospel Tradition and its Beginnings" in *SE*, pp. 43-65). He reminds us that first-century teaching involved memory work. Every rabbi made his pupils commit large sections of his teaching to memory. Any student worth his salt was expected to remember things accurately, and some phenomenal feats of memory have been recorded. There is nothing improbable in the suggestion that Jesus perpetuated the essential features of His teaching by getting His followers to learn part of it by heart. Riesenfeld's contention is that it is essentially this that lies behind the traditions recorded in the Synoptic Gospels. He can say, "And this implies that Jesus made his disciples, and above all the Twelve, learn, and furthermore that he made them learn by heart"; "what was essential to his message he taught his disciples, that is, he made them learn it by heart" (*ibid.*, pp. 59, 61). What Jesus thus began was carried on by oral tradition. The form critics may thus have their say, but Riesenfeld insists that the origin is in the instruction given by Jesus and memorized by the disciples.

But a rabbi did more than one thing. In addition to his formal teaching, systematically committed to the memories of his students, there was instruction of a more informal kind, delivered under less exacting conditions. There was the sort of scholarly intercourse that takes place when teaching as such is not primarily in mind but when one mind takes fire from another. Was there something akin to this in Jesus' relationship with His followers? Riesenfeld thinks that the starting-point of the Johannine tradition "is to be found in the discourses and 'meditations' of Jesus in the circle of his disciples, such as certainly took place side by side with the instruction of the disciples proper, with its more rigid forms" (*ibid.*, p. 63).

It is not necessary to agree with everything said by Riesenfeld and his supporters to see that this is a very suggestive line of approach. A priori there seems no reason why Jesus should not have made His disciples learn certain things, which then formed the starting point of the Synoptic tradition. In addition He may well have engaged in more informal conversations with His friends and disputes with His enemies, which formed the starting point of the Johannine tradition. If this is so it will explain a great many things, and it will preclude us from denying the historicity of John simply because the tradition embodied in this Gospel is markedly different from that in the Synoptics.

My conclusion is that many recent scholars have been too hasty in denying that John is to be taken seriously when we look for history. There are several factors which indicate that this Gospel is reliable, and there is one way at any rate of accounting for the differences from the Synoptic Gospels. I do not suggest that this way is necessarily the right way, but it at least opens up a possibility. This being so, the indications of accuracy which we noted earlier must be given their full weight. John is not careless about the factualness of his narrative, but on the contrary seems determined to make it clear that his work is to be trusted. And in this twentieth century there is still good ground for agreeing.

THE HISTORICITY
OF THE RESURRECTION

Merrill C. Tenney

*Merrill C. Tenney is Dean of the Graduate School of Wheaton College,
Wheaton, Illinois.* *He served Gordon College in New England as
Professor of New Testament from 1930-43, when he was invited to
Wheaton as Professor of Bible and Theology.* *He is general editor
of the* Zondervan Picture Bible Dictionary *and the author of many
books, among them* Resurrection Realities, John: The Gospel of
Belief, Galatians: The Charter of Christian Liberty, The Genius of
the Gospels, Interpreting Revelation, New Testament Survey, *and*
New Testament Times. *He was president of the Evangelical Theological Society in 1951.* *He holds the Ph.D. degree from Harvard University.*

9. Merrill C. Tenney

THE HISTORICITY
OF THE RESURRECTION

THE RESURRECTION of Jesus Christ is the pivotal doctrine of Christian faith, for the witness of the New Testament declares that "if Christ has not been raised, your faith is futile and you are still in your sins" (I Cor. 15:17). Whether it be regarded as veritable history, convenient mythology, or a deliberate hoax, it is inescapable, for one can neither assert nor deny the truth of the Christian gospel without taking cognizance of this fundamental article of belief. If the New Testament message is credible, the importance of the resurrection in its total structure must be acknowledged.

To acknowledge its importance, however, is not the same as accepting its historicity. A legend may sway popular opinion irrespective of its intrinsic verity. The historicity of the resurrection implies that the body of Jesus of Nazareth which had reposed in the tomb of Joseph of Arimathea was revived and released on the first day of the week, and that the living Lord appeared subsequently to certain of His disciples. The resurrection was an event as factual as the discovery of America by Columbus in 1492. With few exceptions every book of the New Testament constantly affirms this fact, and the brief epistles that do not mention it (Philemon, II Peter, II and III John, and Jude) assume its reality.

So astounding a miracle will inevitably be challenged because of its apparent impossibility, apart from any theological considerations. From the apostolic age, when certain persons in the Corinthian Church declared in oracular fashion that "there is no resurrection of the dead" (I Cor. 15:12), to the present day, the historicity of the resurrection has been repeatedly questioned or denied. Opposition has focused at three points: the integrity of the literary sources, the intrinsic historic probability of the narrative, and the scientific possibility of such a phenomenon. Are the records reliable and consistent accounts of an actual occurrence, reported by qualified witnesses, or are they the fabrications of men whose imaginations were excessively active? From the historical standpoint, the witnesses have been impugned for inadequacy of knowledge, lateness of time, and theological prejudice. Scientific opinion, assuming that no evidence for the resuscitation of a corpse could possibly be sufficient to establish such a fact, regards the Gospel narratives as naive, and explains the post-resurrection appearances of Jesus psychologically. Because of these objections, some theologians have remanded the resurrection to the realm of myth, asserting that it represents only the conviction of the early Church that Jesus must have survived death, expressed by the material figure that was current in the mythology of their age.

I. INTEGRITY OF THE SOURCES

Recent literary objections have been largely founded on the *Formgeschichte* method of documentary study. *Formgeschichte*, or "form criticism," advances the hypothesis that the Gospels consist of individual anecdotes of the life of Jesus collected and organized in a theological framework supplied by the writers. The Gospels are thus the products of the Church, designed for homiletical or liturgical purposes, and are in no sense critical biographies. Consequently they contain a large amount of pious commentary and legend which had didactic and devotional value for their time, but which cannot be classed as an exact transcript of "what really happened." For instance, the testimony concerning the empty tomb is dismissed as an ecclesiastical invention of which Paul presumably knew nothing, since he does not stress it in his notable defense of the resurrection in I Corinthians 15 (Rudolf Bultmann, *History of the Synoptic Tradition*, tr. John Marsh [New York: Harper & Row, 1963], p. 290). This use of the argument from silence is quite unconvincing, for Paul's Pharisaic background implies that his concept of the resurrection would be physical, and that he would take for granted that if Christ rose, the tomb was empty.

The literary differences between the various Gospel accounts of the resurrection do not necessarily mean that the evidence is confused or false. Varying perspectives and emphases evoked by different viewpoints and for different audiences may account for them. Mark's statement that the women "said nothing to anyone, for they were afraid" (Mark 16:8) and Matthew's report that "they departed quickly from the tomb with fear and great joy, and ran to tell his disciples" (Matt. 28:8) are not contradictory. The women did not broadcast their discovery to the world lest they should incur suspicion as meddlers with the tomb, but they reported it immediately to the disciples whom they considered trustworthy.

Admittedly the Gospels reproduce the preaching and teaching of the early Church, and represent its elemental faith. In their pages scattered events of the life of Christ are grouped in approximate chronological order, or are sometimes organized topically for didactic rather than for biographical purposes. In all of them, however, the death of Christ and the resurrection are treated as equally historical, and always occur in the same setting. One cannot consistently affirm the factual character of the former and impugn that of the latter without grave inconsistency in literary interpretation.

Furthermore, the accounts of these events in the canonical Gospels bear no trace of such imaginative embellishments as occur in the apocryphal Gospels. "The Gospel According to Peter," which can be dated about the middle of the second century, narrated how the heavens opened, and two men descended from heaven in a great light. The door of the sepulchre rolled open of itself, and the soldiers saw three men emerge, two of them supporting the third, and a cross following after them ("The Gospel According to Peter," X). The grotesque features of this spurious work are absent from the canonical text, which refrains from describing the method of the resurrection, but simply emphasizes the fact. The Gospels exercise so severe a restraint in their descriptions that they understate rather than exaggerate the supernatural quality of the event.

The differences of the narratives indicate that the known facts did not originate with one writer, but that they were reported in various segments for various purposes. Despite the apparent discrepancies which may seem unresolved because the complete picture of "what happened" is no longer accessible, the basic facts are sufficiently in accord to assure a common core of truth and adequate confirmation of the apostolic testimony that Jesus returned from death.

The sincerity of the apostolic testimony cannot be questioned. The same men who had associated with Jesus prior to the crucifixion and who had witnessed His death proclaimed that He had risen. According to the Gospels they had never understood His predictions of the resurrection (Luke 18:34), nor did they expect that He would rise. If they were prejudiced concerning the concept of His resurrection, they

were prejudiced against it. Nevertheless, all of the writings emanating
from them or from their followers assert that Jesus rose, and those who
proclaimed it, including the apostles, were ready to stake their lives on
its verity. Nor can the literary accounts be dismissed as legendary
embroidery created by a credulous community, for something happened
to overcome the initial skepticism of the apostles and to account for
the origin of the resurrection story.

II. HISTORICAL PROBABILITY

The integrity of the literary evidence is founded on the principle of
historical cause and effect. The resurrection is inextricably woven into
the fabric of Christian origins. Whether one believes the Church to be
a supernatural institution or whether he regards it as the accidental product of social and religious forces that combined in the fourth decade
of the first century to create a new religious movement, two facts must
be acknowledged. The first is that the Church was an active social force
in Rome by the time of Nero, not later than A.D. 64. Certainly the Church
cannot be called unhistorical, for the correspondence of Paul, its chief
protagonist, was widely circulated, and its influence was recognized by
secular historians. Tacitus, in discussing the fire at Rome in the latter
days of Nero's reign, alluded to the Christians as devotees of a pernicious
superstition which owed its origin to Christus, who was executed by
Pontius Pilate, governor of Judea (*Annals*, xv. 44).

The second fact is that the existence of the Church demands an historical cause for its origin. According to its own records, its beginnings
are attributed to the resurrection. Peter in his sermon at Pentecost, declared that "this Jesus did God raise up, whereof we all are witnesses.
Being therefore by the right hand of God exalted, and having received
of the Father the promise of the Holy Spirit, he hath shed forth this,
which ye see and hear" (Acts 2:32, 33). The first converts accepted his
word as truth, and their united assembly to hear the apostles' teaching
and to share in the breaking of bread and prayers (Acts 2:42) constituted the Church.

The body of believers was formed on the assumption that Jesus had
really risen from the dead and that the coming of the Holy Spirit was
a direct consequence of His ascension. This assumption was never disproved, although the educated hierarchy of the Jewish nation which had
plotted and had finally accomplished Jesus' death opposed the movement
bitterly. Had His body still been accessible, they could have produced
it and thus have nullified the preaching of the apostles. The priesthood
did not refrain from doing so because they feared popular opinion, for
on several occasions they arrested the apostles and held them in jail for

trial. The obvious inference is that they did not deny the resurrection because they could not refute the fact. The body could not be found, and no other explanation than resurrection could account for its absence from the tomb.

The quality of the witnesses is unimpeachable. The earliest written record of the Church's testimony is probably that of Paul, whose epistles can be dated more exactly than the Gospels, and can consequently be placed more accurately with relation to the development of Christianity. In Galatians, which may be his earliest extant epistle, written about A.D. 48, he spoke of "Christ, and God the Father, who raised him from the dead" (1:1). In I Thessalonians, dated with certainty about A.D. 50, he mentions "the living and true God and His Son from heaven, whom he raised from the dead" (1:10). Paul's outstanding essay on the resurrection in I Corinthians 15 states that "Christ died for our sins in accordance with the scriptures, that he was buried, that he was raised on the third day in accordance with the scriptures, and that he appeared to Cephas, then to the twelve . . ." (vv. 3-5). He places the resurrection on the same historical plane as the death and burial, and claims that he had simply relayed to the Corinthians what he had already received.

Paul was not proclaiming some private theological invention, but was following an established tradition that antedated his preaching and that was generally accepted by the Church. Since I Corinthians was written from Ephesus not later than A.D. 55 or 56, there were numerous living witnesses who could attest the truth of what he wrote; indeed, he refers to more than five hundred persons who had seen Jesus alive after the resurrection, of whom the majority still survived at the time of writing. Furthermore, Paul had been preaching for approximately twenty years, so that the message was not a novelty to him. If he had obtained the particulars concerning the resurrection from Peter (Cephas) and James, who are mentioned in this context (15:5, 7), the facts were imparted to him not more than five years after the event occurred.

The objective nature of the resurrection appearances has been challenged on the ground that Paul's vision of the risen Lord was subjective. "Last of all," he said, "as to one untimely born, he appeared also to me" (15:8). If, as seems probable, this vision may be equated with his conversion near Damascus, he was the only one of his company who saw and recognized the figure of Christ, though his companions saw a light but not the person (Acts 9:7). If this vision was purely inward and subjective, why should not the "appearances" to the other disciples have been also subjective? May not the contact with the Lord have been genuine, though the appearance could not have been recorded by a camera or on video tape?

The converse of this argument for the subjective character of the resurrection appearances is equally valid. If the manifestations to Peter, James, the apostles, and others were objective, why should not the appearance to Paul also have been objective? The objectivity or subjectivity of these experiences cannot be settled wholly on the basis of comparisons; some further criteria are needed.

Historicity, of course, is not completely identical with objectivity, since subjective experiences can be real. Even a hallucination is objective in the sense that it may occur at a definite time and place. In another sense it is unreal, for it does not correspond to any external fact which can be corroborated by external witness or by subsequent experience. The resurrection of Christ, however, was no hallucination. Its external objectivity was attested by Jesus' audible speech, by visibility to many people under differing conditions, by His ability to break bread and to eat, and by the tangibility of His material body. The Gospels, insofar as they describe His appearances, deny that He was a ghost or a dream (Matt. 28:9; Luke 24:36-43; John 20:20, 27).

This objectivity is confirmed by the earliest history of the Church, the book of Acts. Although it was probably not written before A.D. 60/62, it recounts the preaching of Peter and Paul at a much earlier time. In the majority of their public addresses the resurrection is mentioned explicitly as the central point of faith. Peter's inaugural presentation at Pentecost of the messiahship of Jesus was founded on the assertion that God raised Him from the dead (Acts 2:22-34). The reiteration of this theme (3:15; 4:1; 10:33; 5:30-31) confirms the impression that the resurrection was the primary message of the Christian Church.

Not only was the resurrection central to the preaching of the apostles in Jerusalem, but it was also the chief subject of the missionary testimony to the Gentile world. The sermon of Paul in the synagogue of Antioch of Pisidia (13:26-41) is a sample of the message that reached out to the proselytes and from them to the pagan population of the Roman provinces. Paul stressed the resurrection (13:30, 34, 38), as he did also before the Greek philosophers of Athens (17:18, 31). The distinctive message of Christianity was not a new application of the Old Testament law, nor even the fulfilment of prophecy, but the astounding fact of the resurrection of Jesus.

Obviously the resurrection was an integral part of the apostolic testimony which became the belief of the Christian community. To assert that the community created the event to account for their faith would be a reversal of the proper psychological order. Such an hypothesis cannot explain the origin of the faith. The Pharisees believed in a personal resurrection and immortality before Jesus began His ministry, and a conviction that men would rise at the last day was a commonplace of popular belief (John 11:24). Neither in the learned circles of the

Pharisees nor among the less erudite people of the land did any concept of personal resurrection emerge, nor was it connected in their minds with the Messiah. Assuredly the Christian community accepted and preached the story of the resurrection, giving it such application as immediate circumstances may have required; but the idea of Jesus' resurrection was not the creation of the community mind.

The four Gospels represent a stage of preaching later than that recorded in Acts. Although they are not biography in the modern sense of the term, since they do not furnish a consecutive account of the life of Jesus from birth to resurrection, their usefulness would certainly have been impaired if they presented information that was false or distorted. Even if they manifest different theological trends, the trends themselves may well reflect what Jesus Himself taught. Undeniably the Gospels were composed to meet the needs of their generation, but they were not thereby so altered that they failed to convey truth. Mark merely records the bare initial facts in his undisputed though fragmentary ending (Mark 16:1-8); Matthew offers a defensive explanation of the false rumor that the disciples had stolen Jesus' body (Matt. 28:11-15); Luke connects the resurrection with the fulfilment of messianic prophecy (Luke 24:25-27); and John discusses its effects on individuals (John 20:1-29). All four differ in content, emphasis, and style, yet all agree that the tomb was empty, that the followers of Jesus were unprepared for the event, that Jesus had actually risen, that He appeared later to the disciples either individually or as a group, and that He gave them a commission to fulfill. The sources differ on details; they agree on the major facts.

The Gospels are the fullest extant sources for information concerning the life of Jesus. Even if they are regarded as secondary echoes of communal belief they are rooted in the primitive events which initiated that belief. It is inconceivable that members of Christian community should have risked their lives for legends which they themselves had created gratuitously. Behind the narrative of the resurrection was the conviction that Jesus had risen, and the conviction must be traced back to an adequate cause.

III. SCIENTIFIC POSSIBILITY

The scientific objection to the historicity of the resurrection is founded on the axiomatic principle that death is terminal. The objection is not new, for Paul asked the Corinthians, "How can some of you say that there is no resurrection of the dead?" (I Cor. 15:12). The syllogism may be formulated as follows: Dead men do not rise again; Jesus was unquestionably dead; therefore He could not have risen.

While it is true that according to ordinary observation death is final, such an argument is unsound, for it assumes the impossibility of resurrection before any proofs are offered. A truly scientific attitude would investigate all the pertinent phenomena and evaluate them rather than to exclude arbitrarily any evidence that might bear upon the subject. Asserting that dead men do not rise, and then rejecting the resurrection of Christ for that reason is arguing in a circle. Of course the dead usually do not rise, for if they did, the miracle of Christ's resurrection would lose its distinctive quality and become only one more of a series of common occurrences. If the resurrection proves to be an exception to the ordinary cycle of human life, it must be treated as a fact which may call for a new explanation of experience.

On the assumption that the resurrection experiences were real, in what ways were they objective, or were they essentially subjective? Did those who encountered Christ in the post-resurrection hours really see and hear a tangible person who had returned from death, or were they only describing a memory of Him or possibly an inner vision stimulated by the excitement or desire of the hour?

Modern writers who realize that the resurrection cannot be explained as an illusion tend to accept the hypothesis of an objective impression created in the minds of the disciples by projected contact of the risen Lord. Foremost among authors of this persuasion is Michael C. Perry, whose work, *The Easter Enigma,* attempts to answer this problem:

> Jesus died on the cross, but was raised from the dead by his Father. In His new state he was no longer clothed by the old body of his incarnate life, but by some kind of spiritual body such as St. Paul attempts to describe for us.
>
> Without a body of flesh, Jesus wished to convince His disciples that he was alive and had transcended death, and to continue the teaching which Calvary had interrupted. He could not do this merely by impressing their minds with the certainty of His survival. Nobody else would have believed them and they would not have had enough conviction to continue to believe in the face of opposition. (*The Easter Enigma* [London: Faber & Faber, 1959], p. 194).

Perry contends that the image of Jesus was stamped upon the minds of the disciples without any intervening physical media. Vision and hearing were unnecessary; the impression of the living Lord was conveyed directly to their consciousness by extrasensory impulse. They "saw" Him as truly as if His physical person had stood before them, and they projected a mental picture of His body as they had known Him.

Perry's view is not wholly convincing. It is directly counter to the teaching of the Gospels that the risen Lord possessed flesh and bone which still carried the marks of the crucifixion (Luke 24:39, 40). Furthermore, if they "projected" His body as they had known Him, why did they fail to recognize Him when He appeared to them (Luke 24:16: John 20:15)? Why should they not recognize an image of their own projection?

This concept of the creation of an image by extrasensory perception is controverted by the stubborn fact of the empty tomb. Perry attempts to account for the disappearance of the physical body of Christ by assuming that it was annihilated when Christ entered into a "spiritual" existence. To assume that the body of Christ which had been dead in the grave was instantly dissipated into nothingness is merely to substitute one miracle for another. The chemical process of disintegration after death is never that rapid, and such a rapid disintegration would be as phenomenal as the change which the resurrection implies.

The transfiguration may afford a clue to the nature of the resurrection, for the accompanying change of Jesus' appearance implies that a parallel phenomenon occurred; in fact, the analogy is so close that Charles E. Carlsten has called the transfiguration a misplaced resurrection appearance ("Transfiguration and Resurrection," *Journal of Biblical Literature,* Vol. 66 [1961], pp. 233-240). Such a transposition in time is not necessary; it can rather be called a sample of the resurrection life. Jesus had promised His disciples that some of them would not see death until they witnessed the Son of man coming in His kingdom (Matt. 16:28). The next sentence of the text states that after six days Jesus took Peter, James, and John into a high-mountain and was transfigured before them. The transfiguration involved a physical transformation, for the account says that His face shone like the sun and His garments became white as the light (17:1, 2). Neither the body nor the garments were annihilated and replaced by a different substance, but both were activated into incandescence by the power of deity. As an ordinary electric lamp made of glass and metal becomes luminous when power is applied, so the physical apparel of Christ took on new properties and luminosity.

Paul stated that flesh and blood cannot inherit the kingdom of God, thereby implying that the kingdom of God involves the opening of a different realm with new conditions of life. Those who inherit the kingdom enter it only by the resurrection. Presumably, then, the resurrection entails a transformation of the present body that will fit it for a more glorious existence.

Nowhere does the New Testament state how the resurrection took place, nor does it offer any scientific definition of the process involved. By refraining from any explanation it avoids restricting the scientific interpretation to the terms of any one era. Probably no theory that could be advanced would be fully or permanently satisfactory, for the resurrection belongs to a world of dimensions different from ours, although it did occur within the bounds of time and space.

The evidence is sufficient to demonstrate from a literary, historical, and scientific viewpoint that something happened that can be classed as an objective event, and that left an ineradicable imprint on the lives and faith of the early believers. Their attitudes, characters, and careers were transformed, and the Church which resulted from their new faith still persists as a movement in history. The Easter faith must logically presuppose an historical event which underlies it.

"ON THE THIRD DAY"

Clark H. Pinnock

Clark H. Pinnock is Associate Professor of Theology at New Orleans Baptist Theological Seminary, Louisiana. Formerly he was assistant lecturer in New Testament in the University of Manchester, from which he holds the Ph.D. degree.

10.   Clark H. Pinnock

"ON THE THIRD DAY"

WHY IS IT thought incredible by any of you that God raises the dead?" (Acts 26:8). It is primarily a philosophical question which Paul addresses to his hearers. The factual basis for resurrection preaching was transparently clear to his mind — for this event did not happen "in a corner" (v. 26). More than human testimony was required to enable King Agrippa to overcome his native skepticism and succumb to the force of the evidence. For the category of resurrection refused to fit neatly into his world view. It was as customary in the ancient world as it is today to sneer at the idea as something less sophisticated than belief in a vague immortality loosely defined. Many sectors of modern theology have shared this skepticism in the physical miracle of the resurrection. Liberal theologies, old and new, virtually agree in their conviction that the bodily resurrection is more an offense than an aid to genuine faith today. Out of loyalty to the New Testament it is necessary to reply to this objection, and from there to explore the bearing of this unique event upon the Christian understanding of redemption.

Many historians of the origins of Christianity insist on starting with the experience of Easter, the rise of the resurrection faith, as constituting the only truly historical datum we have access to. The resurrection itself does not belong to the continuum of historical events which may be subjected to verification. Man is denied the right to extrapolate backwards in time and inquire about the prior history of this belief. This sheltering of the resurrection event from critical scrutiny is often accompanied by the view that a bodily resurrection, although it is a possible explanation of the Easter faith of the disciples, is not a necessary prerequisite to it. It is impossible, however, to remain satisfied with this approach. Besides creating a riddle at the genesis of Christianity, this attitude of indifference to the fact of the miracle of resurrection endangers the central thrust of the scriptural proclamation, namely, that this saving act of God took place in the midst of world history, on the same time line. It is easy to capitulate to the current secular mood which cannot accommodate itself to the bodily resurrection, and so lose the heart of the gospel. Our task must be to swim against the stream if necessary, in order to preserve the integrity of the gospel, and then to draw out if possible the implications of our faith for Christian thought and witness.

One of the biggest obstacles to overcome in recovering the New Testament pattern of fact and faith has been something called "Lessing's ditch." Should the security of faith be in any way related to or suspended upon historical occurrences only probably known? "Certainly," writes Bornkamm, "faith cannot and should not be dependent on the change and uncertainty of historical research" (*Jesus of Nazareth* [New York: Harper and Row, 1960], p. 9). Often in the history of rationalism history has been frowned upon in favor of scientific disciplines thought to be more precise and reliable. By detaching Christianity from too intimate an association with historical facts some hoped to preserve its message from the acid bath of destructive criticism.

Unfortunately, however, exponents of Lessing's dictum have failed to notice how his attitude destroys *all* historical and empirical knowledge. All statements about facts are assertions of probability. The only absolutely certain logical statements are tautologies — assertions which say the same thing twice. But if God cannot reveal Himself in the empirical probabilities of history, He cannot reveal Himself at all in history! The objection may be carried further. If the fact of the resurrection is difficult to the liberal Christian because its uncertainty *as a fact* is an embarrassment to faith, then by the same token the very existence of Jesus of Nazareth is problematic for him. Better to banish Him altogether from the stage of history that that faith should suffer from uncertainty! In that case the Easter faith is fully irrational, having neither the resurrection nor Jesus to rest upon.

The biblical picture is quite different. God reveals Himself and redeems man with factual reality, in the flesh and bone of history. Without the bodily resurrection, the Christian message is simply discredited. But the non-absolute character of historical revelation should not make us squeamish, for (1) all of our knowledge of factual reality is of a probable nature, but (2) the probabilities in support of the Christian claim are much stronger than the evidences we accept gladly in support of other events. Once the necessity that divine revelation be historical is recognized, it is not difficult to proceed.

I. DISENGAGEMENT FROM HISTORY

This specter of uncertainty has haunted modern discussions of the resurrection, so that theologians of widely differing perspectives have taken offense at the resurrection as a fact. Johannes Weiss, for example, takes offense in this "myth" and sees it as having no bearing upon the "inner truth" of Jesus' teachings. In this he is merely voicing the classical liberal concentration on ethical principles as the germ of the gospel. But incidentally, as if to ease his conscience, Weiss offers his opinion that for the original disciples faith in the resurrection was only a spiritual thing anyway and did not involve an empty tomb. By this device he seeks to smite down the miracle at the objective level and reintroduce it again on the subjective (see *Earliest Christianity* [New York: Harper, 1959], I, 87, 100-104).

From a similar angle Maurice Goguel attempts to retain something of the dynamism of the Easter faith without allowing any miraculous element in the discussion of Jesus' body (*Birth of Christianity* [London: Allen & Unwin, 1953], pp. 29-86). He devotes sixty careful pages to proving the impossibility of probing behind the psychical experiences of the disciples. As his solution he concludes that, although the cross shattered the confidence of the disciples, by faith they were nonetheless able to surmount the tragedy. Obviously Goguel reverses the message of the New Testament, and prefers his riddle to the gospel miracle. But it is difficult to understand how this triumphant conviction was conceived in the hearts of broken men, unless Christ actually rose.

The offensive character of the resurrection as a literal event reversing the normal course of nature in the decomposition of a body in death remains equally strongly for the new theology. The insistence of both Tillich and Bultmann on its symbolic non-literal meaning is well known. Tillich admits the existential encounters which led the disciples to apply the resurrection as a symbol to Jesus crucified. He even lists the physical theory as a possible explanation for faith in the New Being. But candidly he regards it as a crude rationalization developed rather late in the first century. He much prefers a new theory of his own, which he wishes to distinguish from a simply psychological explanation. The real miracle was the creation of faith in the New Being. The orthodox alternative he treats with disdain as "absurdity compounded with blasphemy." Perhaps it is more apt to turn this pejorative expression onto the implications of his own thesis which depicts the disciples confusing their inner experience with an event in the past, deceiving both themselves and Christians since (cf. Paul Tavard, *Paul Tillich and the Christian Message* [New York: Scribner's, 1962], pp. 133-139).

Bultmann's position offers the same irrationality. To him the resurrection is a mythopoeic idea expressing the meaning of the cross. The tragedy of Calvary was overcome in this view in the minds of the disciples by a sheer leap of faith unwarranted by any objective event. Taken alone the cross could only convince the disciples about the hopelessness of living in a world where heaven is deaf to the cries of faith, justice, and love. No motivation was present to transform despair into hope. Giovanni Miegge asks, "Is it possible that faith in the resurrection should become incarnate in a man, unless he believes that on Easter morning Jesus of Nazareth really left the sepulchre empty and appeared before the eyes of his disciples, astonished, doubtful, and reluctant to be persuaded as they were?" (*Gospel and Myth in the Thought of Rudolf Bultmann* [Richmond, Va.: John Knox Press, 1960], p. 50). Any retreat from history into the realm of bare experience is disastrous for the Christian faith. Belief in the resurrection involves far more than belief in the raising of a body but it does not involve less. If Jesus had been still held by death no gospel proclamation would have been issued to the world. The Christian message and experience depends upon the prior fact of Easter (D. Cairns, *Gospel Without Myth?* [London: SCM, 1960], p. 163).

Immunity from proof is not a biblical virtue in the act of personal faith as Bultmann intimates. The offense of the cross is not belief in a resurrection which is impossible to prove simply because it did not happen in history. Faith embraces but does not create its object. The New Testament does not present the resurrection as a symbol for something else. The event proclaimed is a real victory over death. The powers of the age to come have broken into time. The Person of Christ is powerfully vindicated. A fragment of the old cosmos has been redeemed, a foretaste of the new creation to come. The drift to irrationalism represented by any attempt to disassociate the resurrection from history must be arrested. An indispensable element of the gospel is lost, and a new edition put forward. It is historical and semantic nonsense to speak of resurrection unless a physical miracle is referred to.

II. RESURRECTION AS HISTORICAL

In his Areopagus address Paul appealed to the resurrection as a piece of evidence which vindicated Christ's claims and laid upon His hearers an intense responsibility to respond to the gospel (Acts 17:31). Jesus regarded His own miracles in this light. His healing miracles proved the presence of the kingdom in power (Matt. 12:28). His mighty acts laid a deeper obligation upon those who observed them because they more explicitly pointed up His credentials (Matt. 11:21).

Because the New Testament classifies the miracles as evidences for the truth of the gospel, their verification is in principle possible. The resurrection, because of its central importance and impact on history, is especially open to investigation. Obviously some non-Christians when confronted with the evidences may prefer to evade their force, rather than to accept any supernatural implications. But the historian cannot escape from involvement in the situation he is examining when it threatens to alter his entire world view. Positivism was wrong to imply that history was a pure science yielding certainty which no one could dispute. Yet at the same time, one cannot be entirely indifferent to the factual element in a historical meaning situation.

In lifting the resurrection above the time line altogether, into the region of bare experience, modern theology has become Docetic with regard to history. The Bible does not contrast revelation and history. Gnostic systems delight in shielding their mysteries from the eyes of the general observer. In contrast, biblical revelation is open to the man with eyes to see (Josh. 2:9-10). It does not gain any validity because a man believes in it. The objectivity of its saving events is the basis for its binding universal claim. In biblical thought salvation occurs through the contemplation of redemptive acts in the past. The moment the connection of the gospel with history is severed, the heartbeat of the message stops.

In answer to Lessing, we pointed out that it is impossible to speak of absolute certainty about any events in the historical realm. To reject investigation of the resurrection on the grounds that it cannot yield certainty is an argument against any empirical study of the factual world. Existentialist theologians brush aside the historical question by appeal to caricature. *No* event is absolutely certifiable. If the resurrection can provide a high degree of probability, this is enough to make the preaching of the event legitimate. Otherwise, the gospel becomes an attractive fairy story whose validity hangs solely upon the experiences it can excite. But the apostles appealed, not to their encounter with Christ, but to God's saving action as its background and basis. It is our contention that the bodily resurrection is the most rational historical explanation for the birth of Christianity.

Often the complexity of detail present in the various resurrection accounts is thought to cast doubt upon the literary evidences for the event. It is more likely that this polyphony, which is by no means incoherent, gives testimony to a deposit of eyewitness accounts. The two sets of appearances, the one set in Galilee (by Matthew and Mark) and the other in Jerusalem (by Luke), present no intrinsic contradiction, for they seem to be brought together in John 20-21 and in I Corinthians 15:5f. The brute fact always remains that the central miracle of the gospel, when first believed, occurred in the very recent past, and it was handed down and believed as an event in the stream of history. It cannot therefore be insulated from the factual question, or withdrawn from analysis. The result of such inquiry will produce in the impartial mind a firm confidence in its historical integrity. The first preaching of the resurrection circulated in the same generation, indeed within a few months of the time, in which the event took place. It sprang into existence already fully grown. An outsider like Paul was able to satisfy himself of its historicity with numerous testimonies from people who actually saw the risen Lord.

The resurrection then is an event which clarifies human existence, not an experience which creates a "happening." Still the attempt is made to drive a wedge between the fact and meaning of Easter, in order to salvage the experience and dispose of the scandal. The common device consists in implying that the empty tomb did not belong to the earliest stages of resurrection preaching, and is quite unnecessary to the gospel. It is taken to be a later apologetic detail invoked to support a materialistic view of Easter. This criticism is faulty on two counts: it is semantically absurd, and it is historically incorrect.

In the first place, no theory of resurrection which has nothing to say about the fate of the physical body is known to the New Testament. Paul could indeed use the term spiritually in reference to our new life in Christ (Rom. 6:4, Col. 3:1), but only because our Saviour really rose, making the image available and forecasting our own resurrection on the last day. The narratives which do introduce the detail about the empty tomb with explicitness never do so with overt apologetic intent, as though the idea were not known otherwise. It merely occurs in the accounts of sufficient length to accommodate a fuller treatment of the gospel theme. It is pseudo-biblical, a mere modern sophistication, to impute the notion of resurrection without empty tomb to the first disciples. The bare miracle of Easter can be equivocated by the unbeliever if he prefers to remain in unbelief. A mere empty tomb cannot "prove" the Christian claim. But it is certain, that if the tomb was not empty on the third day, this fact would have *disproved* it. It remains an insoluble mystery for a non-Christian to explain why the original enemies of the gospel did not succeed in exploding the fantasy of the resurrection.

As a matter of historical fact, the detail of the empty tomb does belong to the oldest tradition of the resurrection. Paul's allusion to the burial of Christ before the resurrection can bear no other meaning (I Cor. 15:4). Neither for that matter can the mentioning of His death fit symmetrically with resurrection unless the same body is meant in both cases. The empty tomb witnesses to the continuity of Jesus crucified and the risen Lord. Easter is more than a new perspective on life quickened in the disciples' hearts by a personal encounter. For this new outlook is focused on Jesus Christ, and if His history ended on the cross then faith in His "resurrection" is sheerest illusion. It is true that existentialism tends to delight in believing the absurd, but this is never a condition in biblical faith. Man bows in creaturely humility before what God has certainly wrought in His grace for him.

Faith in the risen Lord arises out of the work of the Spirit in the mind of a man considering the claims of the gospel. The Spirit acts upon the evidence to accredit the message. This evidence consists chiefly, as historical evidence does, of the personal testimony of those close to the event. If at the outset a person excludes the miraculous as a possibility, no amount of persuasion would be sufficient to necessitate belief. The problem then concerns, not the adequacy of the evidence, but the openness of the man to admit this fact. There is little doubt about the New Testament view on evidences. For Paul the resurrection marked a powerful corroboration of the divine status of Jesus as the Lord (Rom. 1:4). When he invokes the list of witnesses who saw the risen Lord (I Cor. 15:5-11), his obvious intention is to undergird the factual basis to his resurrection preaching. In that chapter he sets out to dismiss the notion that one may have true faith in the resurrection without the event itself (v. 14). The mere claim to mystic experience of Christ has no real value in his mind apart from a sturdy connection to the factual miracle. Critics often point to the alleged materialistic details introduced in Matthew and Luke in support of the bodily resurrection. But why should we suppose these authors to be so mistaken about the true character of the resurrection? In fact it is the modern disjunction of fact and meaning which creates the confusion which could never arise in the mind of the New Testament reader. This is a matter of greatest importance. Faith does not claw the air. It lays hold upon saving verities planted in the fabric of history.

III. THE MEANING OF THE RESURRECTION

The fact and meaning of the resurrection stand together. It is wrong to suggest a false dichotomy here. The same probability which accredits the fact of the resurrection also offers the best clue to its meaning. For it was Jesus the Messiah who arose from the dead. The full transcript of its meaning can be scanned in His own teachings regarding His person and death, and in the teachings of His apostolic band who were trained by Him and who encountered Him risen. Our faith then does not lend meaning to the event. Its significance is contained within the fact itself. True resurrection faith must be open to both fact and interpretation.

The bodily resurrection was not an arbitrary miracle. It has deep meaning within the biblical understanding of creation. Neither was it a concession to the limited thought forms of the disciples, to aid their faith in a manner which our own does not require. The glorified body of Christ speaks of the new creation. The New Testament view of redemption includes the transformation of the natural order (Rom. 8:21). Salvation as it affects man does not limit itself to ethical change but aims at the redemption of his body too. For the body, though at present the vehicle of sin, is the good creation of God, and is to be raised in power (I Cor. 15:43). This is the deliverance *of* the body, not *from* the body. Salvation honors man in his wholeness. The resurrection of Jesus is an anticipation of a wholly new mode of existence in the age to come. This is the cosmic significance of the Easter event. Without the bodily resurrection the meaning of the gospel is radically altered, and faith of no avail.

The stuff of this creation is to be changed. J. A. Schep writes, "In Scripture the resurrection of the body as a glorified body of flesh is inseparably tied to the renewal and glorification of the cosmos" (*Nature of the Resurrection Body,* [Grand Rapids: Eerdmans, 1964], p. 218). Behind modern embarrassment over the bodily resurrection lurk at least two alien presuppositions: a lingering naturalism which denies God any verifiable activity in the world, and a refusal to concede to the type of redemption the Bible proclaims. Skepticism about the possibility of a violation of "natural law" is a curious vestige of the older rationalism which can still be heard but which scarcely requires refutation. In the biblical view, the whole world is the product of God's creative breath and is upheld at every point by Him (Col. 1:17, Heb. 1:3). Nature is no stranger to Him, but part of His total discourse. In the resurrection it is only the *mode* and not the *fact* of divine activity which alters. Even more seriously, rejection of the bodily resurrection implies a negative verdict on God's creation. God would save the whole man, body and soul, but man will not rest content with his status as an embodied creature. Resurrection destines man to eternal creaturehood. Men wish to be as gods, but the gospel offers no ontological promotions. Modern man wants to be released from his finitude (involving an ontological change), not from his guilt (involving a moral change). The gospel of the resurrection offers to redeem him from the disastrous effects of sin and acquit him of his weight of guilt. The resurrection is offensive to the sinner because it exposes his need in categories he will not accept and offers him a solution he does not want. Notwithstanding, "if any man be in Christ there is new creation."

The fuller implications of the resurrection carry beyond itself also to the ascension. If Bultmann employs the resurrection as a symbol about the meaning of the cross, many others employ the ascension as a symbol of the resurrection. But these three are knitted together. It is a procedure of reduction to eliminate the ascension, when the latter is an unavoidable sequel to the bodily resurrection. The ascension marks the transition from the seen to the unseen world. This distinction between two realms is made by the apostle. "We look not to the things that are seen but to the things that are unseen; for the things that are seen are transient, but the things that are unseen are eternal" (II Cor. 4:18). The clue which Scripture gives of the difference between these two realms is framed in the visible/invisible form, rather than the spirit/matter form. We know nothing of the substance (if that is the right word) which goes to make up the invisible world, only certain of its properties. The body of the resurrection is described by three attributes — imperishableness, glory, and power. Even in our own experience, visibility is not a necessary property of matter. At a certain temperature water becomes invisible.

For this realm, however, all models are imperfect. Until the "perfect" is come our partial knowledge will never become complete (I Cor. 13:9-12). For the present we simply acknowledge the ascension as the passing of Christ's glorified body to this transempirical realm. It is unfair to ridicule the ascension as a journey into space, when the critic is uncertain what he should expect to see and what the witnesses needed to see in their cultural setting. Christ proceeded to the center of God's dominion in the new creation He is preparing for His people. From thence He will return to judge and redeem the world. This is the event of our patient watch and hope.

Modern theology faces its hour of decision. From its bewildered uncertainty it must forsake its neglect of history, and recommit itself to historical revelation. The resurrection is a critical point where clarity ought to be unmistakable. Elusiveness here calls into question the slogan repeated so often in current theology that "God acts in history." Belief in the bodily resurrection affirms the biblical realism of objective revelation in history. The event-character of the resurrection is unaffected by faith or unbelief. The miracle of the resurrection stands grandly in absolute priority to faith, which is oriented to it in a wholly receptive and not creative fashion.

Gemeindetheologie :
THE BANE OF
GOSPEL CRITICISM

Everett F. Harrison

Everett F. Harrison is Professor of New Testament in Fuller Theological Seminary, Pasadena, California. He is author of The Son of God Among the Sons of Men *and* Introduction to the New Testament. *He is also editor of* Baker's Dictionary of Theology, *co-editor of* The Wycliffe Bible Commentary, *and a frequent contributor to religious journals. He holds the Th.D. degree from Dallas Theological Seminary and Ph.D. from University of Pennsylvania.*

11. *Everett F. Harrison*

Gemeindetheologie :
THE BANE OF
GOSPEL CRITICISM

*G*EMEINDETHEOLOGIE — the formidable-looking German word
meaning "church theology" — has come to be associated closely with the
approach to the Gospels known as form criticism. A companion term,
Gemeindebildung, indicates the process by which this theology has
become crystallized. In contrast to source criticism, which concerned
itself with the literary relationships between the Synoptic Gospels,
form criticism has sought to trace in the oral period that preceded the
Gospels the influences that determined the choice and content of the
materials used.

Form criticism makes a sharp distinction between the post-Easter
faith of the Church and the understanding of Jesus held by His immediate followers during the days of His flesh. Because of their faith that He
had risen from the dead, it was no longer possible to think of Him merely as the teacher-prophet of Galilee, but as the Messiah. As the words
and deeds of Jesus were passed on, first in oral and then in written
form, this heightened conception of Jesus was supposedly read back
into the period of the ministry. It becomes the task of the critic to
make a separation between the original materials which can provide
a basis for the knowledge of the historical Jesus and those for which
the Church has been responsible as a molding, and even to some extent
a creating, influence.

159

About two decades before the rise of form criticism, in the year 1901, Wilhelm Wrede published a book entitled *Das Messiasgeheimnis in den Evangelien*, in which he set out to explain how it happened that the disciples did not have this post-resurrection faith in Jesus as the Messiah during His ministry. Wrede found in Mark the device of the messianic secret. Jesus' messianic dignity was carefully concealed and thus kept from the disciples and others. The net result for the critic is that the confession of Jesus' messiahship by Peter is no longer to be regarded as historical but must be treated as something read back into the life of Jesus. This opened the door for a similar treatment of other aspects of the tradition that could be suspected of belonging to the Church's development. So *Gemeindetheologie* became firmly entrenched as part of the methodology of form criticism. It was aided substantially by the insistence of Wellhausen that "a literary work or a fragment of tradition is a primary source for the historical tradition out of which it arose, and is only a secondary source for the historical details concerning which it gives information."

One of the leading advocates of form criticism, Rudolf Bultmann, reveals the extent to which this approach to the Gospels has shaped his thinking when he says in the opening paragraph of his *Theology of the New Testament* that the Church "frequently introduced into its account of Jesus' message, motifs of its own proclamation." He is convinced that one must distinguish between the words and ideas of Jesus and those imputed to Him by the Palestinian Jewish-Christian community and that one must recognize a further layer of tradition as coming from the circles of Hellenistic Christianity in which the Synoptic Gospels took their rise.

Bultmann finds Jesus' message to be sharply eschatological but not lacking in ethical thrust. "The Reign of God, demanding of man decision for God against every earthly tie, is the salvation to come." He cannot accept the messianic consciousness of Jesus as historically grounded, and from this vantage point he deals summarily with items touching this theme. Peter's confession "is an Easter-story projected backward into Jesus' life-time, just like the story of the Transfiguration." Though Jesus was baptized, the account of it is legendary. So is the temptation. The predictions of the passion are dismissed as *vaticinia ex eventu*. Some of the teaching is challenged as inappropriate to Jesus, for example, Matthew 5:17-19, which is alleged to be in conflict with other sayings of the Master and with His own practice (more of this later). Enough has been said here to indicate the radical nature of Bultmann's handling of the Gospel materials.

In recent years some scholars who are sympathetic to his general position have become distressed over the chasm left between the procla-

mation of the early Church (kerygma), which is all-important to Bultmann's thinking, and the historic background for it in the ministry of
Jesus. As a result, there is increasing effort to find materials in the
Gospels that can be properly assigned to the ministry rather than to the
early Church, which can aid our understanding of Jesus Himself and
measurably prepare the way for the formulation of the kerygma.
Bornkamm, for instance, in his *Jesus of Nazareth* (London: Hodder and
Stoughton, 1960), finds that Jesus does not fit altogether the pattern
of what would be expected of a teacher in His age — the places where
He teaches, the people whom He makes His audience, the authority of
His utterances, His "astounding sovereignty in dealing with situations
according to the kind of people he encounters." "Again and again his
behaviour and method are in sharp contrast to what people expect
of him and what, from their own point of view, they hope for." These
are helpful insights, but the broad position is left unchanged. Much is
still assigned to intrusion into the record by the hand of the earthly
Church.

I. GENERAL PROBLEMS FACING THE EMPHASIS
OF *GEMEINDETHEOLOGIE*

Some general observations should be made at this point. If *Gemeindetheologie* is to be allowed a major role in criticism, it should be capable
of demonstration beyond all cavil as a legitimate tool of historical research. What impresses one in reading Bultmann, however, is his great
facility in translating premises into propositions and propositions into
certainties. He is ready to explain too readily in terms of the Church
that which can with equal or greater propriety be explained in terms
of the historical Jesus.

A half-truth is hard to resist; it is so easily acknowledged as the
whole truth. A half-truth is also hard to refute, for the element of error
tends to find an advocate in the element of truth that is in it. The
matter could be put this way. Any writer, however objective, finds it
difficult, if not impossible, to avoid reflecting his own situation to
some extent. He cannot write in a vacuum. This is the truth in
Gemeindetheologie. Our Gospel records are not on-the-spot accounts
by neutral reporters of what Jesus said and did, but are the distillation
of the materials of the life after much reflection and repetition by men
of faith. They are a combination of history and interpretation, the
latter being what has been felicitously called "the web of significance."
If it is permissible to balance these factors one against the other,
one may say that the plurality of Gospels, although it seems to accent
the element of interpretation because of variations in parallel passages,

may actually be urged as an argument in favor of historicity, for the Church would hardly care to advertise its laxity of supervision over the proper understanding of the message by allowing the spawning of divergent accounts for the very purpose of advocating new interpretations. It is hard to resist the impression that the reason for the drawing up of accounts by the many (Luke 1:1) was a burning desire to tell the story of Jesus as it had been apprehended in its many-sidedness by those who had access to the necessary historical data.

But what is one to do about variations in the reported sayings of Jesus? Before concluding that there has been tampering with the original form, one ought to explore the possibility that Jesus repeated Himself sometimes (which is natural in view of the length of the ministry and His movement from place to place) and that the variations in the parallel passages may reflect the actual differences in the form of the teaching on various occasions. There is so little attention in the Gospels to the precise setting for Jesus' teaching that it would be both easy and natural to allocate variations of a saying to what appears as a single incident in the records.

A simple illustration may suffice. Matthew 7:11 reports Jesus as saying, "If you then, who are evil, know how to give good gifts to your children, how much more will your Father who is heaven give good things to those who ask him?" In Luke 11:13 this saying is identical except that "the Holy Spirit" is substituted for "good things." It is widely held that here the early Church, under the influence of Pentecost, has made the substitution for the original statement as it occurs in Matthew. This would be an example of interpretation, based on the realization that the Spirit was the best of gifts. A second possibility is that Luke himself, judging from his interest in the Spirit, both in his Gospel and in Acts, has made the substitution. These options are open, but so is the possibility that Jesus Himself may be responsible for the wording in both cases. If one adopts the first solution, the *Sitz im Leben* would be a reflection of the early Church's current interest, based on Jesus' promise to send the Spirit and the Church's experience of the Spirit, which is a rather different thing from *Sitz im Leben* that involves a creative milieu.

In this connection it ought to be noted that one of the basic assumptions of form criticism has been that the Christian community had a creative capacity that enabled it to fill this role of adapting and even formulating Scripture. This assumption lacks demonstration. Sociologists tell us that groups are receptive but not creative entities. The Christian community was made up of people who had received Christian traditions and accepted them as true. It does not readily appear how such a community could have created these materials.

This idea of tradition as something received by the Christian community figures notably in the prologue of Luke, where it occurs in the verbal form "delivered" (Luke 1:2). The passage teaches that those who were eyewitnesses and ministers of the Word delivered or handed down what they saw and heard as the basis for any accounts of the ministry of Jesus that might be drawn up. The element of creation is not only lacking but is excluded by the very force of tradition. The same word is central to Paul's account of the gospel in I Corinthians 15:3, where the words "delivered" and "received" are correlative, bound together as compounds having the same preposition (παρά). They present a vivid picture of the process whereby the facts of the gospel were handed down to Paul by the Jerusalem Church and in turn passed on to the Corinthians by him. From these two passages it is clear that the leaders of the Church had a lively interest in securing the faithful transmission of the materials relevant to the ministry of our Lord. That they would abdicate their responsibility or permit their constituency to alter the picture of Jesus and His mission that they had treasured and communicated, is simply unthinkable.

The importance of tradition in connection with Gospel origins has been enhanced by the research of Birger Gerhardsson set forth in his book *Memory and Manuscript* (Lund, Sweden: Gleerup, 1961). Emphasizing that Jesus' ministry was carried on in a Jewish setting and that he was considered a rabbi, the author draws upon the known habits of Jewish teachers in relation to their disciples to conclude that Jesus' teaching was a combination of text and interpretation, and that He required at least some of His teaching to be memorized by His disciples. This constituted the substance of the teaching of the disciples in the days of the early Church — the ministry of the word to which they gave themselves with all diligence. Some reservation about Gerhardsson's conclusions may be legitimate, for Jesus differed from the rabbis in His person and teaching at least as much as He resembled them, and, furthermore, there is a lack of uniformity in the reporting of His teaching in the Gospels. Nevertheless the main contention seems valid. The disciples were committed to transmission rather than alteration or origination. As Gerhardsson says, "It is unrealistic to suppose that forgetfulness and the exercise of a pious imagination had too much hand in transforming authentic memories beyond all recognition in the course of a few short decades."

It may not be accidental that Bultmann has no real doctrine of the Spirit in his treatment of the Gospel materials. But this supernatural factor ought to be given at least as much consideration as the conscientiousness of the apostles. One cannot dismiss Jesus' promise of the

Spirit and His assurance that the Spirit would not only illumine and guide into truth but would bring to remembrance what Jesus Himself had spoken. A Church that was supposedly shaping the tradition in terms of its own life situation would hardly invent the saying that the ministry of the Spirit would involve recall of what Jesus had said (John 14:26).

It should be granted that the gift of the Spirit made possible the element of interpretation woven into the fabric of history that constitutes the Gospel tradition, but this interpretative element simply draws out the implications of the history rather than imposing something new upon it. Everyone recognizes the basic distinction between Gospel and Epistle in the sense that the former deals chiefly with event (the Christ-event, specifically), whereas the latter has to do with interpretation and application of that which is historically described in the gospel story. *Gemeindetheologie* threatens to eradicate this basic distinction by overloading the Gospels with interpretative additions.

Finally, Bultmann's insistence that there must have been a radical tranformation of the tradition when it passed from the Palestinian to the Hellenistic communities encounters resistance from our sources, which indicate that a very close relationship was maintained between the two branches of the Church in the period prior to the emergence of the Gospels. W. D. Davies notes, "There was frequent intercourse between figures such as Peter, and other apostolic guardians of the tradition, and Christian communities in various places, so that the transmission and development of the tradition was unchecked. It is not a vague folk tradition, developing over vast stretches of time, that lies behind the New Testament, but an ecclesiastical one, which developed intensively in a brief period" (*The Setting of the Sermon on the Mount* [Cambridge, 1964], p. 417).

Furthermore, we may assume, on the basis of the readiness of our sources to admit the presence of controversy such as developed over the admission of Gentiles, that if any branches of the Church sought to develop and propagate views of Jesus' person and activity that were at variance with the apostolic tradition, the sources would not conceal these cleavages. It will be important to keep this in mind when we examine the titles used of our Lord in the Gospels.

II. CONCRETE OBJECTIONS TO THE POSITION
OF *GEMEINDETHEOLOGIE*

It is in order now to proceed to certain concrete data that make the position of *Gemeindetheologie* dubious.

Schmiedel's Pillar-Passages.

This scholar belonged to a generation that was deeply engrossed in the search for the historical Jesus (a theme with which *Gemeindetheologie* is intimately related). Finding that current methods of literary criticism were of little avail in this search, since every layer of tradition originated with men who revered Jesus, Schmiedel decided to strike out in another direction, namely, to uncover passages which precluded the element of invention by the early Church. He found nine such passages, including, among others, the statement that blasphemy against the Son of man can be forgiven (Matt. 12:32) and that the Son did not know the time of His return (Mark 13:32). In Schmiedel's words these passages "might be called the foundation-pillars for a truly scientific life of Jesus." From this description one may assume that even though Schmiedel was hostile to the supernaturalism in the Gospels, he was prepared to grant that other items in addition to these nine could be found to enlarge the picture. We shall take his chosen passages in that sense rather than as pitiful remnants of a great structure erected by a misguided Church as a memorial to Jesus. The point is that if the followers of Jesus were willing to include in the record such items which were capable of being turned against a supernaturalistic conception of His person, it is certainly arguable that there was no conscious manipulating of the data, and that therefore the rest of the materials were introduced not for the purpose of heightening the impression of Jesus but rather as a faithful reproduction.

The Nature of the Kerygma in the Early Church

The nature of the kerygma of the early church is well known. It centered in the redemptive work of Jesus expressed in terms of death and resurrection. But what of the kerygma that Jesus Himself preached? On *Gemeindetheologie* principles we should expect a reading back into the Gospels of the centrality of Jesus to the kerygma. But when Jesus sent forth His followers to preach, the message dealt with the good news of the kingdom, the same message He had been imparting to the multitudes. Conversely, the overwhelming stress on the kingdom of God in the Synoptic reports of Jesus' proclamation fails to achieve any major place in the preaching of the early Church, as a cursory check of Acts and the Epistles will demonstrate. This disparity between the Synoptic tradition and that of the early Church indicates a sensitivity to the epochal importance of the finished work of Jesus Christ in its effect upon the kerygma. It is not what we would expect if the Church was busy editing the tradition of Jesus' preaching with a view to bringing it into conformity with its own.

The Use of Parables

Parables constituted the most common framework for the teaching of Jesus as found in the Synoptic Gospels. This medium is strangely lacking in the literature of the early Church. Whatever may be the reason for this, it seems to show that there was no tendency to read the practice of the Church back into the ministry of our Lord. Furthermore, as Jeremias has pointed out, in many cases the parables have a *Sitz im Leben Jesu* in that they reflect a polemic against His opponents.

The One Teacher

The teaching material of the Gospels, aside from a few words of counsel attributed to John the Baptist, is credited to Jesus. If the early Church is actually responsible for much of this, then it is difficult to account for the assertion that there is only one teacher, namely, Jesus (Matt. 23:8, 10), since the Church would be putting itself or its leaders on a par with Jesus. Whether that passage was spoken by Jesus or not is not the real issue here. If it is genuine, then the Church is guilty of disobedience if it created tradition. If the passage is spurious, the Church would be inconsistent by putting something into the record that condemns its own practice.

Looking beyond this single passage, one can confidently assert that the very loftiness of the teaching points to Jesus rather than to those who confessedly sat at His feet. The enigmatical character of some of His sayings and the difficulty encountered by the disciples in grasping His intent tells the same story. If the Gospels are not trustworthy in their presentation of Jesus as the master teacher, acclaimed by friend and foe alike, then they can scarcely be trusted for anything. To maintain that Jesus was revered almost exclusively because of what He did in death and resurrection is to impose an intolerable dichotomy on His career as a whole. The evidence for the impact of Jesus as teacher is varied and unassailable.

The Use of "Abba"

Jesus' use of *Abba* in the context of prayer has an important bearing on the question in hand. Years of research led J. Jeremias to conclude that no evidence is available that anyone in Palestinian Judaism ever addressed God as "my Father." Jesus taught His followers to use this address as a distinctive mark of their relationship to Him. Jeremias draws this conclusion:

> It has been widely maintained that we know scarcely anything about the historical Jesus. We know him only from the Gospels, which are not historical accounts but rather confessions of faith. We know only

the Christ of the Kerygma, where Jesus is clad in the garb of myth; one need only think of the many miracles attributed to him. What we discover, when we apply historical criticism in analyzing the sources, is a powerful prophet, but a prophet who completely remained within the limits of Judaism. This prophet may have historical interest, but he has not and cannot have any significance for the Christian faith. What matters is the Christ of the *Kerygma.* Christianity began at Easter. But if it is true — and the testimony of the sources is quite unequivocal — that *Abba* as an address to God is *ipsissima vox,* an authentic and original utterance of Jesus, and that this *Abba* implies the claim of a unique revelation and a unique authority — if all this is true, then the position regarding the historical Jesus just described is untenable. For with the *Abba* we are behind the Kerygma. We are confronted with something new and unheard of which breaks through the limits of Judaism. Here we see who the historical Jesus was: the man who had the power to address God as *Abba* and who included the sinners and the publicans in the kingdom by authorizing them to repeat this one word, *"Abba, dear Father"* (*The Central Message of the New Testament* [New York: Scribner, 1965], pp. 29f.).

The Character of the Passion Narratives

One of the most impressive features of the Gospels is the prominence given in all of them to the passion narratives. No doubt this can be understood as an indication of the great importance placed by the early Church on the death and resurrection of the Saviour which formed the heart of its own kerygma. But in the adumbrations of the death attributed to Jesus' teaching, it is the event itself that is emphasized, whether it be from the standpoint of the human opposition that effects it or the will of God that is fulfilled in it. Beyond this there is the teaching that the death will benefit "the many" (Mark 10:45) and also the necessity that the true disciple take up his cross and follow Jesus. All this is what could be legitimately expected if the death was in fact a part of a divinely ordained mission. There is no theologizing of the death such as appears in the Epistles of Paul, to the effect that believers have died with Christ to sin. On *Gemeindetheologie* principles, this whole line of thought could have been imported into Jesus' pre-cross teaching (or even more adroitly into His post-resurrection teaching), for it was current before the Gospels were written. But nothing of this kind is allowed to intrude.

The Gentile Problem

If the contention of form criticism is correct that the Gospels are above all a reflection of the life and interests of the early Church, one would expect that they would contain some endorsement of the principle of Gentile equality with the Jew, particularly since the Church had been led to take this position about the middle of the first century (Acts 15). It would have been highly convenient for the early Church to be able to point to one or more utterances by our Lord that would afford warrant for accepting the Gentile on an equal basis with the Jew. What we find in the Gospels is an avowal by Jesus of having been sent only to the lost sheep of the house of Israel (Matt. 15:24). His dealings with Gentiles are rare and marked with some reluctance. The hour of the non-Israelite had not yet come. The Church's policy toward the Gentiles developed as a matter of the guidance of the Spirit rather than as something justified by the Master's instruction. "It is of the utmost significance that the Apostle to the Gentiles was not able apparently to appeal to any specific word or act of Jesus during his ministry which would justify his championing of the Gentile Christians" (W. D. Davies, *Christian Origins and Judaism* [Philadelphia: Westminster, 1962], p. 53). In line with this, one fails to find any discussion of circumcision in the Gospels, a subject that engrossed the Church in its struggle to find the answer to the Gentile problem.

The Distinction Between Church Teaching and Jesus'

It has been pointed out by a number of scholars that the Church distinguished between Jesus' teaching and its own. Perhaps the clearest case is in connection with Paul's discussion of divorce (I Cor. 7), where he is careful to state the Master's teaching and then his own in areas which Jesus' teaching did not cover.

The Relevance of Jewish Traditions

The inclusion in the Gospel records of the Corban discussion (Mark 7:11) could hardly be for the sake of its relevancy to the early Church, which was preoccupied with preaching the gospel rather than discussing Jewish traditions. The same could be said for the prominence given to the Sabbath controversy. As far as is known, the Palestinian Church kept the day faithfully and did not antagonize their Jewish brethren at this point. Later there were sporadic attempts to Judaize Gentile converts, including the imposition of the Sabbath (Col. 2:16), but these attempts could hardly account for the large place given to the Sabbath in Jesus' ministry and teaching. This question had a far more distinct bearing on His situation than on that of the Church.

The Permanence of Law

Matthew 5:17-19 offers a notable testing ground for the *Gemeinde-theologie* theory. Bultmann detects the atmosphere of debate in the opening words, "Think not," and concludes that the passage "records the attitude of the conservative Palestinian community in contrast to that of the Hellenists" (*History of the Synoptic Tradition* [New York: Harper and Row, 1963], p. 138). In an elaborate study of this pericope, W. D. Davies (*Christian Origins and Judaism*, pp. 31-66), finds ample ground for taking a different position. For one thing, the occurrence of Matthew 5:18 in a slightly different form in Luke 16:17 establishes the fact that the kernel of the verse, with its insistence on the permanence of the law, is not a creation of Matthew or his Church, for it is plain that Luke cannot be accused of Jewish-Christian sympathies. Davies goes on to expound the view that a legitimate place for the elements in the passage can be found in the actual life situation of Jesus' ministry. It is clearly recognized that the problem of the passage lies in its apparent ambivalence, since on the one hand the permanence of the law is affirmed, and affirmed in such a way as to suggest that some people believed Jesus' attitude was rather loose at this point, and on the other hand the antitheses that follow indicate a free handling of the law that does not comport readily with the strong affirmation of its permanence.

The solution of Davies is that the necessity for the denial of any purpose to destroy the law (v. 17) is grounded in suspicions that had been stirred by Jesus' rather free attitude toward certain of the demands of the law, such as observance of the Sabbath rest. Jesus is prepared to deny any purpose on His part to annul the law. On the other hand, He seems to envision the day when the law will give way to a new order, and this is suggested in the qualification placed on the permanence of the law — "until all things come to pass" (v. 18). Jesus may well have in mind a distinction between the period before His death, when the authority of the law continues to hold, and the period after His death, when the barrier of the law will be removed, making possible the oneness of Jew and Gentile in Himself, such as came to pass after His death and resurrection.

Explicit Christian Influences

The early Church was a worshipping as well as a witnessing community. Snatches of hymnody, prayers, and brief confessions of faith dot the Epistles. All these elements of worship reflect the distinctive Christian position of the Church and reveal the centrality of Christ to its faith and life. If *Gemeindetheologie* is well grounded, the Gospels should reflect this distinctively Christian influence at appropriate places. A test case for the position is the Lord's Prayer. But, as C. F. D. Moule points out, this great prayer contains no word or phrase that is explicitly Christian. Its content remains true to its original setting.

III. DIFFICULTIES OF *GEMEINDETHEOLOGIE* IN VIEW OF THE TITLES OF JESUS

Some of the matters already considered deal with the theology only in a marginal sense. At this point it is in order to take at least a glance at some of the titles accorded Jesus in the Gospels, whether by Himself or by others, since here we confront the *Gemeindetheologie* problem head-on.

Messiah

Probably the most central title accorded to Christ, especially from the standpoint of Jewish backgrounds, is *Messiah*. It is clear from Acts 2:36 and other passages that the Jerusalem Church, in the light of the resurrection and exaltation of Jesus, looked on Him as the Messiah. In the missionary proclamation of the Church in the synagogues of the Graeco-Roman world, this was the central point in the appeal to faith (Acts 17:3; 18:5, 28; cf. John 20:31).

But a rather different situation is encountered in the Gospels, for the one who is so confidently regarded by the early Church as filling this role seems here to be hesitant about it. It should be borne in mind that hesitancy is not the same thing as doubt, and it is certainly not to be interpreted as denial.

An explanation for the data has been offered by Wrede in his messianic secret theory, which has been readily accepted by many, especially those in the tradition of radical German scholarship. Bultmann, for example, thinks that the Evangelists have imposed their own belief in the messiahship of Jesus on the traditional material. Cullmann expresses the reluctance, felt by others, to go along with this procedure when he asks, "But is it not illusion to think that we can have the same faith as they in the early church if we accept its Christological views, but still assert that Jesus himself had no 'self-consciousness' of being what we confess him to be?" (*Christology of the New Testament,* [Philadelphia: Westminster Press, 1959], p. 8).

The situation becomes greatly clarified once the popular conception of Messiah is grasped, together with the tense political situation in the Palestine of Jesus' day. To adopt the title for Himself under those circumstances could lead to serious misunderstanding of the nature of Jesus' mission. On certain important occasions, namely, at Caesarea Philippi and before the Sanhedrin (Mark 8:29, 31; 14:61, 52) He substituted for the term Messiah that others had used, His own chosen term Son of man.

Cullmann seems to be on the right track when he observes, "Precisely the fact that we have to do here with restraint and not with rejection seems to me to be the best proof of the fact that we are concerned with history, not with early Christian theory" (*ibid.,* p. 125). Further, he states that Jesus could not well reject the title *per se,* as distinct from its current use, because it had great value for expressing a continuity between the task He had to fulfil and the Old Testament. In line with this, one could point to Luke 24:46, which constitutes a natural link between the situation in the Gospels and that which prevailed in the early Church (Acts 2:36).

Son of Man

This title presents a situation almost exactly the reverse of that in connection with Messiah, for the Lord did not avoid the term Son of man, but preferred it to any other when referring to Himself. Along with this fact we have to reckon with the indication from our sources that others did not use the title of Jesus (Stephen is the one exception — Acts 7:56). Bultmann, recognizing that in Daniel and Ethiopic Enoch the title indicates an eschatological figure, is prepared to accept passages in the Synoptics as spoken by Jesus when they refer to eschatological manifestation, but thinks Jesus had no intention of designating Himself, but rather another who was to come. He will not accept those passages which occur in the context of suffering and death, since he rules out Jesus' predictions of the cross as editorial additions by the Church. So, says Bultmann, Son of man in this class of passages is an instance of *Gemeindetheologie.* He fails to note that the predictions of the passion are not detailed or artificial, therefore not suspect of being supplied by later hands. They comport with the whole atmosphere of opposition in which Jesus moved. Furthermore, the uniting of the Son of man terminology with the motif of servant-suffering, as in Mark 10:45, is far more likely to belong to Jesus than a reflecting Church. Our sources make clear that the perceptiveness of the followers of Jesus in the area of messianic prophecy owed its impetus to Him. It is entirely credible that the Church respected His use of the title Son of man and chose to retain it only as a self-designation of our Lord. On the other hand, if the title in the Synoptics is due to the Church, then the cessation of its use in the remainder of the New Testament appears both arbitrary and inexplicable.

Son of God

It is part of Bultmann's reconstruction that this title, like Lord, became applied to Jesus in the Hellenistic communities and then was read back into the earthly life of Jesus. This minimizes the strength of the evidence that the title was at home in a Judaistic milieu and depended on Old Testament usage. More seriously, it fails to see that the application of the term in the Synoptics rarely comes in a context of a marvelous miracle worker, as in the pagan usage from which the Hellenistic churches supposedly derived it. On the contrary, the point of its use in the temptation, for example, is the refusal of Jesus as the Son of God to exercise His supernatural power in such a way as to call attention to Himself as a superman. Rather, He insists on maintaining full dependence on the Father.

Servant of God

Here also the *Gemeindetheologie* advocates assume that the Church is responsible for the identification of Jesus with the picture of the servant in Isaiah, especially in His suffering role. If this were so, one would look for a far stronger presentation of Jesus as the suffering servant in the Christology of the early Church. The evidence points to the fact that it characterized the early Jerusalem community to a considerable degree (Acts 3:13, 26; 4:27, 30; 8:30-35), but in the remainder of the New Testament it is either present to a minimal degree or absent altogether. The slight place accorded to it in Paul is particularly important. The situation in I Peter is somewhat different and this is what one would expect in view of the place given to the servant concept in the early part of Acts, where Peter is prominent.

Jeremias notes that of the servant passages in the latter part of Isaiah only Isaiah 42:1-4, 6; 49:6; and 52:13-53:12 were interpreted messianically in the New Testament, and that these are the very texts that Palestinian Judaism, as opposed to Hellenistic Judaism, interpreted messianically (Jeremias and Walter Zimmerli, *The Servant of God* [Naperville, Ill.: Allenson, 1957], p. 93).

With some confidence we may place the origin of the identification of Jesus with the servant in His own mind and ministry, beginning with the baptism (Mark 1:11; Isa. 42:1), coloring His announcements of the passion (Mark 10:45), and controlling His thoughts on the eve of His suffering (Luke 22:37; Mark 14:24). No doubt He carried over the representative force of the expression in Isaiah into His own situation as He made Himself available as a sacrifice for sinners, dying in the place of the many.

IV. CONTINUITY AND DISCONTINUITY IN THE NEW TESTAMENT MESSAGE

In conclusion, it is fitting to note that much would be gained in the debate over *Gemeindetheologie* by clarifying the distinction between the period of Jesus' ministry and the period of the early Church from this standpoint: that the epochal death and resurrection of Christ must necessarily affect the thought and life of the Church in a way that was not possible for the followers of Jesus prior to these events. Even in the case of Jesus there had to be a certain reticence in speaking of how His own work would shape the future. If the Gospels presented their material anachronistically, we could more readily go along with *Gemeindetheologie*. But lacking this, we do well to accept them as they ostensibly intend to be taken, as history, and as history that is crucial for faith. The gap between the Jesus of history and the Christ of faith is an unbridgeable chasm only if one fails to appreciate the factors that provide a continuum between them.

FAITH AS
HISTORICAL
UNDERSTANDING

James P. Martin

James P. Martin is Associate Professor of New Testament in Union Theological Seminary, Richmond, Virginia. Formerly he was Assistant Professor of New Testament in Princeton Theological Seminary. He is author of a volume on The Last Judgment. *He holds the Th.D. degree from Princeton Seminary.*

12. *James P. Martin*

FAITH AS HISTORICAL UNDERSTANDING

This essay seeks to explore the understanding of the *Heilsgeschichte* in the New Testament first of all with respect to its bearing on the historical place and the nature of faith, and then with respect to the understanding brought to faith by the "object" of faith. The object of faith in the New Testament Church is the God of Israel known in the work of Jesus of Nazareth, the Christ. We assume that the meaning of faith and the understanding of Jesus Christ apprehended by faith cannot be defined by any kind of philosophical a priori as to the nature of religion or the nature of faith as some general human capacity. As J. C. K. von Hofmann of Erlangen pointed out in his 1860 lectures on biblical hermeneutics, faith in the biblical sense belongs to the realm of *Heilsgeschichte,* and the novel feature of New Testament faith is that the community was formed by faith. Since, according to the New Testament, Christ is the essential content of all *Heilsgeschichte,* faith in Jesus involves necessarily some kind of historical understanding.

We wish to investigate this understanding along several lines of thought. With Paul as a fixed starting point, we shall examine the place of faith in Paul's theology of history, with particular reference to the eschatological history inaugurated in Jesus the Christ. This leads to a more extended investigation of the way in which the faith in Jesus of the New Testament Church involved historical understanding; in particular this is opened up by the description of Jesus as *archēgos* and *teleiōtēs* of faith. This way of thinking will be seen to

177

demand a *Heilsgeschichte,* which faith apprehends in Jesus. Also, some consideration will be given here to the importance that the insistence of the early Church on the continuity of her experience of Jesus and the risen Christ has for faith and its understanding. Proceeding from these matters, we shall discuss the uniqueness of faith itself as a phenomenon in the history of religions, in order to prepare the way for an examination of the important question about the origin of this renewed intensity of faith in early Christianity. The origin is discovered to be Jesus Himself, not the post-resurrection community. What He taught about faith will then be related to the question of historical understanding. This essay is not an exhaustive discussion of the nature of historical understanding, but seeks rather to provide some biblical materials for such discussion by showing that faith, which is so central in the life of the New Testament Church and which is centered on the work of Jesus the Christ, apprehends in Jesus the *Gestalt* of history.

I. THE PLACE OF FAITH IN THE PAULINE
THEOLOGY OF HISTORY

The importance for Paul of the historical priority of faith to law may be seen in the emphasis he gives (in Galatians 3 and Romans 4) to the historical argument from the Abraham narrative. Paul's insistence on this historical priority seems, however, to be contradicted by his equal insistence that in Jesus Christ faith has come as a historical reality. "Before faith *came,* we were confined under law . . but since faith *has come,* we are no longer under a custodian" (Gal 3:23, 25). The verb "come" is a remarkable verb to use of faith Nevertheless, its use in these Galatian texts intimates to us the dimensions and centrality of historical understanding for Paul. The *Heilgeschichte* which appears in these texts in condensed form is later fully developed in the theology of history set forth in the letter to the Romans.

If faith preceded the law, what does it mean to assert that faith has nevertheless "come" in and with Jesus the Christ? This way of speaking is not incidental to Paul for it is supported by the technical use of the term "now" in his theology, when he speaks of the event of Jesus Christ as inaugurating a new time in *Heilsgeschichte,* a time which provides the believer with a perspective from which to judge religious man and his history. The technical Now of Romans 3:21 (cf. Rom. 8:1; 5:9, 11; 3:26; 2 Cor. 6:2) marks off the new time in which Paul lives and from which he, as a new man in Christ, analyze and judges the religious situation of man now brought under the certainty of divine judgment (note the stress on judgment and its re lation to gospel: Rom. 1:24, 26, 28; 2:2, 3, 5, 16; 3:6, 19, 20). The Now of which Paul speaks is the period of *Heilsgeschichte* commencing with the ministry of Jesus and lasting until His parousia. Faith is explicitly associated with this Now in the argument of Romans 3:21-26, and this argument leads directly to the historical discussion of Abraham and the temporal priority of his faith as the pattern of all justification. Although the words "it was reckoned to him" were written of Abraham, they were not written for his sake alone but for ours also (Rom. 4:23, 24). For the same righteousness, as right relationship to God, is reckoned to us who believe in the God who raised Jesus from the dead, who was put to death because of our transgressions and was raised for our justification (Rom. 4:25). Here also, although faith begins with Abraham, it is renewed, revitalized and reaffirmed in the death and resurrection of Jesus the Christ. Since this death and resurrection are historical, the renewing of faith as receptivity to God's act is the consequence of a temporal event and therefore temporal itself. Paul describes the results of this renewal of faith in the succeeding argument of Romans 5:1-3 in terms of faith's benefits.

However, here where Paul speaks strongly of the present benefits of faith, he speaks also of sufferings, endurance, approved character and hope. Faith then is not a historical phenomenon appearing briefly in a punctiliar event and then disappearing, but involves obviously larger historical dimensions by which it reaches out into the future toward the attainment of hope (Rom. 8:24, 25). Faith also has a dimension which reaches into the past and links up with the pattern of Abraham's obedience (Rom. 4:1, 16, 23, 24). By believing in the God who raised Jesus from the dead the believer is brought into this history which faith grasps. By faith the believer enters into *Heilsgeschichte* and the past and future of historical understanding thus granted include the wandering Abraham and the coming consummation of a new heaven and a new earth. It is in fact remarkable that Paul should, in writing to the church of the capital city of the Graeco-Roman world, say so much about an obscure ancient Semite, mention an equally obscure oriental prince, David (Rom. 1:3), express a longing expectation for a new heaven and a new earth (Rom. 8:19-24), and actually center all of this history in the life of a Jew crucified by the Roman state.

When any man attaches himself by faith personally to the history of Jesus of Nazareth, he enters into *Heilsgeschichte*. By this, he confesses that he understands that the meaning of his own existence and that of all men, and the cosmos, is offered in this same Jesus. This Jesus is to faith the risen Lord, who alone has the power and authority, by virtue of His resurrection, to bring men into this holy history and to bring this history forward through time to its goal and consummation.

The vision of Revelation 5 has this as its theme. It is proper so to regard faith in Jesus as the crucial matter in interpreting the historical consciousness of the New Testament, because He is proclaimed by the primitive Church primarily in the context of the history of Israel. He is the obedient servant of God (Acts 3:13; 4:30) who has opened Israel's history to the nations through faith.[1]

Faith and law are not primarily rival systems of morality or mutually exclusive psychological attitudes, but periods of *Heilsgeschichte* reflecting the essential tension of promise and fulfillment in pre-Christian Judaism. Paul's own conversion to Christianity must also be understood first of all in light of this tension of promise and fulfilment in its bearing on the interpretation of Israel's past. Paul's conversion makes little sense when interpreted in terms of a tension of legalism vs. liberty. Whatever truth there is in this tension, it is clearly secondary (cf. R. A. Longenecker, *Paul Apostle of Liberty* [New York: Harper and Row, 1964], p. 84). In its proclamation therefore, the early Church preached Jesus as fulfilment. But the Church did not reduce the sense of fulfilment to a one to one correspondence between Old Testament letters and New Testament events, because it proclaimed Jesus also as promise of a new future. This expectation of the new future is present in the earliest speeches in Acts 2 and 3. The eschatological proclamation is not the result of a crisis, nor is it an unnecessary addition, but it is essential to the form of historical consciousness in the New Testament Church. J. A. T. Robinson's argument that the whole structure of New Testament theology is to be built upon a shift of perspective between Acts 2 and Acts 3 is an impossible reconstruction, on critical as well as on theological grounds.[2] For it was the resurrection of Jesus which *demanded* the futuristic eschatological expectation. Resurrection means cosmic salvation, and this had not occurred with the raising of Jesus; therefore it is expected to come. The question of the time-psychology of the primitive Church should not blind us to the central fact that the early Church expected a future, final revelation of the one taken up into heaven

---

1 The nature of Jewish Christianity is the important, albeit complicated question, for understanding the history of the primitive Church. Bultmann's supposition of a pre-Pauline Hellenistic Church is a construction of the imagination and must be rejected. See Dom Gregory Dix, *Jew and Greek* (London: Dacre Press, 1953) and H. J. Schoeps, *Paul: The Theology of the Apostle in the Light of Jewish Religious History*, tr. Harold Knight (Philadelphia: Westminster Press, 1961).

2 J. A. T. Robinson, *Jesus and His Coming* (New York and Nashville: Abingdon Press, 1957), pp. 136, 147, 152. The ingenious exegesis by which Robinson seeks to transform Acts 3 into a Jewish parousia expectation is as fantastic as his misinterpretation of the eschatology of Hebrews (*ibid.*, p. 157f.). The exegesis tells us more about what Robinson cannot believe than it says about the eschatology of the New Testament Church.

(Acts 3:20, 21), as a fulfilment of what was already begun and given in the ministry of Jesus of Nazareth. The realities of the new age: salvation, life, forgiveness, resurrection, which God has offered man in Jesus, were not proclaimed solely and totally within the category of fulfilment. The new event of Pentecost is brought within the scope of the meaning of Jesus' work and interpreted in terms of a continuing activity of the exalted Lord in and through His Church in order to prepare for the consummation of the kingdom (Acts 2:23, 33 and 1:6-8). Jesus' ministry, death, resurrection, and exaltation are announced as eschatological event, that is, as the event which promises a new future for history and at the same time because of this pledged future reveals the present to be also eschatological. In the name of Jesus the Christ men are called to believe *for,* that is, with an end to, salvation, which, according to all the New Testament writers still remains future because of its cosmic scope.

II. THE HISTORICAL UNDERSTANDING OF THE NEW TESTAMENT CHURCH'S FAITH

In his address in Solomon's porch, Peter proclaims Jesus as the *archēgos* (pioneer, inaugurator) of life, whom the men of Israel had killed. God, however, raised Him from the dead and to this event the apostles are witnesses (Acts 3:15). "The God of Abraham, Isaac and Jacob, the God of our fathers, glorified his servant Jesus" (Acts 3:13). But this glorification does not consist in total and instant accomplishment of the promised salvation, because Jesus by His resurrection has become an *archēgos* of a "process" (history) which opens up a future to the final completion of God's purpose. The tension of fulfilment-promise in the work of Jesus is clear in the remainder of this sermon, when Peter speaks directly of fulfilment (Acts 3:18) and at the same time of the sending of the Christ appointed for you, namely Jesus, whom heaven must keep until the time for the final fulfilment of the promises. Between the initial and the ultimate fulfilment, Jesus is known and believed in as the *archēgos.*

Archēgos may mean either a leader, ruler, prince, or one who begins something as first in a series and thus supplies the impetus and opportunity for others to follow. In profane Greek usage, it may also mean originator or founder, for example, the hero or founder of a city. In the Septuagint, *archēgos* is usually used to refer to the military or political leader of the people. First Maccabees 10:37 exemplifies the superiority of the *archēgos,* who alone makes it possible for others to act at all. It appears that the second meaning of the *archēgos* as initiator, or pioneer, provides the best sense for the term in Acts 3:15. The concomitant idea of ruler, leader, or prince inheres also to this sense of course, but it is not primary. The *archēgos* is qualified more precisely in this text as the *archēgos* of life (τῆσζωῆς). The resurrection of Jesus has opened the door to eternal life to all who believe in Him. He is therefore by His resurrection the *archēgos* of our participation in the life to come by the general resurrection of the body. In this sense the term *"archēgos* of life" is equivalent in meaning to the designation of the resurrected Christ as *aparchē* (firstfruits) of those who sleep (I Cor. 15:20). Whereas *aparchē* speaks directly of the resurrection of the dead (I Cor.. 15:23), *archēgos* is a term which relates to the activity and future of the living. Just as *archēgos* implies an inclusion of others in the process opened up by the action of the *archēgos,* so also *aparchē* includes within itself an anticipation of completion. The *aparchē* is the part of the sum total already present, and as the first installment is the pledge and guarantee of the reward to come. In his argument in Romans 8 Paul links in eschatological tension the present adoption, the firstfruits of the Spirit, to an adoption yet to be consummated, namely, the redemption of the body. Redemption of the body does not mean deliverance *from* the body but resurrection *of* the body. Paul's term is probably not to be restricted to the living who await transformation at the parousia but simply expresses the destiny of all who have received the Spirit, whether or not they are alive at the parousia. In I Corinthians 15:23 and 52, he is speaking expressly of the transformation of the living at that time. It is probably incorrect to make a rigid distinction between *aparchē* and *archēgos* by referring them to the dead and the living respectively, but nevertheless some distinction of spheres of reference seems plausible. In Acts 5:31, the absolute *archēgos* coupled with the title *sōtēr* (Saviour) describes the functions of the exalted Jesus with respect to the continual enlargement of the community of believers through repentance and forgiveness of sins. But forgiveness of sins cannot itself be detached from the future salvation and isolated as present religious experience only.

The importance of the idea of initiation in the term *archēgos* is supported by other designations of Jesus as the 'first.' He is called the first of the resurrection of the dead (Acts 26:23); the beginning, the first-born of the dead (Col. 1:18), and the first-born of the dead (Rev. 1:5). To these might be added "I am the first and the last" (Rev. 1:17); "the first and the last" (Rev. 2:8); and "the beginning of the creation of God" (Rev. 3:14). The resurrection of Jesus is certainly not to be understood as a seal of His past alone, but an event which in itself is soteriological and which reveals the scope of the salvation God intends for His creation. The resurrection is not just evidence or proof of the quality of the atonement, but as the basis of justification, opens the way into a new totality of life which will reach its consummation in the general resurrection. Paul's argument concerning the reign of Christ as a conquest of God's enemies, the last of which is death, is pertinent to this perspective (I Cor. 15:25, 26). The concept of Jesus as first of a new creation is also related to the theology of Christ as the second or last Adam (Rom. 5:12ff. and I Cor. 15:45ff.); this theology provides the indispensable background for the interpretation of the Christological hymn in Philippians 2:6-11. But our concern in this essay is to try to discover the implications of the eschatology implicit in the designation of Jesus as the *archēgos* for faith as historical understanding.

In Hebrews 12:1 Jesus is called the *archēgos* of *faith*. He is also called in the same text the *teleiōtēs* (perfector, consummator) of faith The two terms indeed are employed as a unit; the readers are to look unto Jesus, the initiator and consummator of faith. In Hebrews 2:10, Jesus is described as the *archēgos* of salvation. This language, like that of Acts, manifests an eschatological perspective of present and future. Attached to what is popularly called the Easter-faith of the primitive Church, it illuminates very much the historical dimensions of the work of Jesus and therefore the historical understanding implicit in faith in Jesus.

Since, as Paul says, faith has come to fulfil the promise (to faith!) which antedated the law, we may summarize the result of this coming of faith by saying that the people of God are no longer under a *paidagōgos* but under an *archēgos*. This *archēgos* is Jesus. God's purpose has passed from the law as *paidagōgos* to Jesus as the new *archēgos*. It is important in this connection to insist that the designation of Jesus as *archēgos* by virtue of His exaltation does not denote an honorific title of a deity now escaped from history into timelessness, nor the final title of victor at the end of a race, but, paradoxically, the title of one who by his exaltation initiates a new stage in the historical process which has all the attributes of finality. Jesus the *archēgos* calls the community of faith to a new historical existence as the community which is to inherit the future of God. (To say that we are under an *archēgos* also corresponds to the meaning of the term as hero or guardian; Christ being the eponymous hero of the Christian's heavenly citizenship.) The series of generations of the people of God follow in the path pioneered by the *archēgos*, and this conception demonstrates clearly that the meaning of Jesus is grasped only in faith. The author of Hebrews is explicit on this point. When he comes to apply to his readers the examples of and witnesses to faith and perseverance under the old covenant (Heb. 11), he urges his readers also to run the race, looking away unto the inaugurator and consummator of faith, Jesus. In Hebrews 2:10 also, we meet similar ideas together; Jesus as *archēgos*, and His own perfecting as essential to the saving of those who would believe in Him. "For it pleased him [God], on account of whom are all things, and through whom are all things, in leading many sons into glory, to perfect the Pioneer of their salvation through sufferings." Because Jesus has been perfected Himself He has become the perfector (consummator) of the faith of those who believe in Him.

There is a similarity between Paul and the author of Hebrews at this point, for both are concerned to relate the newness introduced by Jesus to the past faith of Israel. We are told that the heroes of the old covenant all died in faith, not having inherited the promises, but having seen them from afar (Heb. 11:13, 39). The perfecting of the elders awaits in turn the perfecting of the whole people of God. The past of *Heilsgeschichte* is thereby taken up into the new future inaugurated by Jesus the *archēgos*. The entire course of *Heilsgeschichte* will be consummated by the work of Jesus because He is also the perfector (*teleiōtēs*) of faith. The perfecting of the faithful of all the ages of holy history, before and after Jesus, is guaranteed by the personal perfecting (*teleiōsis*) of Jesus in His obedience as a Son. It awaits the future of His appearing apart from sin unto salvation (Heb. 9:28). The language in Hebrews of pioneer, perfector, faith, and perfecting is of a piece with the eschatology of the Epistle which exhorts the people of God to move out and forward, toward the approaching day of the Lord (Heb. 10:26), the city with foundations (Heb. 11:10, 16), the city to come (Heb. 13:14), the remaining rest (Heb. 4:1, 11), the inheritance of all the promises (Heb. 6:12; 11:39; 6:18), and the end (Heb. 3:14; 6:11, cf. 10:36). The running of the race points also, of course, to the goal of the race (Heb. 12:1f.). Faith, therefore, as acceptance of the history of Jesus the Son, anticipates the future of Jesus and lays hold of His past. The perfecting of Jesus through His obedience has opened up the new and living way both into heaven and on earth, in the renewed history into which God's people are called and in which they are to run, persevere, hold fast, stir up each other to love and good works, all in faith. Jesus is the "hero" of the household of faith; He is the pioneer of the renewed *Heilsgeschichte* which faith embraces as He is also the consummator of this history and thereby the consummator of faith. Characteristically, all the New Testament writers conjoin perseverance, endurance, and patience to faith (Heb. 6:12, 15; 10:36, 39; 11:27; 12:1-11; Rom. 5:1-3; 2 Thess. 1:4; Col. 1:11; James 1:3, 4; 2 Peter 1:6; Rev. 2:2, 3, 19; 3:10; 13:10; 14:12; Mark 13:13).

The definition of faith as the *hypostasis* (substance, confident reliance) of things hoped for, the *elenchos* (a proving of, a conviction about) things not seen, relates faith to the future of history, not merely to a presently existing invisible world surrounding the one who has faith. Heaven and the hidden paradise are, to be sure, not excluded from the embrace of faith, but faith is a desire toward the invisible and unknown quite different from the desire of mysticism. Faith, in the New Testament understanding of the term, never wants to stop time and escape from the historical process into timelessness. Faith rather awaits the coming of the invisible world and consequently while it waits, it works, bears, endures, suffers, hopes, and runs. The certainty that there will be future revelation of the hidden which will come does not rest upon some power of wishful projection, or on emotional attachment to invisibility or mystical absorption, but upon the historic work of Jesus of Nazareth, who by taking on Himself "flesh and blood" (Heb. 2:14-17) and being perfected through suffering (Heb. 2:10) and obedience (Heb. 5:7-9), has become the *archēgos* of faith. Just as time and history have received heaven and paradise and eternity into themselves because of the work of Jesus, so also because of the resurrection and ascension of Jesus, heaven has received time and history into itself, so that faith does indeed embrace both realms. The citizenship of the Christian is already in heaven where Christ is; the dead are with Him in the hidden paradise now; but faith does not expect a consummation of these realities by mystical escape from history, nor even at the moment of personal death, but only at the last day. The last day is supremely the day of complete salvation, and men are brought to that salvation only through the work of Jesus the Christ.

Hebrews 2:10 is particularly instructive in revealing how the primitive Church's faith involved historical understanding or historical consciousness. Eschatology, Christology and historical consciousness are indissoluble in the theology of Hebrews (Heinz-Dietrich Wendland, *Geschichtsanschauung und Geschichtsbewusstsein im Neuen Testament* [Göttingen: Vandenhoeck und Ruprecht, 1938], p. 40). Hebrews maintains the realism of apocalyptic; its theology cannot be pressed into a Platonic-Hellenistic scheme of coexisting worlds. The historical consciousness of the author of Hebrews certainly emphasizes the crucial importance of the present as the day of salvation because of the effective work of Jesus the great high priest. This work is not an end in itself, but the guarantee of the coming day of salvation and the last judgment (Heb. 10:25f., 12:25f.). The continuing work of the exalted Christ and the work of the "historical" Jesus are comprehended as a unity. The continuity of historical understanding thus given to faith means that faith itself is eschatological. Faith accepts the future fulfilment promised by God because it knows that that for which it hopes already exists invisibly in God. (C. K. Barrett, "The Eschatology of the Epistle to the Hebrews," *The Background of the New Testament and its Eschatology*, ed. by W. D. Davies and David Daube [Cambridge University Press, 1956], p. 381). The center of faith and of its historical understanding is the perfecting of Jesus as the *archēgos* of salvation. The future goal of God's will, to lead many sons into glory, is inaugurated by the perfecting of Jesus through sufferings. The term salvation in Hebrews 2:10 used as a modifier of *archēgos* does not mean only the sum total of individuals who believe, but in keeping with the general apocalyptic outlook of the New Testament, it means the cosmic salvation of the end-time. The perfecting of Jesus initiates the process of God's leading many sons to glory. The aorist participle, *agagonta* (Heb. 2:10) is to be understood as an ingressive aorist, denoting an action viewed absolutely, yet initiating a process. The term process does not demand a mechanical or impersonal or evolutionary mode of action; it simply denotes the whole history of the personal interactions of God and man. Glory is a term reserved for the ultimate destiny of God's creation. As Paul reminds us, already Christ in you is the hope of glory (Col. 1:27). The perfecting of Jesus through sufferings is another way of describing an aspect of His way of obedience culminating in the finality of His sacrifice (cf. Heb. 5:9). The priestly theme is also joined elsewhere to the motif of the Way (Mathias Rissi, "Die Menschlichkeit Jesu nach Hebr. 5, 7-8," *Theologische Zeitschrift*, Vol. 11 [Jan.-Feb., 1955], pp. 29f.). In Hebrews 6:20 Jesus is designated as the forerunner implying that other runners are to follow in the new and living way.

This language reminds us of the technical use of the term "the Way," "those of the Way" employed by Luke to describe the early Christian community (Acts 9:2; 16:17; 19:9, 23; 22:4; 24:14, 22; cf. 18:25, 26). "The Way" describes a group who know the goal of history, who understand *Heilsgeschichte* as a Way, and who confess that their pattern of life in this Way (history) is the Way of the ministry of Jesus of Nazareth in His going to His cross. His humiliation as the prerequisite to His exaltation provides the pattern for the mind of the Church. Luke's travel narrative in his Gospel (9:51-19:45) introduces this way of Jesus to His cross by speaking of its goal as ascension and exaltation. The way to Jesus' exaltation by ascension lies in His obedience to suffering by setting His face to go to Jerusalem where as the Son of man He submits to the judgment of men and fulfills the work of the servant of God. This way of Jesus becomes in turn the event which originates the new way of the community of faith. The early Church insisted that the risen Christ whom she worshipped was not a psychological experience, nor a myth patterned after Hellenistic mysteries, nor a supernatural *x* of unknown quantity and quality but really and actually Jesus of Nazareth. Faith in the risen Lord provides access to the Jesus offered to us in the Gospels. The early Church saw herself not as the creation of apostles but of Jesus. She understood the work of Jesus not as the work of a self-appointed revolutionary or a messiah-hopeful but as the work of the God of Abraham, Isaac, and Jacob. The Church was profoundly aware of the continuity of historical life between Jesus and old Israel on the one hand, and, on the other hand, between Jesus and the new community of faith emerging as the Israel renewed by God into public history following Pentecost. In Hebrews, Jesus is called Son in all the stages of His existence, yet it is remarkable that the epistle says that He inherited the name (Heb. 1:4). The idea of inheritance relates His sonship to a precise point of time (Rissi, *op. cit.,* p. 29). The letter describes the exalted high priest at considerable length, yet it emphasizes in its own distinctive way the real humanity of Jesus and His life in this humanity as the way to His inheritance of Sonship (Heb. 2:9, 14, 17, 18; 3:2; 5:7, 8; 9:26b; 10:19, note the term "blood of Jesus"; cf. John 19:34, 35). The exalted high priest is not an idealized priesthood figure, but, again, Jesus. The early Church did not dig an abyss between Jesus of Nazareth and the risen Christ; the resurrection did not induce mass amnesia nor did it create indifference as to just exactly who had risen. The modern embarrassment at this point was not shared by the apostolic Church. Luke very carefully structures both his Gospel and the Acts in terms of the continuity of the ministry of Jesus and the ongoing history of the Church. The events of the ministry have come to fruition in the Christian society (Luke 1:1) and what Jesus began to do and to teach according to the record of the Gospel, He continues to do and teach in the record of the Acts of the Apostles (Acts 1:1).

Although Paul concentrates the kerygma concerning Jesus into Christ crucified (I Cor. 1:23; 2:2) and Christ raised (I Cor. 15:14), this concentration does not exclude the fact that crucifixion and resurrection are the fulfilment, and in a sense, the epitome, of the ministry of Jesus. The ministry as a whole is epitomized in such formulary texts as "he made him to be sin who knew no sin" (II Cor. 5:21), "he became poor" (II Cor. 8:9), "crucified in weakness" (II Cor. 13:4), "of the seed of David according to the flesh" (Rom. 1:3), "the form of the servant, found in appearance as a man, in the likeness of men" (Phil. 2:5ff.). The form of the servant seen in the obedience of Jesus is the pattern for the mind of the Church in its service to its members (Phil. 2:1-5). John placed the story of the empty tomb (John 20:1-10) before any narrative of resurrection appearances in order to stress the fact that the Jesus whom he saw dead on the cross (John 19:34,

35) was not in the tomb on the morning of the third day. It was the body of Jesus that was gone. The appearance to Mary Magdalene immediately following serves to emphasize in turn the recognition of the risen Christ as Jesus (John 20:11-18). The appearance to Thomas has the same purpose (John 20:24-29). The confession is that the crucified Jesus is now Lord and God. According to the theology of John's Gospel, such a confession is not mere intellectual recitation of a formula; the faith which utters it is a faith which experiences Jesus through the Spirit in such a way that He becomes for the present believer what He was for the Church behind this Gospel. John's well-known avoidance of the noun "faith" in preference for the verb form expresses the dynamic character of faith. It is nothing less than entering into the life of Jesus who is the Way to the Father. Since John too shares the apocalyptic framework of the New Testament, the coming to the Father through Jesus is not completely fulfilled in the initiatory experience of rebirth, but in the day of resurrection. Regeneration is entrance into life; not a life of mystical escape from history, but life in a history transformed by present fellowship with Jesus and the Spirit; a life of service, rejection by the world, obedience and mission (John 14-20). Exactly where Jesus reveals that whoever believes in Him has eternal life, He stresses the promise that He will raise up the believer in the last day (John 6:39, 40, 44, 47, 54). John's theology has of course reflected at this point the experience of death in the primitive Church but the problem did not create the theology, rather it called it forth from the tradition about Jesus through the process of remembrance (James P. Martin, "History and Eschatology in the Lazarus Narrative John 11:1-44," *Scottish Journal of Theology*, Vol. 17, No. 3 [Sept. 1964], pp. 332-43).

Historical study of the faith of the New Testament Church, no matter with what particular writer the scholar is concerned at the moment, cannot commence by assuming a radical discontinuity between the Easter faith, as it is commonly called, and the prehistory of this faith in the ministry of Jesus of Nazareth. That the Easter faith had a prehistory is the common witness of the New Testament theologians and must be kept in view in any discussion of how the Proclaimer became the Proclaimed. The risen Christ reveals Himself to men in the environment of the present age as Jesus, the man approved of God by His good works. "Who are you, Lord?" Saul asked on the Damascus Road. The answer was not, "I am the Redeemed Redeemer" or "I am the Christ-principle" but "I am Jesus, whom you are persecuting." From this time on, Paul bore about in his body the death of Jesus so that the life of Jesus might be manifested (II Cor. 4:10f.). The message and life of Jesus are not presuppositions of New

Testament theology, but its major concern, because faith in Christ the Lord is at the same time faith in Jesus' work.

The homologues of the early Church, Jesus is Christ and Jesus is Lord, show that we have to do with the meaning and content of both terms, Jesus and Christ (Lord). Christian understanding cannot restrict itself to the content of the titles. The primitive Church maintained this confession first of all against the hostility and unbelief of Judaism, and had to give reasons for its faith that Jesus of Nazareth, not John the Baptist or Judas the Galilean (Acts 5:37), was the Christ (Acts 5: 42). The evidence for the claim of the early Church is the ministry of Jesus of Nazareth according to the traditions deposited in our written Gospels. The period of His life between baptism and passion is decisive for this claim; Jesus is He who came by water and by blood (I John 5:6).

III. THE UNIQUENESS OF THE NEW TESTAMENT
VIEW OF FAITH

The biblical concept of faith requires more careful analysis than is often given to it even by those who stress faith as the only way to God and emphasize its difference from works of the law. Philosophically engendered definitions of faith, such as those employed by Schleiermacher, Bultmann, and Tillich, show a curious inability to relate faith to the historical reality of Jesus. Negatively, these theologians reinforce the view that faith belongs to the realm of *Heilsgeschichte*. From the point of view of the history of religions it is in fact astonishing and unusual that faith should be regarded, as it is in the New Testament, as the special relationship to God. It is surprising that salvation is "communicated" by faith alone. *Sola fide* is not the creation but the rediscovery of the Reformers, and it needs to be renewed again today for it has become encrusted with the barnacles of tradition. The *sola fide* belongs with the *solus Christus* because the historical achievement of Jesus was the faith of the disciples in Him and indeed the continuing faith of men in Him. In the garish day of nineteenth-century moralism when justification was man's achievement and the kingdom of God his private building, Adolf Schlatter in his work *Der Glaube im Neuen Testament* (Göttingen: Vandenhoeck und Ruprecht, 1885) demonstrated the centrality of the concept of faith for the writers of the New Testament. Schlatter's ideas are presented in briefer compass in his only translated work, *The Church in the New Testament Period* (tr. Paul P. Levertoff [London: S. P. C. K., 1955]). He remarks that in contradistinction to Jewish and Greek piety, the centrality of faith became the hallmark of Christianity. Both Judaism and Hellenism had some knowledge of the concept, but the central form of Jewish piety remained righteous-ness and the central form of Hellenistic piety remained gnosis. When the rabbis extolled faith, they extolled it as the highest religious achievement, and Judaism divided men into the righteous and the unrighteous on the basis of achievement. The characterization should be partly qualified by distinguishing between nomism and pure legalism (Longenecker, *op. cit.*, p. 79f.), but in the main it is not inaccurate. Greek thought, for which gnosis represented the dominant ideal, divided men into philosophers and ignorant (foolish). The Christians however, were not an assembly of righteous or of gnostics but of believers.[3]

The concept of faith was weak in late Judaism because of the loss of genuine historicalness (G. Ebeling, *Word and Faith*, tr. J. W. Leitch [Philadelphia: Fortress Press, 1961], p. 221). Bultmann writes that in late Judaism history is brought as it were to a standstill and a real sense of being bound up with it is lacking. The present can no longer continue history in a living way but is merely a medium for transmitting canonized tradition. Faith thus appears as some-thing static and constant (Bultmann, *TWNT*, Vol. VI, p. 201). In view of this it might appear that when Paul declared that faith has come in Jesus Christ, this means that Christianity has broken the static attitude of late Judaism and returned to the Old Testament understanding of faith. This, it would seem, would help us to see why at the same time he speaks so insistently about Abraham's faith. However, while the understanding of faith in the New Testament does recover the historicalness of existence reflected in the Abraham narrative, the New Testament faith in Jesus is no mere restoration of an Old Testament attitude but genuine renewal because Jesus is the eschatological Saviour. Jesus cannot be placed in the pantheon of the heroes of faith (Heb. 11). He is not one of the many elders whose life reveals the historicalness of existence in faith. Jesus is removed from them because He has become the *archēgos* of faith itself who alone can bring the historical existence of all believers of all ages to its intended goal. Because He is also the consummator of faith Jesus does not stand alongside Abraham as another example, but above Abraham as his perfector (cf. John 8:39ff.). Apart from the history of Jesus, Abraham himself and all his sons have no hope of the final salvation; they all died not having received what was promised (Heb. 11:13, 39). Abraham and all the faithful remain in the hidden

---

[3] More complete treatment is provided on πίστις (faith) in Kittel, *Theologisches Wörterbuch zum neuen Testament*, Vol. VI, pp. 174-230. Much of this article appears in translation in *Bible Key Words*, Vol. III (New York: Harper and Brothers, 1961).

paradise (Luke 23:43) until the resurrection and creation of the new
heaven and new earth. In a sense therefore they are not yet delivered
from the effect of death, since death is the last enemy to be destroyed;
they all died in faith not having inherited the promises. The difference between the faith of Abraham and that of the Christian is
that because of Jesus the Christ Christian faith actually apprehends
the eschatological future. This is why faith in the New Testament is
inseparable from hope. Hope is not mere wishful thinking; it possesses
content; it is a reality offered concretely to us. This reality comprises
the coming of the Son of man, the resurrection of the dead, and
cosmic redemption. The blessings of salvation now apprehended by
faith are already the eschatological gifts; the proleptic realization of
the final gifts. Justification, adoption, redemption, are all proleptic
eschatological gifts (cf. *TWNT, loc. cit.*). Faith, then, is the act in
which man turns completely toward God's future in response to His
eschatological revelation in Jesus Christ. Faith constitutes the existence
of the believer; it completely characterizes his life. Thus the New Testament can use *pistis* and *pisteuein* absolutely as the designation of the
"Christian religion" (Bultmann, *TWNT,* Vol. VI, pp. 217, 218). Christ
is God's last deed, including the future in its scope. We must insist,
however, that the historical future which faith expects is not futurity
in the sense of possibility as it has been so interpreted in existentialist
theology, but the future as temporal future, as the completion of
Heilsgeschichte.

Nevertheless, despite the new eschatological dimension to faith in
the New Testament which arises from the fact that Jesus is the
Christ of Israel, there are elements in the Old Testament concept of
faith which belong also to the New Testament concept (see G. Ebeling,
op. cit., 207ff. and *TWNT,* Vol. VI, pp. 182-197). Against the indispensable background of the primeval, universalized history of Genesis 1-11,
Abraham marks the beginning of *Heilsgeschichte* and the characteristic
note of his piety is faith. In Genesis 15:6 we read that Abraham "believed the Lord." There is not a passage in the Old Testament which
relates believing directly to a fact. To say that Abraham "believed
the Lord" means that the idea of faith expresses the attitude of man
toward God which corresponds to the claim of God. Faith applies
to the whole of man's relationship to God (A. Weiser, *TWNT,* Vol.
VI, p. 185). The term "believed" in Genesis 15:6 expresses the ac-
knowledgment of the promise and of the power of God to perform
it. The promises and commands of God are therefore not merely
statements of fact but claims for the future. Consequently faith is
the only possible response for man who cannot penetrate or control
the future nor yet escape it. In faith man takes God with complete

seriousness as the one who claims faith because He is the living God who alone has the power of the future. Abraham said "Amen" to God with all the consequences for God and for himself.

Since reality, according to the Old Testament view, is not static existence but that which comes into being, faith therefore arises on the ground of the initiative of God who speaks His word of promise or command and thereby wills that it shall so come to pass. In the Old Testament faith does not mean primarily thinking something about God but expecting something from Him, although the two ideas are certainly not mutually exclusive. But the basic attitude of faith is not believing that a God exists, but believing in the coming of God, who wills to act according to His promise (Heb. 6:13-18). Man lives in faith when his own future is yielded up to God and at the same time is expected from God (Gen. 22). This distinguishes the life of faith from a life based in a surrender to a chain of causality. At the same time faith is not directed to any old future, or even to future things, but to Jesus the Christ because He is the essential content of *Heilsgeschichte*. As Bengel has remarked, the Christian should not expect death as the goal of Christian life, but the appearance of Jesus. This event transcends personal death and the dimensions of individual existence.

IV. THE TEACHING OF JESUS AND THE NEW TESTAMENT EXPERIENCE OF FAITH

The origin of the renewed power of faith in the New Testament must be sought, I believe, in the deeds and words of Jesus Himself. It is highly probable that Paul's statement that faith "came" pertains to Jesus first of all, not first of all to the post-resurrection community. Enough has already been said about the continuity of this community with the historical Jesus. Bultmann in his article in *TWNT* does not discuss whether or not Jesus made a claim for faith, although he had spoken of this in his earlier work, *Jesus and the Word*. The question calls for fresh discussion. It cannot be explored here in all its depth, but the argument that faith brings historical understanding which is centered on Jesus demands that something be said even in a preliminary way about Jesus' call to faith. Two extremes of approach are obvious. If we believe that nothing can be known historically except the sudden emergence of the Easter faith and its results, then the Gospels will be approached as evidence of the effects of the Easter faith upon the record of Jesus and everything will be viewed as the product of a *Gemeindetheologie*. This statement is not meant to prejudice the obvious effect of the resurrection upon the disciples' understanding of Jesus, or upon the Jesus tradition. The other extreme is to historicize Jesus so as to exclude the possibility of relating Him to the Easter faith, so that the faith of the community is loosely attached to a historical basis. The proper method is to accept the early Church's consciousness of the continuity of her experience of Jesus with her resurrection faith and to inquire into the initial aspect of this experience. This method has been intimated above and needs to be followed somewhat further at this point.

According to Synoptic tradition Jesus did not speak openly about His own faith but was concerned to awaken in others faith in God. This faith in God, however, is directly associated with the action of Jesus Himself and is not to be detached from Him. At the cursing of the fig tree Jesus counselled the disciples to have faith in God. While this faith has to do with the action of God toward Israel in the present crisis, the action of God takes place in and through the actions of Jesus. Furthermore, the faith which appears so strikingly in the healing narratives is a faith which expects Jesus to act. The men who let the paralytic down through the roof acted in faith toward Jesus' action; as did the woman who touched His garment (Mark 2:5; 5:34). The faith of the centurion is a luminous example that faith is expectancy that Jesus can and will act in a situation calling for an act of God (Matt. 8:10). The familiar saying about faith moving the mountain shows that faith has to do with what God alone can perform; it is letting God go into action. Since the healings and other miracles, such as the storm on the lake in which Jesus rebukes the disciples for having no faith (Mark 4:39), are signs of the inbreaking kingdom, faith is related directly to the opening up of the eschatological future through the action of Jesus. On the other hand, absence of faith restricts the activity of Jesus. Jesus marveled because of the unbelief in Nazareth and could do no mighty work there (Mark 6:5, 6; Matt. 13:58; cf. Luke 4:23b). Apart from faith, which involves personal acceptance of Jesus, Jesus does not act. Faith, then, is not a mental attitude which exists irrespective of a personal response to Jesus. To speak of faith is to speak of what one expects to happen, and for the New Testament Church, one does not expect anything to happen apart from Jesus (cf. Acts 3:6, 16!). We may conclude that faith is always related to the expectation of God's acts in which He will manifest the promised salvation. Faith as a special gift of the Spirit in the early Church is also associated with gifts of healing and so related to events which are expected as signs of the eschatological salvation (I Cor. 12:9).

Although Jesus does not speak in so many words of His own faith in God, the fact that faith is always associated with the action of

Jesus in which He performs what is expected from God indicates that Jesus' work cannot be understood apart from faith. Since the eschatological salvation is brought by God to men only through the work of Jesus, then the ministry of Jesus is a work which makes faith possible as *the* relationship of men to God. Jesus' own faith in God is normally described in the Gospel tradition as His obedience to the will of His Father. Even the mocking of those who passed by the cross, "He trusts in God," is a witness to Jesus' manifest sense of obedience. The obedience of Jesus has made faith possible for man; this is true whether one wishes to speak of faith in Jesus before His passion or faith in the risen Lord following the resurrection. The resurrection has made public and universal what was proleptic and anticipatory in the public ministry, and has revealed once for all the depth of the eschatological perspectives inherent in the ministry of Jesus. It is futile to argue that the faith of those healed by Jesus in His public ministry is different than the faith of the post-resurrection community, and worse than futile to confuse the question with remarks about saving faith and ultimate salvation. The *Heilsgeschichte* of the New Testament preserves the historical and real value of faith wherever and whenever it occurs with respect to Jesus, and relates all faith to the eschatological future salvation.

Another figure which illumines the demand of faith, according to the Gospel tradition, is the call of Jesus to men to follow Him. Following Jesus means first of all following Him to His passion, but beyond that, since the entire work of Jesus is taken up into the cosmic eschatology opened up by His resurrection, following Jesus means to follow Him until the parousia of the Son of man. This is particularly clear in the enigmatic saying preserved in the tradition of the Fourth Gospel about the Son of man and walking in the light (John 12:34-36). The meaning seems to be that if men will walk with the Son of man in the little light they now have concerning Him, by virtue of what the Son of man will do for them in His being lifted up they may become sons of light and no more walk in darkness.[4] The Synoptic use of the term "follow" denotes something new and unique, without parallel in Greek and Jewish writings (E. Schweizer, "Der Glaube an Jesus den 'Herrn' in seiner Entwicklung von den ersten Nachfolgern bis zur hellenistischen Gemeinde," *Ev. Th.* [1957], pp. 7-21). Israel,

---

4 Since we have referred here to the Fourth Gospel, it might seem that an argument on Jesus' claim to faith could be settled immediately by quoting such texts as John 14:1; 6:40, 47. But in all fairness, this would call for a discussion of the Johannine tradition which would take us beyond the purposes of this essay. In any case, the Johannine tradition does not contradict the Synoptic tradition on the matter of faith but rather reinforces it.

to be sure, knew of the danger of going after false gods, and the picture of devotees walking behind images and idols seems to have prevented Israel from applying the same term to Yahweh. The thought of following God appears also difficult to reconcile with His transcendence, especially if transcendence is emphasized as it was in pre-Christian Judaism. It is no accident that the New Testament never speaks of following God but does speak concretely about following Christ. To follow Jesus means to participate in the salvation offered in Him and it also implies a participation in the fate of Jesus in the world (Kittel, ἀκολουθέω, *TWNT,* Vol. I, p. 214). Although the word "to follow" is not used outside the four Gospels and is not used with respect to the exalted Lord, it is certainly implied in the description of the community as "those of the Way." It is the action, not the concept, which is important. To follow Jesus does not mean to imitate Him in the sense taken by the later Church, rather it means to share the fellowship of the servant of God in His sufferings in this world. The sayings of Jesus about the similar fate which will befall His disciples in the world describe the action of the word "follow." In this fellowship the community is, like Jesus, to assume the role of the servant; to have this mind, which was given in Christ (Phil. 2:5ff.). Here too the demand which faith makes upon the total life and for the future is obvious.

Healings of the lame in the Gospel records contain a summons by Jesus to the lame person to rise up and walk. Usually the term does not bear any technical or symbolic meaning, although the events are signs of the inbreaking time of salvation (Mark 2:9; John 5:8-12; Isa. 35:6; cf. Luke 7:22 and Acts 3:6f.). The healing of the man by the pool of Bethesda is an act of prophetic symbolism in which the action of the man in walking is a rebuke to Israel's refusal to heed the word of Jesus and follow Him to the messianic age. The thirty-eight years symbolize the wandering in the wilderness, and the question, "Do you want to be healed?" is the question Jesus puts to Israel of His day reminding them of the unwillingness of their fathers to enter the promised land. Paul uses the term "walk" in a technical sense to denote the moral and religious actions which should characterize the newness of life in Jesus Christ. "As you have received Christ Jesus the Lord, so walk in him" (Col. 2:6; see also Gal. 5:16; I Thess. 2:12; Col. 1:10; Eph. 4:1; 5:8; Rom. 14:15; II Cor. 4:2; Phil. 3:17. All these references contain the verb περιπατέω.). While Paul does not bring out any sense of direction in the figure of walking, the term takes on meaning only within the new eschatological situation created through Jesus. This is particularly clear from the association of walking with the Spirit. In Johannine theology, the figure of walking is more obviously directional since it is associated with the action of following and with the revelation of Jesus Himself as the Way to the Father. In John 8:12 following and walking are conjoined, and the life which gives light is the life offered to man in Jesus. This life attains its fulness in the resurrection on the last day (John 5:28). The revelation of Jesus as the Way is given in a discourse concerning His going and coming, with the final goal being the attainment by the disciples of the place where Jesus is (John 14:1ff.). According to John, walking is an activity of faith; an expression of fellowship with Father and Son (I John 1:6f.). It is possible to walk in darkness or in light; the latter is the way Jesus walked (I John 1:7). Light is not a symbol of gnosis or of moral perception, but of eschatological realism. Believers are in the light because they know the goal and destiny of life; they understand where they are going. He who hates his brother is in darkness, and walks in darkness and does not know where he is going. This text illustrates the fact that the so-called moral duties have eschatological sanctions, for all men are going to the day of judgment. Already the light of the eschatological age has dawned and believers therefore keep the commandment of Jesus and walk as He walked because they know the destiny of life (I John 4:17). John's exhortations to love and to do the truth are comprehensible only to him who knows the eschatological situation, that it is the last hour (I John 2:18). Faith, which is the sole means of access to Jesus, brings historical understanding therefore, for in faith we grasp the eschatological situation brought about by Jesus' obedience to the will of His Father.

The revelation of Jesus as the Christ brought the world into eschatological time. The only possible response to this revelation event is faith. Faith is personal response and surrender to the total historical claim which Jesus the Christ makes upon us. By faith we enter into the history of Jesus, accepting the efficacy of His historic work in His ministry because the attestation of this work by the Spirit of God is itself an eschatological event by which we confess that we expect the future which God has offered to the world in Jesus the Christ. Since Jesus as the Christ cannot be understood except in the context of the *Heilsgeschichte* of Israel, faith in Jesus is participation in this *Heilsgeschichte,* and therefore "is" historical understanding.

We are not able to find a neutral vantage point from which we may judge the *Heilsgeschichte* through Israel. Rather, *Heilsgeschichte* is the vantage point from which we judge all history. Since Jesus Christ is the personal revelation of the meaning and goal of this *Heilsgeschichte,* faith in Him involves an historical consciousness and, we may claim, historical understanding. This understanding is frankly a matter of faith. Men are not compelled to accept it. Yet those who profess faith in Jesus Christ cannot escape the implications of this faith for historical understanding. The New Testament never restricts this understanding to individualistic historicity; it relates it everywhere to the history of the people of God who are called to work towards and to inherit a cosmic redemption. The history of Jesus the Christ therefore is not merely a recapitulation of the personal "history" of every individual. Indeed, the word history does not fit the individual at all. Since the history of Jesus cannot be confined to the temporal limits of one's personal existence, then faith can only mean the surrender of one's personal existence to the temporal limits of the personal history of Jesus the Son of God. The Western Christian (or any other Christian for that matter) cannot deny his historical roots in Israel renewed through Jesus the Christ. Since he cannot escape this history, he can only follow it to its future and lay hold of this future in faith because it is already given to Him in the resurrection of Jesus from the dead. It is clear furthermore that the word history cannot simply refer to the past, or even the study of the past, but must mean the *Gestalt* of temporal existence in its totality understood as a unity because it has a goal. Temporal existence is not a fate imposed upon man by a demiurge, but a destiny graciously offered to him by the God of Salvation who is the God of Creation. Time is the expression of the activity of God in the world; it is therefore not essentially evil, although evil has certainly endeavored to thwart and oppose the activity of God and thereby appears also as time-related. The answer the biblical revelation gives to the mystery of evil is not primarily a creational one, but an eschatological one; the Bible does not point us to the origin of evil but to its destiny. It too will be revealed in the future and will be unmasked and overcome by Jesus Christ. Because of this expectation, the historical understanding given by faith is not equivalent to an idea of progress, or evolutionary betterment. History is understood rather as an arena of personal conflict; and apart from the consummation of the work of Jesus Christ, there can be no victory or resolution of the conflict.

To sum up, the God who revealed Himself in Jesus is, according to the New Testament, not the God of philosophers but the living God of Abraham, Isaac, and Jacob. Faith therefore has to do with the future because God is the God of promise. Jesus is central to this future because by His resurrection He has become the *archēgos* of life, salvation, and faith. The process inaugurated by the ministry of Jesus is continued by Him until the goal of history arrives, for He is also the *teleiōtēs* of faith. The resurrection of Jesus is the crucial event for understanding Jesus and the nature of the faith to which He calls men. Apart from the resurrection, the kerygma of the Church has no content, faith has no object (I Cor. 15:14), Christian activity is futile, and honesty would lead us to embrace the Epicurean philosophy (I Cor. 15:32). The assurance that labor for Christ in this world is not futile rests upon the resurrection, which thus serves as an eschatological sanction for faith's work (I Cor. 15:58b). Furthermore the New Testament Church did not see the resurrection as a radical discontinuity in *Heilsgeschichte,* and so the risen Christ is for the Church no other than Jesus. The historical understanding mediated in faith in Jesus confesses Him as Lord in the present time, assumes the form of His obedience in fellowship with Him, and confidently looks toward the full revelation of the Son of man in His parousia. To believe in Jesus Christ is to apprehend the *Gestalt* of history. This understanding is not gnosis, but faith. It confesses what it cannot see; yet it does not believe that the future ends in darkness, because the one to whom the future belongs is the *archēgos* and *teleiōtēs* of faith.

FACT AND FAITH
IN THE KERYGMA

Paul Althaus

Paul Althaus served from 1925 until his recent retirement as Professor of Systematic and New Testament Theology at the University of Erlangen, Germany. A critic of the dialectical theology of Karl Barth and of the existential theology of Rudolf Bultmann, he is author of numerous works. The book translated under the title Fact and Faith in the Kerygma *of Today contains lectures critical of Bultmann's theology. Professor Althaus studied in the Universities of Göttingen and Tübingen, and in the theological seminary at Erichsburg, Hannover.*

13. Paul Althaus

FACT AND FAITH
IN THE KERYGMA[1]

P RESENT-DAY kerygma theology considers itself to be a resumption
and justification of theses which were first propounded in 1892 by Martin
Kähler in his famous book, *Der sogenannte historische Jesus und der
geschichtliche biblische Christus* (Leipzig, 1892; henceforth cited as
Historische Jesus). It is no accident that this book was recently (1956)
republished [München: Chr. Kaiser Verlag]. In it Martin Kähler protests
against the contemporary "Lives of Jesus," and particularly against the
kind of historical relativism which claimed by the use of scientific historical method to resuscitate the so-called "historical Jesus," and to offer this
to the Christian Church as the ground and object of its faith. This procedure, Kähler asserts, is an error both from the standpoint of faith and
from that of historical scholarship. "My intention is not merely to defend faith's independence of theology, but also, very definitely, to establish the right scholarly method" (*ibid.,* p. 96). In relation to faith,
the claim of the historian that he alone can provide faith with its object
and ground, is an assault upon faith's independence of theology. Faith
in this manner becomes dependent on the scholars, and grows perplexed
in view of the difference of their results. The ground and object of faith,
Jesus Christ, must be immediately accessible to every Christian. "Faith
must not be dependent on the uncertain conclusions about a reputedly
reliable picture of Jesus which is tortured out of the sources by the meth-

---

1 This material is excerpted from Professor Althaus's *Fact and Faith in the Kerygma
of Today,* tr. by David Cairns (Philadelphia: Muhlenberg Press, 1959), and is used by
permission of Fortress Press.

ods of recently-developed historical investigation. . . . For in relation to
the Christ in whom we have the duty and the privilege of believing, the
most learned theologian must be no better off and no worse off than the
simplest Christian" *(ibid.,* p. 73) . . . .Thus, "it is today the task of the
dogmatic theologian, as representative of the simple faith of Christians,
to set limits to the papal pretensions of the historians" *(ibid.,* p. 73).
This is the religious, the evangelical significance of Kähler's protest. He
was resisting the encroachments of historical scholarship upon the rights
of simple Christian men. . . .

At the same time Kähler shows that in point of scholarship the "Lives
of Jesus," and "the search for the historical Jesus," were following a
blind alley. For of the "Lives" it is true that "It is for the most part
these gentlemen's own views which they see reflected in Jesus" *(ibid.,*
p. 57). The descriptive biographer is a concealed dogmatic theologian.
But leaving out of account this characteristic of the artistic and imaginative attempts to produce a "Life" of Jesus, there is one fundamental observation which must be made. This Jesus, whose picture is to be reconstructed from the tradition by means of historical investigation, is
not really the historic [i.e., *geschichtlich*] Jesus at all. It is in his work
(Werk) that a person is historic *[geschichtlich].* But Jesus' achievement
is the faith of His disciples in Him, and the confession of this faith
(ibid., p. 63). But this faith was not elicited from the disciples by the
historical Jesus "as He lived and walked," but only by Jesus the risen
and living Lord. "Without this we would know nothing at all of Him."
According to the documentary sources the certainty of the disciples and
apostles that "Christ is Lord" is inseparable from the other certainty that
"He is the living crucified and risen Saviour" *(ibid.,* p. 64). But this risen
Saviour is not "the historical Jesus *behind* the Gospels, rather is He the
Christ of the apostolic preaching, the Christ *of the whole New Testament.*
The real Christ is the preached Christ, and the preached Christ is the
Christ of faith" *(ibid.,* p. 66). Only the whole biblical Christ is the real,
historic *[geschichtlich]* Christ. The biblical Christ is the only historically
credible and accessible Christ *(ibid.,* p. 96).

The search for the "historical Jesus" also contradicts the character of
the Gospels, and vice versa; the latter supports the thesis that the real
Christ is the Christ who is preached, the risen, living Christ. The Gospels
are not in the least like historical sources, as the historian understands
the term; the Evangelists are "preachers" — John (20:31) acknowledges
openly that this is true of himself, and "the other evangelists are in truth,
preachers no less than he" *(ibid.,* pp. 80ff.) . . . . "The portrayal given by
the gospels does not merely find its climax in the Easter story; from the
beginning its perspective is the perspective of Easter" *(ibid.,* p. 108) . . . .

I. BEHIND THE APOSTOLIC MESSAGE

Now in [the] thesis that we must make our theological beginning
with the kerygma, as the ultimate datum accessible to faith in Christ,
and that we must not go behind it, there is doubtless one real insight
that we must never again lose. And that is the knowledge that there is
not, and that there never has been, any other gospel than the authentic
gospel *about* Jesus Christ. To attempt to get behind "Christ" to "Jesus,"
as theological liberalism did, is utterly out of the question. Today there
is almost complete agreement on this point among all schools of theology.
Research carried out principally by liberal theologians — research of a
historical character uninfluenced by dogmatic considerations — has itself
led to the conclusion that the gospel did not come into being until Easter.

And yet, certain though it may be that dogmatic theology is forbidden
to try to get behind the kerygma and the Christ proclaimed by it, the
question still arises whether in another sense theology must not go behind the kerygma; that is, whether it must not inquire what is *the relation of the kerygma to the history* about which it informs us and to
which it bears witness. We cannot naively stop our ears to the question
whether we are not, in the apostolic kerygma, dealing with a *myth,* the
picture of a Saviour which, as so often happens in religion, is a wish-
fulfilment arising from the longings of the human heart. Critical
inquiry has shown to how large an extent primitive Christology applied
to Jesus Saviour-names and concepts lying ready to hand both in Jewish
and Gentile tradition; this is evident not only in the Epistles but in the
Gospels. The language of Christology is to a great extent mythological.
Is the thing itself not also a myth? We cannot evade this question. This
means, however, that we cannot accept the apostolic kerygma in this
sense as an ultimate datum for theology. To use Günther Bornkamm's
language, "We must look for the history in the kerygma" (*Jesus von
Nazareth* [Stuttgart, 1956], p. 18). Only thus shall we do justice to the
fact that in the New Testament we have not only the thoroughly kerygmatic apostolic writings, but before them, and along with them, the
Gospels, which indeed owe something of their form to the kerygma, but
are relatively distinguished from the Epistles by their narrative character.
The Church did not only proclaim the gospel and listen to its proclamation, but also repeated and preserved the remembered tradition of
Jesus' words and His story, interpreted, of course, in the light of Easter.
This fact, that alongside the Epistles stand the Gospels, with their narratives of the story of Jesus which preceded the first Easter, distinguishes
the gospel sharply from a myth. In its own way it anchors the Easter
kerygma in history, certainly quite differently from the way in which
a modern historian would do so, but quite clearly enough. In so far as

they do so, the Gospels are historical sources, admittedly not solely, and not primarily, but secondarily.

While it was necessary for Martin Kähler in his day, in reaction against the writers of the "Lives" of Jesus, to emphasize the fact that the Gospels are not *primarily* sources, but testimonies of faith, today the emphasis must be placed elsewhere; the Gospels are *also* narratives and sources. Accordingly, the retrospective historical question as to the historical basis of the kerygma is unexceptionable and theologically legitimate. By the character of the Gospels, the New Testament itself invites us to such historical reflection. Ernst Käsemann says: "Nor can we deny the identity of the exalted Lord with the incarnate Lord without falling into docetism, and depriving ourselves of the possibility of distinguishing the Easter faith of the Church from a myth" (in *Zeitschrift für Theologie und Kirche*, LI [1954], p. 141). Elsewhere Käsemann says: "The whole New Testament claims that the disciples at Easter did not recognize any heavenly being, much less an abstract content of knowledge like dogmatic propositions, but Jesus Himself. The Christ who since the first Easter has been the object of faith and the theme of preaching, is continuous with the so-called historical Jesus, a continuity without which faith and preaching, in the opinion of the primitive Christian community, would be meaningless. To apprehend with certainty this continuity is an inescapable theological necessity. A theology which, from historical skepticism or on strange dogmatic grounds, attempted to surrender this continuity, would not be worthy of the name" ("Probleme der neutestamentlichen Arbeit in Deutschland," in *Die Freiheit des Evangeliums und die Ordnung der Gesellschaft,* Beiträge zur evangelischen Theologie, BD, XV, 1952, cited in Diem, *Dogmatik,* p. 78f., Eng. tr., pp. 85f.). Käsemann rejects the proposal of a particular theology "to veto on theological grounds the attempt to ask what happened before the Easter event. To make a virtue out of necessity is much too facile a solution to give us any satisfaction."

Kähler himself did not refuse to ask questions of a historical character. He does not evade the question whether the picture which the Gospels give of Jesus may not be wholly legendary, a pious fiction. He answers it thus: "All the biblical descriptions produce the irresistible impression of the completest reality. One might venture to predict how Jesus would have acted in this situation or in that — indeed, even what He would have said. Therefore we can have converse with this Jesus, and need for this purpose nothing more than the biblical representation" (Kähler, *op. cit.,* p. 78). "The picture of Him, so full of life, so singularly beyond the power of invention, is not the idealising creation of a human mind; here His own being has left its imperishable impression" (*ibid.,* p. 79). "He Himself is the author of this picture. . . . Out of these fragmentary traditions, these uncomprehended memories, these descriptions coloured by the peculiarities of the writer, these confessions of the heart, and these sermons about His power to save, there looks at us the lifelike, coherent, and repeatedly recognizable picture of a Man. Thus one must come to the conclusion that here the man in His incomparable and mighty personality, with His unparalleled actions and experiences, culminating in the appearances after His Resurrection, has etched His picture into the mind and memory of His followers so sharply and so deeply, that it could neither be erased nor distorted" (*ibid.,* pp. 87, 89). . . . "Although Jesus . . . appears quite incomparable, His whole figure is perfectly clear and real, these traits themselves are not portrayed merely in negative and superlative terms; and thus we may be sure that this picture is not the product of poetic invention. His contemporaries, by their own express and involuntary confession, did not understand Him and His life. If, in spite of this, the sources agree on all sides to give us a consistent picture of Him, we may conclude that its features and character are not the creation of the inadequate comprehension of His contemporaries. We get the overwhelming impression of His person as a self-coherent, authentic, and quite singular whole," of a "clearly defined personality" (*Wissenschaft der christlichen Lehre,* 3rd edition [Leipzig, 1905], p. 323). All these statements contain unquestionably historical judgments, though perhaps of a prescientific kind. We are not dealing here purely with judgments óf faith. Kähler's opinion is rather that everyone who has a sense of reality will agree with his judgments. He declares himself that "to receive the impression of fullest reality" a man must have a mind that "has enough modesty and patience, to live, as it were, with the person, and enter sympathetically into its particular life" (*op. cit.,* p. 78, n. 1). In order to do this faith is not essential; such a sense is independent of faith, and can precede it — though certainly historical judgments of this kind become even more clear and certain through the believer's intimacy with the picture of Jesus. Thus Martin Kähler himself asks the retrospective question, and makes historical judgments, and directs us to seek for historical assurance.

But it is just this search which is forbidden today by those who in other respects appeal to Kähler's fundamental thesis, and seek to renew it in the contemporary situation. I refer to the kerygma-theology of R. Bultmann, with which F. Gogarten has declared himself in fundamental agreement. Here Kähler's proposition that we cannot theologically and dogmatically go behind the kerygma is affirmed. But in contrast with Kähler, the retrospective question as to the historical ground of the kerygma is also vetoed. Here we have to do with an outlook indifferent to, or rather hostile to, history.

Bultmann forbids faith and theology to ask what is the reality of

Easter, the Easter event which stands behind the Easter kerygma. "Christ, the crucified and risen, meets us in the word of preaching and nowhere else. It would be an error if we were here to ask what was the historical origin of the message, as if this origin could justify its legitimacy. That would mean that we were wishing to establish faith in God's word, and when we confront it we cannot ask any questions as to its legitimacy. Rather does it ask us whether we are willing to believe or not" (Bultmann, *Offenbarung und Heilsgeschehen*, pp. 66f.). "The Christian Easter faith is not interested in the historical question. To ask retrospectively whether the claim of the apostolic preaching is historically justified, is tantamount to rejecting it. This question must be exchanged for the question which the questioner has to put to himself. Will he acknowledge the lordship of Christ?, a lordship which puts to him the decisive question, 'How will he understand his own being?' " The event of salvation is "nowhere present except in the word of preaching which addresses us. A report of memory, i.e. a report referring to a past happening, cannot make the salvation event visible" (Bultmann, *Theologie des Neuen Testaments* [Tübingen, 1948], p. 300). The last sentence is certainly true. But what of the previous ones?

The quotations from *Offenbarung und Heilsgeschehen* reproduce Bultmann's own theological convictions. The sentences from *Theologie des Neuen Testaments* occur within the exposition of the Pauline theology. Thus it is implied that this is what the apostle thinks. But in truth it is not Paul who is speaking here, but Bultmann. When he is dealing with the subject of the Easter kerygma, Paul has no thought of vetoing the question of historical legitimation. He expressly appeals to a tradition *(paradosis)* which he has received, of course from the primitive Church (I Cor. 15:3), and emphatically and earnestly appeals to witnesses to whom appearances of the Lord were granted — *witnesses* of the fact of which preaching speaks. In his exposition of I Corinthians 15 Karl Barth tried to explain away this clear significance of the passage (Barth, *Die Auferstehung der Toten* [Munich, 1926], pp. 75ff.). Bultmann rightly refuses to let this pass, but now Paul is criticized for his "fatal argument" in I Corinthians 15:3ff. (Bultmann, *Offenbarung und Heilsgeschehen*, p. 64). "The argument in this passage is fatal, because it seeks to give a proof of the credibility of the Kerygma" (Bultmann, *Kerygma und Mythos* [Hamburg, 1948], Vol. I, p. 144). In fact, Paul's line of argument is in flat contradiction with Bultmann's thesis. Nor does Paul in other passages renounce legitimation. In the introduction to his Epistles he presents himself to the churches — and so he will have done also in his missionary preaching which led to the foundation of the churches — as a man called and sent by Jesus Christ, as a messenger with authority who was called in a concrete historical event. Thus he decisively refers behind the kerygma to the historical data, that he is a witness to the appearing of the risen Lord, and an ambassador commissioned by Him.

II. THE HISTORICAL CONTENT OF THE APOSTOLIC MESSAGE

If this holds good in Paul's case biblically and theologically, the question of historical fact is essential in all Christian preaching, and refuses to be silenced. Bultmann formulates his position thus: "The word of preaching meets us as God's word, in relation to which we can raise no questions of legitimation. Rather does it ask us whether we are willing to believe or not." That sounds very illuminating; of course one cannot raise questions of legitimation when confronted by what bears witness to itself as the word of God, one can only believe or disbelieve. But the formula "word of God" is here too simple, and conceals the real problem. The problem is this: preaching has a double content in inseparable unity; it is a report of things that have happened, happened in our human history at a determinate place and time. And secondly it is, in the indicative and imperative, a witness of the significance of this event for salvation and judgment. The kerygma of the apostles and of the Church has always also historical content, it is always in addition witness to historical facts. It is different in the case of the word of God proclaimed by the prophets. Here the moment of witness to historical event is missing. The question of legitimation is a different one in the case of the apostles from that in the case of the prophets, precisely because of the relation to past history. . . .

The question is: In the case of the apostolic and Church kerygma, which is witness to an historical revelation, is it not a part of the authority of the preaching as word of God, that it can claim to have its source in genuine history? To repeat our thesis once more, the formula used by Bultmann — "word of God" — conceals the problem which is set for us by the double character of the apostolic witness both as a report of determinate facts and as preaching which appeals for a decision. The case is different with the word of the prophets of the Old Testament. There Bultmann's principle does apply. But it cannot be simply applied to the preaching of the apostles and the Church, because we have here to deal with the witness to things that happened in history. Here preaching, in view of its historic content enclosed in the kerygma, requires "legitimation," and here the question of that legitimation must be raised. Bultmann's principle holds for what we may call in the narrower sense the kerygmatic content of preaching, for the confession of the saving significance of what has happened, a confession which appeals for decision, and calls on men to acknowledge that significance.

If preaching says to me: "The death and resurrection of Christ concern you in your existence, He died for your sin, and was raised for your justification: acknowledge that fact, and let yourself be reconciled in Christ to God," then in fact in this case I can only say "Yes" or "No." Here I must believe; to question here the right of such preaching, i.e., its right to relate what has happened to my existence, is already a decision of unbelief.

Here there is no legitimation except that which is constituted by the message itself. Here my conscience is touched, and I sin if I begin to ask for legitimation instead of knowing that I am touched and questioned. But it is different when we consider the historical content of the message. If I say "Yes" or "No" to the question whether the events of Good Friday and Easter touch *me,* then in every case I presuppose, consciously or unconsciously, that the event of which the message speaks is a real, consequently also an historical, event. Thus I presuppose that the messengers of Jesus Christ, who call me to decision, have trustworthy knowledge about this Jesus and can impart it to me; that "Jesus Christ" is consequently not the name of a mythical figure, that the accounts in the gospel which purport to tell of Him are not the deceptive projection of a myth into history; that He really was crucified because of His preaching and His claim to authority, and that the report of His showing Himself as risen from the dead is credibly attested. This side of the matter — that is, the question of the historicity of the historical content of the message — short circuits Bultmann's talk about the illegitimacy of the question of legitimation. Here legitimation *is* necessary. It does not need to be said that this legitimation of a historical kind cannot prove the character of the preaching *as word of God,* nor does it claim to do so. . . . The revelatory character of the history of Jesus is not known by means of historical reflection or historical reasoning. But on the other hand, it is not known *without these.* For the gospel deals with facts which, it is claimed, happened in this history of ours; it has "historical facts" as content, and its foundation in history is a part of its credibility. . . .

The veto on questions about the historical basis of the kerygma is particularly hard to understand when it comes from a man like Rudolf Bultmann, who is a historian, and has written a book about Jesus. We must ask whether there is not a wide gulf between Bultmann the historian of the book on Jesus, and the systematic theology of the kerygma theology. What, in his opinion, is the relation between the work of historical criticism which he has achieved in the *Geschichte der Synoptischen Tradition* and in his *Jesus,* and kerygma theology? Has the former only a negative significance for the latter, or is there a positive significance also? Hermann Diem concludes that historical study has no positive significance for faith in the thought of Bultmann. Bultmann "tries persistently to get behind the kerygma of the texts [in the gospels] by critical methods, in order to establish what in fact happened, and he does so with the same resources (although sharpened by the methods of form-criticism) as the whole of historical-critical research before him. But he does not do so — and here is the decisive difference — in order to base faith on the historical conclusions attained, but, on the contrary, in order to make impossible any such basis for faith, and thus he has greater scope for the most radical results than any of his predecessors. Always, for him, faith must be made insecure and all historical founda-tions withdrawn from it. That historical criticism (at any rate in regard to the history of Jesus) might have another, positive, significance is not apparent" (*Dogmatik,* p. 83, Eng. tr., p. 90). . . .

[Bultmann] does indeed declare: "I do not deny the close relationship of the Easter *kerygma* to the earthly and crucified Jesus" (*Kerygma und Mythos,* I, 149). But this remains for him an absolutely general and ab-stract statement, which receives no concrete expression whatsoever in the kerygma theology. There is no concrete continuity in Bultmann's theolo-gy between the historical Jesus who was the subject of his historical work, and the apostolic preaching. Various writers have made this criticism of Bultmann. Eduard Ellwein declares that in Bultmann "the bridge between the historical Jesus and the preached Christ has, so to speak, col-lapsed" (in *Zur Entmythologisierung,* p. 23). Does the *Person* of Jesus with its concrete characteristics play any part in the kerygma theology? Günther Bornkamm declares: "Jesus has become a mere fact of salvation and is no longer a person" ("Mythos und Evangelium," in *Theologische Existenz heute,* n.s. XXVI [1951], p. 18). The fact that the person of Jesus as such (of whose concrete characteristics we can, in Bultmann's words, "now know practically nothing" [*Jesus* (Berlin, 1926), p. 12]) has no place in the kerygma, leads to serious theological consequences. The power of the gospel to overcome our unbelief depends on the fact that the kerygma includes the Gospels with their concrete picture of Jesus. In the picture of the man Jesus we lay hold of the character of God, in the spiritual countenance of Jesus we behold the countenance of God. The living eyes of a man look at us out of the Gospels, and compel our faith. The kerygma is a statement, a dogma, if we do not see it filled out by the living picture of Jesus as the Gospels portray Him. Without this, how can the kerygma compel us to believe? If, as Bultmann says, it places before us the question of decision, then, sundered from the picture of Jesus, it meets us as *law.* I am confronted with a decision, I am questioned, I must answer; but of the power that can compel me to believe, there is not a word. And how can the kerygma, emptied of the historical personality of Jesus, have this power? Thus the gospel meets me only as law, as a demand for belief. But the New Testament tells us that the Word became flesh, a human personal life, in whose features we should seek the features of the Father (John 14:9). In the kerygma theology the word has become — kerygma! Kerygma Christology has no need of the actual features of the earthly Jesus. . . .

In defence of its veto on the question of the historical legitimation of the gospel, kerygma theology appeals also to Luther, and claims, in contrast with its "ecclesiastical" critics, to take seriously Luther's view of the Word of God and faith. . . . But we must not overlook — as so often happens when appeal is made to Luther's doctrine of the Word of God — that Luther, in his doctrine of Holy Scripture as the Word of God, always presupposed, usually tacitly, the credibility of the book as a whole as the product of the Holy Spirit. . . . It is not enough to say that because the Word is the word of God, it has its authority in itself. This by no means fully expresses the specific authority of the apostolic preaching. In addition to the distinguishing mark of its particular content — to use Luther's expression, "it deals with Christ" — it has this other characteristic, that in it we have to deal with the "first witnesses," with a witness given in historical proximity and immediate relationship to the history of Jesus. The general concept of the word of God does not underline this special content. So it is not enough to say, in relation to the apostolic kerygma: "The word, just because it is the word of God, has its authority in itself." For this statement does not do justice to the historical element in the authority. Nor may this historical element be overlooked even in the contemporary preaching of the Church; its authority depends on the fact that the present word of preaching is interpretation of the apostolic witness, whose authority depends on its "authenticity" — that is, on the historical reference, that it goes back to the witnesses of the history of Jesus, including the resurrection. . . .

It is strange and inconceivable that the kerygma theology wholly, as it seems, misses this side of the matter. Has then the whole historical enterprise of introductions to the New Testament and history of the canon no theological, no dogmatic significance? Is theology meddling in other people's concerns, or is it doing necessary work when it undertakes to investigate and to prove the authenticity of the New Testament writings, and their origin in the times of primitive Christianity, from the hands of the apostles or the pupils of the apostles, that is, their origin in the genuine tradition? Is it a theological undertaking or not, to pose the question of historical originality or authenticity? There can be no doubt that Bultmann and Gogarten consider these endeavors of introductions to the New Testament necessary and indispensable. But if so, they must concede that the question as to the authority of the kerygma is disastrously simplified if it is thought that everything necessary has been said when the thesis "the word has its authority in itself" has been enunciated — unless the factor of genuine tradition is tacitly included in the phrase "in itself." A doctrine of "the word of God" in the New Testament sense is inadequate if the historical factor of tradition in the doctrine is suppressed. . . .

If theology, in the name of the Reformers' doctrine of the Word of God and of faith, were to neglect the historical question of the authenticity of the apostolic preaching, and thus no longer to ask for the credentials of the message, it would be rejecting the true humanity and the *kenosis* of Christ. For the latter means that God's Word has submitted itself wholly to the law of historical time, and comes to us in the very human form of tradition, of historical witness passed on from mouth to mouth, and thus, as tradition, must submit to the question of legitimacy, in the sense of authenticity. . . .

III. FAITH AND ITS FOUNDATIONS

For Luther, the principle *sola fide* is inconceivable without previously assumed certainty about Holy Scripture, its reliability, and consequently the historical reality of the history to which it bears witness. This certainty, it is true, is not expressly stated when Luther speaks about faith; it was a wholly self-evident presupposition for Luther, as it was for all his contemporaries. But it is always taken for granted. So Luther cannot be appealed to, when the principle *sola fide* is severed from that presupposition, and when the principle in isolation is turned against the presupposition and it is suggested that *sola fide* demands the removal of historical certainty — as if such a skepticism were the necessary implication of the assurance of faith and the *sola fide* principle. But in its dogmatic content also this thesis is beside the mark. When it speaks of "the security of faith," that is in truth only a euphemism for the destruction and surrender of the grounds of faith. For its ground is not a "kerygma" which has no reference to history, but the kerygma in its retrospective relation to history that actually happened, and thus in part its ground is this history itself.

We, too, say that faith in Jesus Christ must bear the weight of irremovable uncertainty about many things in the history of Jesus. But it can only do so because the figure and history of Jesus is not, in decisive matter, problematical, but historical. . . . The faith whose security has been removed in the manner that kerygma theology sets out to do, would be faith without foundations. But is a faith which in this sense is without foundations still faith? . . . Is not the certainty that the event of Golgotha, the death of Jesus on the cross, was historical reality, an essential part of the faith which alone can perceive the salvation event?

Does this historicity belong to the things that "concern" faith, and can faith, in obtaining this certainty, dispense with the way of historical verification? In a word: faith confesses that Jesus the Christ (i.e., the mediator between God and man) died as such on the cross. It is decisive that He dies as the Christ, for all of us; and faith alone knows this. But it is not less essential for faith that this so-called Christ-event is not a myth, but that the real man Jesus died. That is an historical question. Faith cannot declare it a matter of indifference. It cannot undertake to answer it from its own resources. Here it is driven to ask the retrospective historical question. And for this question the Gospels, without any detriment to their character as witnesses of faith, must also be considered as historical sources.

The revelation, the presence of God in Jesus Christ, is known only in faith. It cannot be cogently deduced from the historical facts as such. But faith, though unquestionably the miracle of the Holy Spirit, arises nonetheless in relation to witnessed history. . . . Our "Yes" to the message about Jesus Christ includes a rational judgment, that is, an impression of such reality in the figure and essential characteristics of the story of Jesus as is beyond the power of invention. And this is a judgment which is possible even for the unbeliever, and which, as experience shows us, he is constantly making, consciously or unconsciously.

The believer himself, so long as he does not reflect theologically, does not distinguish this moment of "rational" certainty included in his affirmation of the message, from the certainty which his faith possesses as to the presence of God and His salvation in Jesus Christ. But theological reflection singles this out as a distinct factor, and brings it to consciousness. It asks also the critical question as to the ground and justification of the judgment of "reason," just as it does in the case of faith's certainty about the presence of God. In any case the former is independent of the latter. The former we share with every man who, with whatever intentions, concerns himself with the Person and story of Jesus in the narratives which tell of it: the latter is the concern of the Church alone, and distinguishes it from all other communities.

BULTMANN'S
HISTORIOGRAPHY

Gordon H. Clark

Gordon H. Clark is Professor of Philosophy in Butler University, Indianapolis, Indiana. He is author of many works, among them A Christian View of Men and Things, Thales to Dewey, Karl Barth's Theological Method, *and* Religion, Reason and Revelation. *He served as Instructor in Philosophy in the University of Pennsylvania, from which he holds the Ph.D. degree, and then as Professor of Philosophy in Wheaton College, Wheaton, Illinois.*

14.   Gordon H. Clark

BULTMANN'S HISTORIOGRAPHY

I N 1926 BULTMANN published his volume *Jesus;* the English translation of its second edition, under the title *Jesus and the Word,* appeared
in 1934. Nowhere has Bultmann given a better or more extended account
of his understanding of the nature of history than in the Introduction of
this early book. Therefore a criticism of Bultmann's historiography can
afford to confine its attention to this one volume.

I. THE SETTING OF BULTMANN'S THOUGHT

Properly to appreciate the intricacies of Bultmann's thought and to
disentangle what inconsistencies there are it is necessary to have in mind
the type of theology that prevailed before 1920 and its defects as Bultmann saw them. The liberalism of the nineteenth century, with the
Life-of-Jesus movement, the naively optimistic view of human nature,
the influence of Hegelian pantheism in the then current presentation of
the immanence of God — all this prevailing theology Bultmann attacked,
following the lead of Karl Barth.

It is also necessary to uncover those assumptions relative to New
Testament criticism that Bultmann has never thought of questioning.
These assumptions have restricted Bultmann's thought within a narrow
range of choice, whereas another scholar without these assumptions
could have proceeded in a very different direction. Note must also be
taken of the philosophical guidelines which Bultmann accepted from

Heidegger. This existential philosophy as well as the unquestioned axioms of criticism are most obvious in Bultmann's New Testament interpretation, but they definitely affect his view of history too.

II. BULTMANN AND HISTORICAL SCIENCE

One must remember that Bultmann is not interested in history as a
professional historian, nor is he a philosopher with a consuming desire
to write a philosophy of history. The problems of history entered his
thought more as a side issue blocking his path. He had to dispose of them
before he could proceed with New Testament criticism. Therefore, from
the standpoint of thoroughgoing historiography, his remarks appear
somewhat disjointed. To combine them into logical clarity is a considerable task. But if a student begins his reading of Bultmann with
historiography mainly in mind, this task is the immediate one. Therefore the surest procedure is to take the Introduction to *Jesus and the
Word* and go through it phrase by phrase.

The text reads,

> The essence of history cannot be grasped by "viewing" it, as we view our
> natural environment. . . . Our relationship to history is wholly different
> from our relationship to nature. . . . When [a man] observes nature, he
> perceives there something objective which is not himself. When he turns
> his attention to history, however, he must admit himself to be a part of
> history. . . . He cannot observe this [living] complex [of events] objectively
> as he can observe natural phenomena. . . . Hence there cannot be im-
> personal observation of history in the same sense that there can be im-
> personal observation of nature (p. 3).

This opening paragraph is intended to make a sharp distinction between history and nature, and between the methods of investigation
proper to each. They are said to be "wholly different." Such a position
is extreme. On any reasonable definition (and Bultmann substitutes
none of his own) history and science are not *wholly* different. There
are similarities between them. Doubtless there are dissimilarities too;
but, what is worse than the overstatement "wholly different," is the
failure of Bultmann's attempt to describe what the differences are.

When a man observes nature, he perceives something not himself;
when he turns his attention to history, he also perceives something not
himself. He perceives emperors, wars, economic conditions, and even
parts of nature. These are not himself. If at the same time he must
admit himself to be a part of history, he also cannot avoid admitting
that he is a part of nature as well. In this Bultmann has not hit upon
any difference between science and history.

Further, Bultmann would have a hard time proving that "there cannot be impersonal observation of history in the same sense that there can be impersonal observation of nature." Regrettably Bultmann does not explain in what sense there can be impersonal observation of nature. Since World War I there has been a philosophy of science, operationalism, that insists on the personal involvement of the scientist in his problem — a problem too that is dictated by the demands of society. Even among scientists who are not operationalists there is widespread agreement that the formulations of science depend in part on the aesthetic preferences of the formulator. Pure, objective impersonal observation of nature is not well accepted today as a description or as a goal of science. It may turn out therefore that Bultmann makes his obscure contrast between science and history only because he has retained an outmoded nineteenth-century view of science, while at the same time adopting and modifying Martin Kähler's revised view of history.

If Bultmann is relying on non-scientific common opinion for his assertion of impersonal observation of nature, on this basis there is also an impersonal observation of history. Bultmann himself obliquely admits it, when in the sentence immediately following the previous quotation he hopes that his volume *Jesus and the Word* will be for the reader "more than information on interesting occurrences in the past, more than a walk through a museum of antiquities."

No doubt an impersonal observation of history, or, as J. H. Hexter put it, a love of the past for the sake of the past, is history on a low level; perhaps it is very superficial history; but unless history is arbitrarily defined as one's personal involvement in present controversies, the possibility of impersonal or disinterested observation remains.

So far, then, Bultmann has asserted a difference between history and science. There are many differences; but Bultmann has failed to mention any because of a defective view of science and an as yet unclear notion of history.

The better form of history, or, if Bultmann insists, the only form of *history,* is to see "Jesus [or presumably any historical figure] as a part of the history in which we have our being, or in which by critical conflict we achieve being, [in which case history books] must be in the nature of a continuous *dialogue with history"* (pp. 3f., italics in original).

This language is the echo of existential philosophy and needs to be demythologized. If this means merely that a student's character can be altered, if he can come to himself, if he can develop his personality — and so "achieve being" — by a critical examination of the past, well and good. Even those historians who are most insistent on objectivity would approve such a "dialogue" with history. But whether Bultmann would agree that this demythologizing had preserved the essential truth of his thought is another matter. It is indeed a doubtful matter because the explanation he offers is unclear.

"The dialogue," continues Bultmann, "does not come as a conclusion, as a kind of evaluation of history after one has learned the objective facts. On the contrary, the actual encounter with history takes place only in the dialogue." Presumably this means that history does not consist in learning that Napoleon reached Moscow only to find the city deserted; after which we conclude that it is poor strategy to invade Russia in the winter. The first half is not the actual encounter with history, and possibly the second half is not the dialogue.

Bultmann's "dialogue is no clever exercise of subjectivity on the observer's part," as it might be if someone decided that a mechanized invasion of Russia would not flounder into Napoleon's predicament. No, Bultmann's dialogue is "a real interrogating of history, in the course of which the historian puts this subjectivity of his in question, and is ready to listen to history as an authority" — an authority apparently that tells us mechanization makes no difference.

Now if we mean by the term encounter the personal adoption of certain principles to guide our own conduct, principles intuited in our study of Napoleon, it makes fair sense to say that "the actual encounter with history takes place only in [or by means of] the dialogue." But if the dialogue is not a kind of evaluation of Napoleon's defeat, it is hard to say what encounter means. It is hard to grasp the meaning of "a real interrogating of history," or to know what to do in order "to listen to history as an authority." Does the continuing quotation clarify this puzzle?

"Further, such an interrogation of history does not end in complete relativism. . . . Precisely the contrary is true: whatever is relative to the observer — namely all the presuppositions which he brings with him out of his own epoch and training and his individual position within them — must be given up, that history may actually speak."

Now it is superficially intelligible to imagine an hypostatized history demanding that we lay aside all presuppositions before it continues its lecture. But whatever would follow would be a lecture and not a dialogue. A dialogue, an interrogation, means that the historian asks questions; but without presuppositions and a personal position no questions can be asked. This is so obvious that Bultmann admits it in the next sentence: "History, however, does not speak when a man . . . assumes neutrality, but speaks only when he comes seeking answers to the questions which agitate him." How true! But, of course, in this sentence Bultmann contradicts what he has just finished saying.

The difficulties grow greater, not less, as we proceed. Having prohibited the personal presuppositions of individual historians, he goes further and prohibits schools of historiography from having common presuppositions. Bultmann admits that the methods of historiography permit an objective determination of chronological sequence; but he claims that this misses the true significance of history precisely because of the presuppositions. "Thus quantitatively it collects many new facts *out of* history, but learns nothing genuinely new *about* history and man. It sees in history only as little or as much of man and humanity as it already explicitly or implicitly knows; the correctness or incorrectness of vision is always dependent on this previous knowledge" (p. 5).

By implication therefore Bultmann will provide us a method of understanding history such that our vision will be independent of our previous knowledge. We shall be limited neither by personal ideas nor by the methods of any school, but shall encounter history directly.

"An example may make this clear." It is to be sure, an example of constrictive presuppositions improperly applied. But whether it demonstrates our ability to write history independently of our previous training and present ideas remains to be seen.

> A historian sets himself the aim of making a historical phenomenon or personality *"psychologically comprehensible."* Now this expression implies that such a writer has at his disposal complete knowledge of the psychological possibilities of life. . . . Making anything "comprehensible" means the reduction of it to what our previous knowledge includes. . . . On this assumption the criticism of the tradition is based, so that everything which cannot be understood on that basis is eliminated as unhistorical (pp. 5f.).

Very likely Bultmann has in mind some nineteenth-century attempts to explain the personality of Jesus. Strauss and the others assumed that the mind of Jesus had to be essentially like our own. Since therefore He could not have had messianic delusions of grandeur, He must have been nothing more than a good teacher of ethics; for only that can be historical which falls within the limits of the historian's present experience.

Possibly Bultmann was here influenced by Martin Kähler. In opposition to the Life-of-Jesus movement (Strauss, Baur, Renan), Kähler pointed out that despite their claims to presuppositionless objectivity the authors filled in the gaps disclosed by historical criticism with the unsupported fancies of their individual psychology. For this and other reasons Kähler concluded that a biography of Jesus is impossible.

Now, Kähler scored a decisive blow against the Life-of-Jesus movement by uncovering the inconsistency between the ideal of objectivity and the practice of reducing Jesus to the personal limitations of His critics. But Bultmann's historiography is not too clear. What follows if it is true that psychological analysis presupposes a "complete knowledge of the psychological possibilities of life?" Would it not follow that historical analysis also presupposes a complete knowledge of historical possibilities? In short, it would be impossible to know anything without knowing everything.

Such a Platonic or Hegelian requirement of omniscience is a serious philosophical problem. It is not to be dismissed thoughtlessly. The meticulous scholar, J. H. Hexter, in his *Reappraisals of History,* castigates historical relativism as a fad and insists on the "rudimentary distinction" between knowing something and knowing everything, but he omits all philosophic justification for this distinction.

Obviously this distinction must be maintained, if a human being is to be able to know anything at all. Make omniscience the prerequisite of partial knowledge, and partial knowledge vanishes. But Bultmann, like Hexter, offers no help: less help in fact, for Bultmann lets the requirements of omniscience stand. Indeed, he says explicitly, "So far as purely psychological facts of the past are the objects of investigation, such a method is (for the psychological expert) quite correct" (p. 6).

Bultmann is not concerned to deny the presupposition of omniscience. The point he makes is the quite different one that psychology does not explain history. "Whoever is of the belief that only through history can he find enlightenment on the contingencies of his own existence, will necessarily reject the psychological approach, however justified that method is in its own sphere" (p. 6). The plain suggestion is that only history can shed light on life's contingencies. Psychology cannot.

If Bultmann had said that the psychological facts of the past are impossible to recover, and that only overt actions can be recovered, his suggestion would be plausible. But to admit that the psychological expert can correctly investigate the past and to deny that his results can give enlightenment is a position most difficult to credit. Yet he insists that "in such a belief this book is written."

On this basis Bultmann prides himself on refraining from pronouncing value judgments.

> A judgment of value depends on the point of view which the writer imports into the history . . . [value judgments] are given from a standpoint beyond history. As against this I have especially aimed to avoid everything beyond history and to find a position for myself *within* history. Therefore evaluations which depend on the distinction between the historical and the superhistorical find no place here. . . . Accordingly this book lacks all the phraseology which speaks of Jesus as great man, genius, or hero; he appears neither as inspired nor as inspiring, his sayings are not called profound, nor his faith mighty, nor his nature child-like. There is also no consideration of the eternal values of his message . . . (pp. 7-8).

Why, then, should we study Jesus? Or, why should any history be studied? If we cannot evaluate one event as important and another as unimportant, if we cannot distinguish a profound statement from nonsense, or a great man from a moron, on what basis does an historian choose his subject? All this is the theory of objective, presuppositionless history, which Strauss and Baur professed but which no one ever practiced.

Bultmann gives something of a verbal answer to such questions. After rejecting the items mentioned, he immediately says, "Attention is entirely limited to what he *purposed* and hence to what in his purpose as a part of history makes a present demand on us." This verbalism, however, does not remove the objection. It does not explain why one should pay attention to Jesus' purpose rather than to Pilate's or to Zebedee's; nor is a value judgment avoided when it is asserted that Jesus' purpose makes a present demand on us. If anyone should reply that we study Jesus' purpose rather than Zebedee's because we have more information about Jesus, Bultmann cuts the ground away by insisting, "I do indeed think that we can now know almost nothing concerning the life and personality of Jesus."

In particular it is impossible to know whether Jesus believed Himself to be the Messiah or not. Without such knowledge, however, is it at all possible to determine what Jesus' purpose was? This point concerning the messianic consciousness is of singular importance, and Bultmann recognizes that "it was really no trifle to believe oneself Messiah, [for] whosoever so believed must have regulated his whole life in accordance with this belief, [and] if this point is obscure we can, strictly speaking, know nothing of the personality of Jesus." Bultmann himself believes that Jesus did not claim to be Messiah; but then to our amazement he continues, "I have in this book not dealt with the question at all — not so much because nothing can be said about it with certainty as because I consider it of secondary importance."

How could it be secondary if one who "so believed must have regulated his whole life in accordance with this belief?" Concretely such a one would have regulated his words and teaching in accordance with this belief, so that the significance of what he said and the purpose of what he did could only be construed in messianic terms.

Bultmann is trapped all the deeper because he holds that Jesus no more than Luther and Napoleon was interested in His own personality. What these men had at heart was their *work,* "the cause to which they surrendered their lives. Moreover, their work does not mean the sum of the historical effects of their acts; for to this their view could not be directed. Rather, the 'work' from *their* standpoint is the end they really sought, and it is in connection with their purpose that they are the proper objects of historical investigation" (pp. 9-10). But if it is impossible to know whether or not Jesus believed Himself to be Messiah, how in the world could we know His standpoint and the end He really sought?

Bultmann tries to evade the force of this consideration by insisting that the purpose of an historical character can be reproduced only in the form of sayings, ideas, or teaching. Of course this is true. We could know whether Jesus believed Himself to be Messiah only if His words clearly indicated it. But we ought not to come to these words with the a priori resolution to read out of them all such claims. Nor ought we to come to them, as Bultmann does, convinced that they do not form a system of general truths, or propositions universally valid apart from the concrete life situation of the speaker. Rather, we must read the words of Jesus and then the words of Plato to see which claimed to be Messiah and which claimed to propound universal truths. Bultmann's a priori judgment that Jesus' words are not such a set of universal truths is all the more surprising in view of his opinion that Jesus did not claim to be Messiah. And the surprise increases when he gives his reason. The reason is not, of course, that a messianic consciousness has things to say beyond general truths, but that so to understand the non-messianic Jesus would be to miss "the essential of history" (pp. 10-11). Ideal systems are judged by standards beyond history, and to learn them from history, as we do when we read Plato's dialogues, is to reduce history to the role of a stimulus to Platonic reminiscence, i.e., a clarification of pre-existing knowledge. "Such a view would be essentially rationalistic; history as event in time would be excluded" (p. 11). So it would, no doubt; but how does this show that Jesus did not teach a Platonic view?

There is a further complication. Bultmann indeed believes that historical criticism can recover a sufficient number of Jesus' sayings. But his criticism is so intricate, his axioms so questionable, and his conclusions so tenuous that one is inclined to question his optimism.

The sources, in his opinion, give the message of the early Church, much of which originated with the Church, and much else modified by the Church. The Gospel of John is not a source at all, and the Synoptics are composed of several layers. The Hellenistic layer must be discarded; Palestinian material remains.

> Within this Palestinian material again different layers can be distinguished, in which whatever betrays the specific interests of the church . . . must be rejected as secondary, [because apparently the church could not possibly have given a correct report]. "By means of this critical analysis an oldest layer is determined, though it can be marked off with only relative exactness [relative to the inclinations of the individual critic]. Naturally we have no absolute assurance that the exact words of this oldest layer

were really spoken by Jesus. There is a possibility that the contents of this older layer are also the result of a complicated historical process which we can no longer trace (p. 13).

With all this skepticism as to what Jesus taught, a skepticism based on an a priori judgment of what Jesus could not have said and what the reporting Church could not state correctly, how can Bultmann determine that Jesus did not teach a system of eternal ideas as Plato did?

But none of this troubles Bultmann. Anyone interested in the personality of Jesus might be troubled, but "for our purpose it has no particular significance. It is precisely this complex of ideas in the oldest layer of the synoptic tradition which is the object of our consideration" (p. 13-14).

Why? Because Bultmann is an impersonal historian and has arbitrarily chosen this layer as an academic exercise? Quite the contrary! "It meets us as a fragment of tradition coming to us from the past, and in the examination of it we seek the encounter with history" (p. 14).

But why should we not seek the encounter with history in the Hellenistic layer instead of in the Palestinian layer? The Hellenistic layer also meets us as a fragment of tradition coming to us from the past. Or, why should we not seek the encounter in Herodotus or Henry Thomas Buckle? The texts of any such authors can be encountered, existentialized, and allegorically interpreted. Any of them can be used for a continuous dialogue with history. Why select one epoch of history rather than any other?

III. REASONS FOR BULTMANN'S FAILURE

Bultmann, I believe, cannot give satisfactory answers to these questions for three reasons. First, his New Testament criticism is as arbitrary as that of Strauss, and his demythologizing is on a level with the allegorical method of the early patristics. Second, his notion of historiography is confused. He tries and fails to separate science from history; he requires and prohibits presuppositions; and he stirs together the objectivism of the nineteenth-century historians with the subjectivism of twentieth-century existentialism. And third, this existential philosophy with the encounter it recommends is unintelligible. I know what it means to learn political lessons from history and to evaluate on non-historical moral grounds the crimes or the virtues of great men, but I haven't the slightest idea of what Bultmann means by encounter or achieving being. Such empty phrases will never furnish a defensible view of historical investigation.

TOWARD A
CHRISTIAN PHILOSOPHY
OF HISTORY

John Warwick Montgomery

John Warwick Montgomery is Professor of Church History in Trinity Evangelical Divinity School, Bannockburn, Deerfield, Illinois. Earlier he served as Head Librarian of the University of Chicago Divinity School and as a member of the University's Federated Theological Faculty. He holds the Ph.D. from the University of Chicago and the Th.D. from the University of Strasbourg, France. His writings include A Seventeenth Century View of European Libraries, Chytraeus on Sacrifice: A Reformation Treatise in Biblical Theology, *and* The Shape of the Past.

15.   John Warwick Montgomery

TOWARD A
CHRISTIAN PHILOSOPHY
OF HISTORY

I N 1950 the English philosopher W. H. Walsh began his Introduction to his *Philosophy of History* with these words: "A writer on philosophy of history, in Great Britain at least, must begin by justifying the very existence of his subject" (*Philosophy of History: An Introduction*, rev. ed. [New York: Harper, 1960]). It is doubtful whether any such justification is required today. The last decade and a half has witnessed a tremendous revival of interest in philosophy of history, as is evidenced by the 1958 Cerisy-la-Salle colloquium on "L'histoire et ses interprétations," which brought together the great thinkers in the field (see Raymond Aron, ed., *L'histoire et ses interprétations; Entretiens autour de Arnold Toynbee,* "École Pratique des Hautes Études-Sorbonne; VIᵉ Section: Sciences économiques et sociales; Congrès et colloques," No. 3, Paris & The Hague, 1961); by a demand for Toynbee's *A Study of History* which has resulted in the publishing of the entire unabridged work in a series of paperbound volumes; by the appearance of the journal *History and Theory;* and by the extensive recent monographic and periodical literature in the field.[1]

---

1 A total of 794 books and journal articles published from 1951 through 1957 are listed in John C. Rule, *Bibliography of Works in the Philosophy of History, 1945- 1957* ("History and Theory Beihefte," No. 1, The Hague, 1961). Items which Rule missed are included as an appendix to M. Nowicki's *Bibliography of Works in the Philosophy of History, 1958-1961* ("History and Theory Beihefte," No. 3, The Hague, 1964); from 1958 through 1961 an average of 35 books and 45 journal articles on

But to conclude from the great interest and activity in philosophy of history that its perennial problems are being rapidly solved would be gratuitous. More effort seems to be expended in pointing up the fallacies of existing comprehensive historical syntheses than in offering new solutions (one notes, for example, the high proportion of journal articles against Toynbee listed in each issue of the quarterly *Historical Abstracts [H.A.] Bulletin*). The reason for this is suggested by a trenchant remark of the French existentialistic historian Raymond Aron: "The meaning of 'total' history is the meaning which we attach to human existence and to the succession of forms that it takes through time" ("Evidence and Inference in History," in Daniel Lerner, ed., *Evidence and Inference; the Hayden Colloquium on Scientific Concept and Method* [Glencoe, Ill.: Free Press, 1959], p. 46). Philosophy of history, in other words, derives from one's general *Weltanschauung;* and the absence of decisive solutions to the great issues of philosophy of history reflects the incapacity of contemporary intellectual life to arrive at a meaningful world view.

It is not really so strange that the central problem of history's meaning should remain murky in an age which, to use the expression of Hans Sedlmayer in his metaphysics of art, has "lost its center" (*Verlust der Mitte,* Salzburg, 1948). Both our philosophies of history and our general philosophies of life have been given classic expression in Camus's diseased city of Oran, which Helmut Thielicke has described thus: "To step . . . into the landscape of Camus's novel is like listening to Bach's *Christmas Oratorio* when your small son has fumblingly turned the knob slightly and allowed the jazz rhythm of a jam session to come yowling into the world of angels and shining skies" (*Nihilism,* tr. John W. Doberstein [London: Routledge, 1962], pp. 96-97). The recent republication of Oswald Spengler's *Decline of the West* (edited and abridged by Helmut Werner)[2] is a commentary both on our current interest

philosophy of history were published annually in the Western languages. These figures, high as they are, do not include writings on "certain major historians, like Toynbee, for whom special bibliographies are projected"; of the latter the Toynbee bibliography (covering 366 treatments of him published 1946-1960) has just appeared in *History and Theory,* Vol. 4 [1965], pp. 212-233.

2 William H. McNeill's stimulating work, *The Rise of the West: A History of the Human Community* (University of Chicago Press, 1963), is a noble effort to present an optimistic-idealistic view of Western history over against Spengler's pessimism. In an invitational paper presented at the meeting of Evangelical Historians, held conjointly with the 79th Annual Meeting of the American Historical Association, Washington, D.C., on December 28, 1964, with Professor McNeill as honored guest, this writer endeavored to show that McNeill's secularistic historical philosophy, by its unsupportable view of human nature, historical significance, and ethical values, theoretically has little more to commend it than Spengler's ("The Christian Church in McNeill's *Rise of the West:* An Overview and Critique," *Evangelical Quarterly,* Vol. 38, No. 2 [April-June, 1966]).

in philosophy of history and on Nietzsche's portrayal of the intellectual climate of our epoch: "The ice that bears weight today has already grown extremely thin; the thawing wind is blowing. We ourselves, we homeless ones, are things that break through ice and other realities which are all too thin" *(Die froehliche Wissenschaft)* .

In such a dispossessed era one might suppose that Christian theologians and historians would stand forth as beacon lights pointing the way to solid historiographical ground. Did not the great Scottish philosopher Robert Flint effectively argue, even before the turn of the present century, that "if history has meaning, this meaning is not historical, but theological; what is called *Philosophy of history* is nothing else than a *Theology of history,* more or less disguised" *(History of the Philosophy of History* [Edinburgh, 1893], p. 62) ? Yet one looks in vain for twentieth-century Augustines. The cry: "Wanted: Christian Interpretation of History" (see Peter DeJong in *Christianity Today,* Vol. 9, No. 12 [March 12, 1965], pp. 13-16), is heard in all quarters, but response is either nonexistent or disappointing.[3] If the need is so great and the Christian responsibility to meet it so clear-cut, why has contemporary theology produced no *Civitas Dei?* In philosophy of history as in medicine, effective treatment of disease requires effective diagnosis; it is therefore to this diagnostic problem that we address ourselves.

I. CONCEPTUAL PERPLEXITY

On one major point virtually all theologians of history — past and present — are in agreement: the meaning of general human history is to be found in Jesus Christ. This conviction is common to such radically different positions as Rudolf Bultmann's neo-Protestant existentialism *(The Presence of Eternity: History and Eschatology; the Gifford Lectures 1955* [New York: Harper, 1957], *passim)* and Hans Urs von Balthasar's sophisticated Catholicism (the final sections of Balthasar's *Theologie der Geschichte* [2nd ed., Einsiedeln, 1959] are appropriately titled, "Christ the Norm of History" and "History under the Norm of Christ"; Karl Barth, in his book, *The Humanity of God,* has acknowledged the Jesuit Balthasar as one of his most penetrating critics) . Reinhold Niebuhr expresses the christocentricity of theology of history with particular effectiveness: "The Christian faith finds the final clue to the meaning of life and history in the Christ whose goodness is at once the virtue which man ought, but does not, achieve in history, and the reve-

---

3 For a valuable orientation to the present state of Christian philosophy of history see Georges Florovsky's essay, "The Predicament of the Christian Historian," in *Religion and Culture: Essays in Honor of Paul Tillich,* ed. Walter Leibrecht (New York: Harper, 1959) , pp. 140-166 (with extensive literature cited on pp. 359-362) .

lation of a divine mercy which understands and resolves the perpetual contradictions in which history is involved, even on the highest reaches of human achievements" (*The Children of Light and the Children of Darkness; a Vindication of Democracy and a Critique of Its Traditional Defense* [New York: Scribner, 1944], p. 188). For the theologian, the answers to the questions posed by the history of mankind are, in the most profound sense, bound up with Jesus Christ — who was Himself an historical person.

But precisely here the crux problem arises for contemporary theology: the problem of the historicity of Jesus the Christ. Vagueness as to what is meant by Christ's historicity must necessarily result in vague and indecisive theologies of history. This atmosphere of confusion and perplexity is well illustrated in the essays contained in the recent composite work, *The Historical Jesus and the Kerygmatic Christ,* and its editors Braaten and Harrisville accurately describe the theological situation reflected in their book as the "winter of our discontent."

Whence arises this "discontent"? Evidently not from the character of the historical evidence for Jesus' life, since the documentary testimonies relating to Him are not qualitatively different from the evidence upon which portraits of other historical figures are built (cf. F. F. Bruce, *The New Testament Documents: Are They Reliable?* [5th rev. ed., Grand Rapids: Eerdmans, 1960]). The issue cuts to the deeper level of the *meaning* of historicity in relation to the Christ. It is thus, to use Enrico Castelli's expression, a question of the presuppositions involved in one's theology of history (*Presupposti di una Teologia della Storia* [Milan, 1952]; this sometimes excessively existentialistic interpretation has been translated into French under the title, *Les Présupposés d'une théologie de l'histoire* [Paris, 1954]). Perplexity in contemporary Christian philosophy of history exists chiefly because of presuppositional ambiguities about the concept of history itself.

A recent article by Will Herberg endeavors to schematize the major uses of the term "historical" in present-day theological discussion ("Five Meanings of the Word 'Historical,'" *The Christian Scholar,* Vol. 47 [Winter, 1964], pp. 237-330). Herberg isolates five fundamental conceptions: (1) History as "past facticity"; this is the "ordinary usage" of the term, and "in this sense the historical is opposed to the fictitious, the fabulous, the mythical, the legendary, and the like." (2) History as temporal enactment, as contrasted with "the timeless and the eternal." Theologians frequently speak of the radical difference between the eternal truths and abstract concepts of the Eastern religions on the one hand, and the concrete historical revelation in Judaism or Christianity on the other. (3) History as *Geschichte* (in contrast with *Historie*). Here theologians such as Martin Kähler have attempted to "go beyond, or even ignore, the element of facticity" by making the historical refer to what we deem to be especially influential on the future course of events (see Martin Kähler, *Der sogennante historische Jesus und der geschichtliche, biblische Christus,* 2nd ed. [München, 1956]). In reference to the historicity of Jesus Christ, this approach argues that "the Christ who is effective in history is he who is proclaimed by the apostles as the crucified and resurrected one, and not an 'historical' Jesus who must first be painfully discovered anew behind the documents by our scientific technique" (thus E. Wolf restates Kähler's thesis: *ibid.,* p. 8). (4) History as the essence of man's being. Theologians such as Reinhold Niebuhr insist that neither individual man nor man in community is to be understood in terms of fixed structures of being; rather, man is what he is because of his historical involvement. (5) History as existential decision in the face of future possibilities. Here man's "nature" is "forever being made and remade by choice, decision, and action, which is what constitutes man's historicity." Rudolf Bultmann provides the best theological illustration of this approach to history; for him, the meaning of history is to be found in "responsibility over against the future" (*op. cit.,* p. 143).

Herberg notes that these five interpretations of the meaning of "historical" run a gamut from history as past facticity to history as future possibility. What he does not observe is the even more important consideration that a radical difference exists between the first two usages and the last three. Usages (1) and (2) assume the subject-object distinction (the distinction between the observer of the past and the past itself) and attempt to subordinate the former to the latter; while usages (3), (4), and (5) increasingly disregard the subject-object distinction and place emphasis not on the objectivity of the past but on the interpretive position of the present-day student of it — whose personal "historicity" is held to be the only key to the meaning of the past. These five approaches to history are thus not as "closely connected" as Herberg claims; in reality, they point to the fundamental cleavage between world views that focus on the objectivity of the external world and those that derive from the subjective stance of the interpreter. In terms of this exceedingly basic presuppositional distinction, where is the present-day post-Bultmannian theology to be located, and what degree of validity is to be attached to its historical aprioris?

II. THEOLOGY OF HISTORY IN THE "NEW HERMENEUTIC"

Tillich has pointed out that one of the chief thrusts in the development of modern existentialism has been the effort to "cut under the subject-object distinction" ("Existential Philosophy: Its Historical Meaning," *Theology of Culture,* ed. Robert C. Kimball [New York: Oxford,

1959], p. 92). Thus Bultmann, who is indebted to existentialism for his philosophical orientation, claims that "for historical understanding, the schema of subject and object that has validity for natural science is invalid" ("Ist voraussetzungslose Exegese möglich?", *Theologische Zeitschrift*, Vol. 13 [1957], pp. 409-417). In place of the subject-object distinction, Bultmann substitutes his "circularity" principle: historical exegesis requires an existential "life-relation" between the past (e.g., biblical subject matter) and the interpreter (on Bultmann's circularity principle, see Armin Henry Limper, "Hermeneutics and Eschatology: Rudolf Bultmann's Interpretation of John, Chapters 13-17," unpublished Ph.D. dissertation, University of Chicago, 1960). In such an approach, the interpreter necessarily assumes first place; thus Bultmann concludes his Gifford Lectures with the reiterated assertion: "Always in your present lies the meaning in history, and you cannot see it as a spectator, but only in your responsible decisions" (Bultmann, *The Presence of Eternity*, p. 155).

As is well known, the current "post-Bultmannian" phase in theology grew out of dissatisfaction with Bultmann's relative indifference to the historical Jesus; Bultmann's disciples found great difficulty in their master's unwillingness to pursue the historical question beyond the perspective of the Church's interpretation of Jesus. Thus, parallel with Barth's introduction of objectifying elements into his theology, Bultmann's students and former disciples have endeavored in various ways to conjoin more meaningfully the Jesus of history with the Christ confessed by the early Church. Does this mean that the post-Bultmannian "New Hermeneutic" has shifted from an existentialistic concept of historical investigation to a presuppositionally objective approach?

The answer to this exceedingly important question is a very definite no. Wherever one turns in the new quest debates, one finds — even when criticism of Bultmann is most severe — unshakable and uncritical adherence to his principle of the "hermeneutical circle" and to the existential "transcending of the subject-object distinction." Indeed, an attitude of superiority and scorn not infrequently characterizes post-Bultmannian theological judgments of "objectivistic" thinking; listen to Heinrich Ott, Karl Barth's successor at Basel, as he dispenses with "the so-called 'subject-object schema' and the view that all thinking and language to a very great extent necessarily have an objectifying character":

> According to this view faith and theology's thinking and speaking are to be basically distinguished, that is, one cannot at all speak of a believing thinking, since in this view all theological talking and thinking always take place from an objectifying distance. I shall refrain from going further into these misunderstandings. The thinking of Martin Heidegger performs the inestimable service of teaching us to see in a more primal way the nature of thinking, of language, and thus of under-

standing. If we listen to him and follow him even only a bit on his way, perhaps the day will dawn upon us when those obscuring premises will fall like scales from our eyes ("What Is Systematic Theology?", in James M. Robinson and John B. Cobb, Jr., eds., *The Later Heidegger and Theology,* "New Frontiers in Theology," Vol. I [New York: Harper, 1963], p. 93) .

On this side of the Atlantic, Roy A. Harrisville's essay "Representative American Lives of Jesus," offered as a contribution to the new quest discussions, purports to show that "apart from an abandonment of the subject-object polarity in the interpretation of history, Jesus 'returns to his own time' as much an enigma as before, and that little more is to be gained from his biography than a portrait of his biographer" (in *The Historical Jesus and the Kerygmatic Christ; Essays on the New Quest of the Historical Jesus,* eds. Carl E. Braaten and Roy A. Harrisville [New York: Abingdon, 1964], p. 196) . To Ott, Harrisville, and the New Hermeneutic in general, the Dilthey-Kähler rejection of objective history is self-evident and axiomatic; and even Dilthey's critic Hans-Georg Gadamer, who is endeavoring to give an "ontological turn" to historical hermeneutic by concentrating on linguistic understanding rather than existential psychology, takes the "hermeneutical circle" for granted and asserts that "historic tradition can only be understood by recalling the basic continuing concretizing taking place in the continuation of things" (*Wahrheit und Methode: Grundzüge einer philosophischen Hermeneutik* [Tübingen, 1960], p. 355) .[4]

What is the effect on Christian philosophy of history when the "obscuring premises" of the subject-object distinction have fallen "like scales from our eyes"? Unhappily, the result is not the promised panacea, but a relativistic, solipsistic chaos. The secular existentialistic interpreter of history, Raymond Aron, frankly admits that out of the marriage of the objective matter of history and the subjective stance of the historian a "plurality of systems of interpretation" comes forth — and his advice to the historian who would "overcome the relativity of history" is that he can do so only by "the absolute of decision," thereby affirming "the power of man, who creates himself by judging his environment, and by choosing himself" (*Introduction to the Philosophy of History,* tr. George J. Irwin [London: Weidenfeld, 1961], pp. 86ff., 334; this translation from the 2nd French edition of 1948 should always be compared with the original, for the translator has frequently obscured the author's meaning) .

---

4 On Gadamer's place in the new quest debates, see James M. Robinson's article, "Hermeneutic Since Barth," which introduces Robinson and Cobb, eds., *The New Hermeneutic* ("New Frontiers in Theology," Vol. II [New York: Harper, 1964], pp. 69-77) . The best introduction in English to Dilthey's philosophy of history is H. P. Rickman's anthology, *Meaning in History: Wilhelm Dilthey's Thoughts on History and Society* (London: Allen & Unwin, 1961) .

Thus an interpretation of the past becomes "absolute" only to the interpreter who chooses it absolutely. As we have seen, this is also Bultmann's conclusion as to the meaning of history.

But whereas Aron and Bultmann at least admit to the existence of objectively verifiable historical facts (though they are quick to point out that concentration on them instead of on our existential "encounter with history" will cause us to "miss history's real nature"), post-Bultmannian Heinrich Ott endeavors to carry the rejection of the subject-object distinction to its logical conclusion; he argues the amazing propositions that "the objective mode of knowledge is entirely inappropriate to historical reality because there are no such things as objectively verifiable facts and, secondly, that all true knowledge of history is finally knowledge by encounter and confrontation" ("The Historical Jesus and the Ontology of History," in Braaten and Harrisville, *op. cit.*, p. 148). Ott introduces God's "seeing" of total history as a device to prevent his position from degenerating into total solipsism, but such a *deus ex machina* is far from successful, since apart from an objectively reliable revelation from God (which Ott's view eliminates *ex hypothesi*), man can never know if one human interpretation of the past is closer to ultimate reality than another.

Relativistic, solipsistic consequences are not accidental when one attempts to transcend the subject-object distinction; they are inevitable. This is the case because a finite, sinful human being is incapable of obliterating the distinction between the reality outside of himself and his own psyche without bending reality in his own direction. "Transcending the subject-object barrier" thus invariably produces, not an experience with higher reality, but a falling back into subjectivism. The more perceptive existentialists have seen this and admitted it; Jean-Paul Sartre, for example, states that what Christian existentialists (such as Marcel) and atheistic existentialists (such as Heidegger and himself) "have in common is that they think that existence precedes essence, or, if you prefer, that subjectivity must be the starting point" (*Existentialism and Human Emotions* [New York: Philosophical Library, 1957], p. 13; tr. by Bernard Frechtman). Gadamer's student Heinz Kimmerle has rendered theology a great service by showing that Dilthey, upon whom Heidegger and Bultmann based their existentialisms, derived his hermeneutic from the later Schleiermacher (cf. Robinson, *The New Hermeneutic*, pp. 70-71);[5] the chain is thus completed from the subjective psychologism of

---

5 Bultmann's dependence on Dilthey in opposing the subject-object distinction is evident from Bultmann's essay, "The Problem of Hermeneutics," which appeared first in the *Zeitschrift fur Theologie und Kirche* Vol. 47 [1950], pp. 47-69, and which has been published in English translation in Bultmann's *Essays, Philosophical and Theological*, tr. J. C. G. Greig [London: Macmillan, 1955], pp. 234-261.

Schleiermacher (from which Ritschlian modernism grew) to the post-Bultmannian New Hermeneutic. The subjective soul of unreconstructed Protestant modernism (ironically rejected by all advocates of the post-Bultmannian era) has in fact transmigrated to the New Hermeneutic of the present decade — with all its deleterious consequences for Christian theology of history.

Will Herberg noted the "futuristic" orientation of existentialistic philosophies of history; this in itself should make us suspicious of them in relation to historical interpretation, for history, after all, has its *raison d'être* in past, not present or future, reality. Thus J. W. N. Watkins pinpoints the inadequacy of pragmatic philosophies of history: "There is something to be said for pragmatism, but it so happens that history is the domain in which it works worst. History is backward-looking, pragmatism forward-looking" ("Philosophy of History: Publications in English," in *La Philosophie au milieu du vingtième siècle,* ed. Raymond Klibansky [4 vols., 2d ed., Firenze, 1961-1962], Vol. III, p. 165). Since "future possibility" is the least knowable aspect of man's life, it is a singularly inappropriate basis for understanding his past; indeed, the "futurity" of existential-subjective approaches suggests the chief reason for rejecting them: their unverifiability. Heidegger's attempt (in his *Was Ist Metaphysik?*) to assert the primacy of existence ("the Nothing") over essence ("the Negation and the Not") has been shown by Rudolf Carnap to consist of analytically meaningless, unverifiable "pseudo-statements" ("The Elimination of Metaphysics through Logical Analysis of Language," in *Logical Positivism,* ed. A. J. Ayer [Glencoe, Ill.: Free Press, 1959], pp. 69-73). Likewise, claims such as Ott's that "all true knowledge of history is finally knowledge by encounter and confrontation" receive decimating criticism by philosophers of religion schooled in analytic and "ordinary language" philosophy; Frederick Ferré, for example, writes:

> If illusion is present sometimes or often in "encounter," what assures us that our experience is not always merely subjective emotion conjoined with personal interpretation? Even if the rapport between persons is sometimes veridical, as seems increasingly likely in the light of contemporary research into para-normal psychology, it is clear from the negative instances that this route to knowledge of other persons is far from trustworthy, and therefore hardly adequate to undergird the entire theological claim to the knowledge of God (*Language, Logic and God* [New York: Harper, 1961], p. 103; cf. C. B. Martin, "A Religious Way of Knowing," in *New Essays in Philosophical Theology,* ed. Antony Flew and Alasdair Macintyre [London: Macmillan, 1955], pp. 76-95).

Endeavors to deal with the issues of Christian philosophy of history by introducing a *geschichtliche* or "suprahistorical" level of understanding fare no better, for, like Heidegger's "Nothing" and Ott's "confrontation," *Geschichte* is subject to no verifiability tests (see this writer's "Karl Barth and Contemporary Theology of History," *The Cresset,* Vol. 27 [November, 1963], pp. 8-14; also published in the *Bulletin of the Evangelical Theological Society,* Vol. 6 [May, 1963], pp. 39-49).

The only way out of the relativistic morass characteristic of the positions we have been considering is a frank acknowledgement of the subject-object distinction as the starting point for all genuine understanding of the past. G. H. von Wright has shown, by a closely reasoned argument, that inductive method, presupposing the subject-object distinction, is the only entrée to verifiable knowledge of the external world: "its superiority is rooted in the fact that the inductive character of a policy is the very criterion by means of which we judge its goodness" (Georg Henrik von Wright, *The Logical Problem of Induction,* 2nd ed. [Oxford: Blackwell, 1957], p. 175; the present writer has related induction to deduction and Aristotelian retroduction in his paper, "The Theologian's Craft: A Discussion of Theory Formation and Theory Testing in Theology," presented at the 20th Annual Convention of the American Scientific Affiliation, August 24, 1965, and published in the *Concordia Theological Monthly,* Vol. 37 [February, 1966], pp. 67-98). To disregard or try to circumvent inductive method in studying the past is to destroy all possibility of objective knowledge of man's history, and therefore to eliminate in principle a Christian philosophy of history. The theologian who thinks he is "transcending the subject-object barrier" becomes like James Thurber, who tells the story that in his college biology course he spent the term meticulously drawing the image of his own eyelash as it fell across the microscopic field. It is this sublime disregard of the self-imposition of subjective categories on biblical material that has vitiated so much of the Bultmannian and post-Bultmannian interpretation of Christian origins. In reality, over against Harrisville, the Jesus of history remains enigmatic to contemporary theology not "apart from an abandonment of the subject-object polarity," but precisely *because* of its abandonment.

III. THE PATH TO SOLID GROUND

The historiographical tradition from Dilthey to the post-Bultmannians has made the great error of reacting too strongly to an erroneous position and thereby falling into an equally grievous error. In opposing nineteenth-century positivistic historicism, which mistakenly endeavored to structure man's history by way of categories derived from Newtonian science, the Dilthey tradition in philosophy and its Bultmannian counterpart in theology radically subjectivized the historical task. Instead of purging historicism of its rationalistic, humanistic scientism, and thus freeing its sound empirical techniques from harmful metaphysical baggage, the anti-positivists threw out the most valuable insight that historicism had to offer: the inductive method. Bultmann's retention of the most reprehensible element in historicism is extremely ironical: he retains its metaphysical assumption that "the whole historical process is a closed unity" and that "this closedness means that the continuum of historical happenings cannot be rent by the interference of supernatural, transcendent powers and that therefore there is no 'miracle' in this sense of the word" ("Ist voraussetzungslose Exegese möglich?", *loc. cit.*). Einsteinian relativity has made this world view hopelessly obsolete. In reacting against historicistic Life-of-Jesus research, post-liberal theology never saw that the real trouble lay not with the heuristic employment of inductive technique based upon the subject-object distinction, but with the humanistic metaphysic of the liberal researchers. Harrisville's article, cited earlier, is a concrete instance of such obliviousness in the interpretation of the Life-of-Jesus era.

In contemporary philosophy of history there are faint glimmerings of light as analytically trained philosophers are turning from the bogs of existential subjectivism to a frank recognition of the necessity of inductive historiography. How unfortunate that contemporary theology is not yet prepared for the logic of such an analysis of the methodological problem as provided by J. W. N. Watkins:

> My own belief is that, while it is no doubt desirable that the historian should be as aware as possible of the sources of potential bias within himself, what really matters, in connection with the problem of historical objectivity, is not so much the historian's mentality as the logical structure of what he writes. The regulative moral and metaphysical convictions, the passion and controversy, which Walsh regards as the causes and symbols of subjectivity in history, have their counterparts in the natural sciences, which Walsh regards as paradigms of objectivity. The objective character of a scientific theory is not a function of its author's temperament and mentality, but of its *criticisability.* Thus for me, the question "How objective can history be?" boils down to the question, "To what extent is a systematic historical reconstruction exposed to criticism?" . . . The informal, common-sense answer is plain enough. There are plenty of excellent historical works in which a previous descriptive interpretation is cogently challenged with the help of fresh evidence or of old evidence presented in a fresh light. It has been done, therefore it can be done.[6]

---

[6] In *La Philosophie au milieu du vingtième siècle,* Vol. III, p. 174. Watkins makes the important point, over against the Dilthey tradition, that recent analytical work by such philosophers as Ryle "dispels the old presumption, to which Hayek, Swabey and others are still inclined, that to understand Ghengis Khan the historian must be someone very like Ghengis Khan" (p. 159). The application to the New Hermeneutic, which makes historical understanding of the Christ of the New Testament dependent upon prior faith in him, should be obvious.

When the Christian philosopher of history is willing to approach the New Testament in this spirit, he finds that the seemingly insurmountable problem of the "historical Jesus" vs. the "kerygmatic Christ" well nigh vanishes away. Objective comparison of the problems in New Testament interpretation with parallel issues in extra-biblical historical and literary scholarship indicates that biblical theology has created its own difficulties through presuppositionalism. "Is it not true that our interpretation of Jesus comes only by way of the early Church?" Certainly, but this in no way forces the conclusion that the Church obscured the real Jesus of history; for we do not similarly relegate to the limbo of the unknowable the numerous other great men of the past who have written nothing (e.g., Alexander the Great, Charlemagne) and who are seen by us through the eyes of their contemporaries. "But should we not assume redaction of Jesus' message by the Church that produced the New Testament documents?" Hardly, when by doing so we are led to employ a technique (the Dibelius-Bultmann *formgeschichtliche Methode*) which proved debilitating in Homeric scholarship decades ago (see H. J. Rose, *Handbook of Greek Literature from Homer to the Age of Lucian* [London, 1934], pp. 42-43) and which has been rejected by students of the English ballad because of the lack of sufficient time periods for oral development — and "no Gospel section passed through such a long period of oral tradition as did any genuine ballad" (A. H. McNeile and C. S. C. Williams, *Introduction to the Study of the New Testament*, 2nd ed. [New York: Oxford, 1955], p. 58).

Indeed, historians who stand outside of the existentialistically suffused atmosphere of New Testament study are frequently at a loss to know what is troubling the Christian historian. Thus A. N. Sherwin-White's Sarum Lectures on *Roman Society and Roman Law in the New Testament* conclude with a section on "The Historicity of the Gospels and Graeco-Roman Historiography" in which we read:

> It is astonishing that while Graeco-Roman historians have been growing in confidence, the twentieth-century study of the Gospel narratives, starting from no less promising material, has taken so gloomy a turn in the development of form-criticism that the more advanced exponents of it apparently maintain — so far as an amateur can understand the matter — that the historical Christ is unknowable and the history of his mission cannot be written. This seems very curious when one compares the case for the best-known contemporary of Christ, who like Christ is a well-documented figure — Tiberius Caesar. The story of his reign is known from four sources, the *Annals* of Tacitus and the biography of Suetonius, written some eighty or ninety years later, the brief contemporary record of Velleius Paterculus, and the third-century history of Cassius Dio. These disagree amongst themselves in the wildest possible fashion, both in major matters of political action or motive and in specific details of minor events. Everyone would admit that Tacitus is the best of all the

sources, and yet no serious modern historian would accept at face value the majority of the statements of Tacitus about the motives of Tiberius. But this does not prevent the belief that the material of Tacitus can be used to write a history of Tiberius. (Sherwin-White's Sarum Lectures for 1960-1961 were published at Oxford in 1963; the quoted passage appears on p. 187.)

The Gospel records of our Lord's life, death, and resurrection do not suffer from these historical difficulties with regard to date, or to primary evidential value, or to internal consistency; how unfortunate, then, that the contemporary Christian theologian is hesitant to go to them and inductively discover there the true grounds of theology of history.

And if one does so? One meets in the primary documents a man who convinces both His friends and His enemies that He regards Himself as no less than God incarnate, come to earth to die for the sins of the world. He places His stamp of divine approval on the Old Testament, as witnessing to Him, and promises His Holy Spirit to the apostles in order that the Spirit may bring to their remembrance all things whatsoever He had said to them (John 14:26).[7] He rises from the dead — bodily — to manifest His *historisch* resurrection even to those such as Thomas who disbelieved. Here we see "historical Jesus" and "kerygmatic Christ" thoroughly united, providing an objective ground — the only objective ground — for an interpretation of total history that is not subject to the limitations of man's sinful situation (see the writer's article, "Where Is History Going?", *Religion in Life,* Vol. 33, No. 2 [Spring, 1964]).

In a moving symbolic novel, *Mount Analogue,* the late surrealist, Sanskrit scholar, philosopher and poet René Daumal has one of his leading characters say:

> "Experience has proved, I told myself, that a man cannot reach truth directly, nor all by himself. An intermediary has to be present, a force still human in certain respects, yet transcending humanity in others. Somewhere on our Earth this superior form of humanity must exist, and not utterly out of reach. In that case shouldn't all my efforts be directed toward discovering it? Even if, in spite of my certainty, I were the victim of a monstrous illusion, I should lose nothing in the attempt. For, apart from this hope, all life lacked meaning for me.
>
> "But where was I to look? Where could I begin? I had already covered the world, poked my nose into everything, into all kinds of religious

---

[7] On the crucial significance of the apostolic "remembering" as the link between the "Jesus of history" and the "Christ of faith," see Oscar Cullmann's "The Resurrection: Event and Meaning," *Christianity Today,* Vol. 9, No. 13 [March 26, 1965], pp. 8-9; this essay is from Cullmann's new book, *Heil als Geschichte,* soon to be published in English translation by Harper.

sects and mystic cults.   But with all of them it came down to the same
dilemma: maybe yes, maybe no.   Why should I stake my life on this
one rather than on that one?   You see, I had no touchstone" (tr. Roger
Shattuck [New York: Pantheon Books, 1960], p. 59) .

For Christian theology of history (as for theology in general and life in
general) the true and only intermediary is Jesus Christ, and the true
and only touchstone is Holy Scripture, which testifies of Him.

THE CHRIST-REVELATION
AS ACT AND
INTERPRETATION

Kenneth Kantzer

Kenneth S. Kantzer is Dean of Trinity Evangelical Divinity School in
Bannockburn, Deerfield, Illinois. Formerly he served as Chairman of
the Department of Bible and Philosophy, Wheaton College, Wheaton,
Illinois. He holds the Ph.D. degree from Harvard University and
has pursued post-doctoral studies in the Universities of Göttingen and
Basel.

16.   *Kenneth Kantzer*

THE CHRIST-REVELATION AS ACT AND INTERPRETATION

I N A FAMOUS essay on revelation Archbishop William Temple strikes the keynote for theological thinking in our day. He writes ("Revelation," *Revelation,* ed. John Baillie and Hugh Martin [New York: Macmillan Co., 1937], p. 83): "The dominant problem of contemporary religious thought is the problem of revelation. Is there such a thing at all? If there is, what is its mode and form? Is it discoverable in all existing things or only in some? If in some, then in which? And by what principles are these selected as its vehicle? Where is it found?   *Or* believed to be found? What is its authority?"

I. REVELATION IN TRADITIONAL ORTHODOXY

This current debate over revelation reflects the concern of modern theologians to rethink time-honored answers to the fundamental religious question: "Can man know God?" Unfortunately, so most contemporary theologians lament, revelation has frequently been misconstrued by a scholastically minded orthodoxy. According to this older view, the object of revelation is a body of "revealed truths." These divine disclosures vouchsafed by God to His chosen prophets and apostles, were handed down in the Bible as divinely inspired propositional truths about reality and about God Himself — the truths which men could not

figure out for themselves and which, therefore, God graciously conde-
scended to communicate to them.

In a forthright statement Emil Brunner gets immediately to the
nub of his opposition to the traditional viewpoint. The idea that God
revealed truths to inspired biblical prophets and apostles is basically
and essentially unbiblical. In loyalty to the Bible, assertedly, he must oppose it. "The way in which the early church spoke of the *logos* and in
which orthodox theological exposition still does," so Brunner declares
(*The Christian Doctrine of God*, tr. Olive Wyon [London: Lutterworth
Press, 1949], p. 26), "betrays an alien influence, not in accordance with
the testimony of the Bible, a train of thought which has been introduced
into Christian thought by Greek philosophers."

To this objection John Baillie adds an additional reason for rejecting
propositional revelation. All propositional apprehension of truth (*The
Idea of Revelation in Recent Thought* [New York: Columbia University
Press, 1956], p. 38) contains a human element and therefore an element
of possible error. To err is human, and it seems to fall but little short
of blasphemy to foist upon the God of truth all the shortcomings and
inadequacies of humanly formed propositions. Particularly does this
objection register impressively on modern men when the entire corpus of
biblical propositions is identified with the truth revealed by God Himself.

The most deeply rooted objection to equating revelation with propositional truths stems from the conviction that such a view of revelation
offers us something less than personal encounter and personal communion with God Himself (Karl Barth, *Das Christliche Verständnis
der Offenbarung* [Munich: C. Kaiser Verlag, 1948], p. 3).

Finally, there are practical objections to the traditional view. Precisely which truths are divinely revealed and which stem merely from
human judgment? How can these divinely revealed propositions be distinguished from others which are only alleged to be so? How can divinely
given truth be understood, interpreted, and adequately conveyed in
human language? Most contemporary theologians consider such questions unanswerable.

II. THE CONTEMPORARY VIEW OF REVELATION

Even though their agreements are frequently disguised by the vigor
with which they debate their differences, an extraordinarily large number
of contemporary theologians are in basic agreement as to the true nature
of divine revelation. By his own searching, so they argue, man can never
find God; but God in His grace has chosen to reveal Himself to man.
This divine revelation comes to man by means of a personal encounter

between God and man in which God unveils Himself to man and in the same act opens man's eyes, spiritually speaking, so that he may see God and know Him in personal fellowship.

Against the traditional view, most contemporary thinkers insist that the content of divine revelation is never truth or a body of doctrine or an inspired book such as the Bible. Divine revelation, rather, always has as its true object God Himself, as a Person. Thus John Baillie sums up the view which he finds to be that of most thinkers of the day when he says (*Idea of Revelation,* p. 29): "From a very early time in the history of the church, the tendency had manifested itself to equate divine revelation with a body of information which God has communicated to man. We must rather think of Him as giving Himself to us in communion. Our examination of New Testament usage . . . amply confirms our conclusion that what is revealed is not a body of information or of doctrine. God does not give us information by communication, He gives us Himself in communion. It is not information about God that is revealed but . . . God himself."

In an authoritative article in Kittel's *Theologisches Wörterbuch,* the German scholar Albrecht Oepke supports this view ("Kalupto," *TWNT* [Stuttgart: W. Kohlhammer Verlag, 1938], III, *in loco.*): "Revelation is not the communication of supernatural knowledge and not the stimulation of numinous feelings. Revelation can, of course, produce knowledge and is necessarily accompanied by numinous feelings. In itself, however, revelation is neither of these things, but is quite essentially a transaction of Jahweh, an unveiling of His essential hiddenness, His offering of Himself in mutual fellowship."[1]

Writing in quite a different theological framework, Paul Tillich declares ("Authority and Revelation," *Bulletin of Harvard Divinity School, Issue Containing the Annual Lectures and Book Reviews for the year, 1951-1952,* XLIX [April 7, 1952], 27): "The content of revelation is not religion but God. Religion is an answer solicited by revelation but given by man."

Archbishop Temple summarizes this position succinctly (*Nature, Man and God* [London: Macmillan, 1960], p. 317): ". . . there is no such thing as revealed truth. There are truths of revelation, that is to say, propositions which express the results of correct thinking concerning revelation; but these are not themselves directly revealed. . . . What is offered to man's apprehension in any specific Revelation is not truth concerning God but the living God Himself."

---

[1] Some of the material in these introductory paragraphs originally formed part of the Griffith Thomas Lectures printed in *Bibliotheca Sacra,* April, 1958, to January, 1959, and it is here restated by permission.

Contemporary religious scholarship is all but unanimously agreed that revelation has as its object God, His Person, not truth or propositions about God. It is also in nearly complete agreement about the method of revelation. Here, too, it takes sharp issue with the traditional view.

According to most contemporary theologians the method of divine revelation consists of the "mighty acts" of God in nature, in history, in conscience, in the human soul, and above all in Jesus Christ. John Baillie speaks for many when he writes (*Idea of Revelation,* p. 50):

> . . . it is one of the points in which there appears a remarkable breadth of agreement in recent discussions about revelation. It is that what is fundamentally revealed is God Himself, not propositions about God. Equally remarkable, however, is the recent agreement on the second, which is this: that God reveals Himself *in action* — in the gracious activity by which He invades the field of human experience and human history which is otherwise but a vain show, empty and drained of meaning.
>
> The Bible is essentially the story of the acts of God. . . . Other sacred books are composed mainly of oracles which communicate what profers to be timeless truth about universal beings or timeless prescriptions for the conduct of life and worship. But the Bible is mainly a record of what God has done.

Tillich adds (*Systematic Theology* [Chicago: University of Chicago Press, 1951], I, 125): "There are no revealed doctrines, but there are revelatory events and situations which can be described in doctrinal terms. . . . the 'Word of God' contains neither revealed commandments nor revealed doctrine. It accompanies and interprets revelatory situations."

Emil Brunner defends the same viewpoint (*Revelation and Reason: The Christian Doctrine of Faith and Knowledge,* tr. Olive Wyon [Philadelphia; Westminster Press, 1946], p. 8): "In the time of the apostles, as in that of the Old Testament prophets, divine revelation always meant the whole of the divine activity for the salvation of the world, the whole story of God's saving acts, of the 'acts' of God which reveal God's nature and His will, above all, Him in whom the preceding revelation gains its meaning and who therefore is its fulfillment: Jesus Christ. He Himself is revelation. Divine revelation is not a book or a doctrine; the revelation is God Himself in His self-manifestation within history."

According to most contemporary thinkers, therefore, the means of revelation consists of God's acts in history. God saved Israel from the angel of doom in Egypt. God saved Israel from the hosts of Pharaoh. God brought Israel into the promised land. God punished Israel for her sins. God saved Israel from her enemies when she repented and turned from their sin. The supreme act of God in revealing Himself is the incarnation of God in Jesus Christ, His miracles, and especially His death and resurrection. God reveals His own Person, and He does so not by dictating truth — not even the true words of the Bible — but by His mighty acts in history, which culminate in His activity in Jesus Christ.

III. THE PROBLEM OF THE NATURE OF REVELATORY ACTS

Necessarily this contemporary view of revelation raises questions. What is the nature of this personal knowledge? How does it differ from ordinary knowledge of fact? What are the "mighty acts" by which God mediates this knowledge of Himself? What is the nature of these mighty acts of God in human history? How are they related to ordinary human history? How may they be known to be true?

Unfortunately, as Langdon Gilkey rightly charges ("Cosmology, Ontology, and the Travail of Biblical Language," *Journal of Religion,* XLI [July, 1961], pp. 194-205), many modern theologians do not appear very eager to clarify the inherent ambiguity in such phrases as "personal knowledge" and "mighty acts of God." Some thinkers seem actually to prefer not to raise these sticky questions; to others, however, these very questions represent the blue litmus paper by which to recognize the presence or absence of what can be properly recognized as Christianity. In any case, the issues rising out of debate over the nature of these "mighty acts" of divine revelation and particularly of the relation between these revelatory acts of God and ordinary human history have occasioned the major theological battles of post World War II Europe.

Karl Barth: Revelatory Acts within History but not Historically Verifiable

Karl Barth, early leader on the contemporary scene, has sought with prodigious energy to rear the structure of an historical Christianity above the ashes of liberal and rationalistic criticism. God, so he argues, really acted in human history to reveal Himself by becoming incarnate in Jesus of Nazareth. As the God-man, Jesus Christ died vicariously for men on the cross, on the third day rose from the dead, leaving an empty tomb as a sign of His resurrection, and appeared to His disciples as His crowning triumph over death in securing the salvation of men. These "mighty acts" of God must be taken seriously; and Barth interprets them as God's acts within the sphere of ordinary human events.[2]

At the same time Barth is unwilling to expose Christianity to the mercies of the secular student of scientific human history. The knowledge of God's activity in history he insists, therefore, remains forever

---

2 Note particularly Karl Barth's "running commentary" directed against the position of Rudolf Bultmann in his *Church Dogmatics,* III, Part 2, 442-447, 451-454, and IV, Part 1, 767ff.

hidden to the eye of a neutral historian or the secular scientist. No doubt such an historian can discover from the data available to him that there once existed a man called Jesus of Nazareth who, as a first-century Jewish rabbi, wandered up and down the land of Palestine. This "Jesus of history," however, could never serve as the foundation of Christian faith and, indeed, appears to be a very ordinary individual and thoroughly irrelevant to the needs of modern man (*The Doctrine of the Word of God,* tr. G. T. Thompson [Edinburgh: T. & T. Clark, 1936], p. 188).

In stark contrast with a Jesus Christ who is the product of historical study (*Historie*) stands the real Jesus Christ of true history (*Geschichte*). The real Jesus Christ becomes known as such only by divine revelation in the immediate encounter through which God in Christ makes Himself known to man as the One who has reconciled man to Himself by the life, death, and resurrection of Christ. In his recent terminology Barth refers to this present work upon the human soul as the witness of the Holy Spirit. By this immediate witness, God validates the truth of Jesus Christ witnessed to in the Holy Scripture and creates the faith that He has actually revealed Himself historically in Jesus. Such faith, as Barth sees it, does not terminate in any sense on historical evidence; it is wholly the product of the divine encounter as God reveals Himself to the individual believer and manifests that He really was, and is, man's redeemer in Jesus Christ. By means of this distinction between the historical Christ (historical meaning that God actually acted in the course of human events) and the non-historical Christ (non-historical meaning that Christ is not and cannot be known by the study of history), Barth seeks not only to preserve the validity of biblical Christianity but also to free it from the erosion of liberal criticism, which could find through diligent historical research no God-man, no virgin birth, no empty tomb, and no bodily resurrection of the Jesus of history (*Church Dogmatics* [Edinburgh: T. & T. Clark, 1956], I, Part 2, 1-202 *et passim*).

Again and again Barth tells us that he is not interested in the Jesus of history in the sense of going behind the New Testament documents in order to discover what the man was actually like who moved up and down the land of Palestine. In one sense the Jesus of history is the Jesus of the New Testament just as He is there portrayed — the virgin-born, miracle-working, vicariously-dying and resurrected incarnation of God. In another sense the Jesus of history is a monstrosity that never existed. For in going behind the New Testament records and building a Jesus that can be substantiated only by historical documents (according to the usual criterion of what makes documents historical), we are led irresistibly to a Jesus who never really lived — to quite a different Jesus from the real Jesus of the New Testament ("Rudolf Bultmann — An

Attempt to Understand Him," *Kerygma and Myth: A Theological Debate,* ed. Hans Werner Bartsch, tr. Reginald H. Fuller [London: S.P.C.K., 1962], I, 83-132).

Rudolf Bultmann: Revelatory Acts not Necessarily Historical or Historically Verifiable

Rudolf Bultmann, who in the years following World War II came to exceed even Karl Barth in theological eminence, holds to quite a different view of the mighty acts of God. True, in the early period of his professional career, he associated himself with Karl Barth in what seemed to be a united opposition against liberalism. With Barth he objected to the manner in which liberals sifted the New Testament documents in order to glean from them the authentic acts and teachings of the real, historical Jesus and thus obtain the essence of the "pure, simple, and original gospel." History, both Barth and Bultmann agreed, does not provide us with the preaching about Christ which we as sinful men desperately need, which forces us to decision, and which thus brings to us salvation in Christ. (See especially his *Existence and Faith,* tr. Schubert M. Ogden [New York: Meridian Books, Inc., 1960].)

Beneath this surface agreement, however, it soon became apparent that a drastic gulf separates the thought of the two men. Although Barth rules out historical study as the basis of the kerygma, he is still concerned to say that the Spirit of God — alone and as a work of pure divine grace — creates in us the assurance that God really did enter the stream of human history, to become incarnate in Jesus Christ, to die on the cross for our sins, and to rise again from the dead for our salvation. Bultmann, by contrast, argues that the kerygma is not concerned with whether or not events described in the Christian gospel actually and literally happened within the framework of human history and in the manner described by biblical statements (*Jesus Christ and Mythology* [New York: Charles Scribner's Sons, 1958]).

In the first place, says Bultmann, a gospel dependent on the literal historicity of the New Testament records would be useless because it would be assertedly unbelievable to modern man. Like other first-century men, the New Testament authors accepted a mythical view of the world. It would be senseless to foist this outworn view upon twentieth-century man because there is nothing specifically Christian in the mythical view of the world as such. It is simply the cosmology of a pre-scientific age. It is, in fact, impossible for modern men to accept such views. "It would demand," Bultmann avers ("New Testament and Mythology," *Kerygma and Myth,* I, 3-5 and 12), "a sacrifice of the intellect which could have only one result — a curious form of schizophrenia and insincerity. It is impossible to use electric lights and the wireless and to avail ourselves of modern medical and surgical discoveries and at the same time to believe in the New Testament world of spirits and miracles." In short, if we had to become interested in what historical studies tell us about Christ because the gospel consisted of what Christ did in past human history, then modern man simply could not believe the gospel, for this gospel would tell us of events which to the modern man are simply unbelievable.

Even if the historical events narrated in the New Testament documents were theoretically possible, moreover, no universal gospel to meet all the needs of men of every age could possibly rely for its validity upon the study of history. Generations ago Lessing taught this lesson to modern man once and for all. Such revelation, bound by time and space, would require a priesthood of historical scholars who alone could know with certainty whether or not such a gospel really fitted the actual facts of history ("The Case for Demythologizing," *Kerygma and Myth,* p. 192).

The most objectionable feature in any attempt to defend a gospel grounded upon the historical validity of the New Testament assertedly lies in the basic misconception this involves as to the true nature of the New Testament gospel. The real value of the New Testament kerygma and, indeed, its real meaning are not to be derived from what happened in Palestine two thousand years ago. The value and meaning lie rather in what this kerygma means to me today. Does it reveal to me today the meaning of life and thus call me to make an ultimate commitment pro or con (*ibid.,* pp. 183, 193, 194).

Once the true nature of the gospel is seen, Bultmann continues, the relative unimportance of the historical question becomes immediately apparent. Either the gospel as preached concerning Christ has ultimate meaning for me by placing me before a moral and spiritual decision, or it does not. The answer to the question, however, cannot be reached through historical study into the facts about the historical life of Christ. Rather, it is reached by self-examination as to the true meaning for me to be gleaned from the stories about Christ (*ibid.*).

As Bultmann sees this, such a right understanding of the gospel delivers me from the anguish of trying to force myself to believe what is actually impossible for any modern man to believe. It clears away the underbrush so that I can see clearly what is the true gospel of the New Testament and profit therefrom. At the same time it shows me also the futility of attempting to create my own gospel by my powers of historical insight and research, in works of intellectual righteousness. It frees me, finally, to arrive at my ultimate good solely by an act of commitment or faith. In this sense, Bultmann claims ("Bultmann Replies to His Critics,"

Kerygma and Myth, I, 210 and 211), he is simply bringing to its logical fulfilment the Pauline and Lutheran doctrine of justification apart from works. "It carries this doctrine to its logical conclusion in the field of epistemology."

The Heilsgeschichte School: Revelation Historical and Historically Verifiable

In sharp opposition to both Barth and Bultmann in their rejection of any historical validation of the gospel, the so-called *Heilsgeschichte* school of theology has argued for a fully historical revelation. Althaus, for example, chides Bultmann for making the gospel a purely subjective affair. He thinks that in the thought of both Barth and Bultmann the Christian message lies at the mercy of individual feelings. It is not so much the extension of the Pauline and Lutheran doctrine of justification by faith as it is an extension in contemporary terms of the liberal theology of feeling fathered by Friedrich Schleiermacher (Paul Althaus, *Fact and Faith in the Kerygma of Today,* tr. David Cairns [Philadelphia: Muhlenberg Press, 1960], pp. 54 and 82).

This denial of the historical nature of revelation, moreover, is decidedly unbiblical. Is it really true, Althaus asks Bultmann, that according to the New Testament there is no interest in historical study as to what actually happened in a certain Palestinian tomb in the year 30 A.D.? Even Bultmann acknowledges, to his own regret, that the apostle Paul in I Corinthians 15 is arguing on the basis of historical testimony for the actuality of the biblical resurrection appearances. Bultmann really gives us, so Althaus charges, not a theology drawn from the Bible but a subjective anthropology drawn from religious experience (*ibid.,* pp. 28, 29 *et passim*).

On the other hand, Barth, who seeks to preserve a kind of objective validity of the events of the gospel history, while denying that they are historically mediated, may be dealing somewhat more faithfully with the biblical gospel; but he does so at the price of a greater inconsistency. Barth's exegesis of I Corinthians 15 simply warps the apostolic teaching to fit his own conviction. He seeks to extract historical truth and the assurance of historical facts out of a subjective experience. This will not do, declares Althaus. The facts of the revelation of God in history must be historically mediated.

Bultmann is wrong when he denies that the biblical kerygma is dependent upon historical facts. Barth is wrong when he denies that these facts of the historical revelation can only be certified through subjective experience. No doubt the significance of these facts of the gospel becomes apparent to men only in the divine-human encounter. We know that it is God who has really spoken to us through these facts only by the results of our personal meeting with God. But the actual facts of the divine revelation in history must be historically mediated and verified through the study of history (*ibid.*, pp. 67-79).

Naturally, so Althaus concedes willingly, if history be defined as a naturalistic history that necessarily rules out a priori the reality of all miracles, then, as Martin Kähler taught us years ago, such a history cannot lead us to the knowledge of the historical facts of the gospel. But if history is defined so as to leave open the possibility of truly miraculous events, then the data of history ought to lead us to the truth of a divine revelation in which God acted in the stream of human events to save men (*ibid.*, pp. 19-37).

To many of us the position of Althaus seems incontrovertible in so far as it goes. It takes seriously the biblical revelation of a God who stepped fully into human history and acted in history. Here is no Docetic incarnation and unsure involvement in the human story. God did not remain "on the rim" of history, in mere juxtaposition to it. The life of God in Christ becomes a part of the facts of human history, the same kind of human history in which the rest of mankind move and have their being — open, public history, seen by eyewitnesses, available for diligent study, able to convince men of good will of its full validity.

IV. THE BIBLICAL VIEW OF REVELATION

A closer analysis of the *Heilsgeschichte* school of thought, nevertheless, reveals a highly significant lacuna in its understanding of biblical revelation. *Heilsgeschichte* presents a sort of halfway house in opposition to the historical subjectivism of Barth and Bultmann. In it we are given a one-sided view of only half of the biblical data concerning the divine revelation in history. While in part grounded firmly upon objective and verifiable history, so ably defended by the *Heilsgeschichte* scholars, the biblical gospel also contains an objective and verifiable divine interpretation of these acts.

Certainly, as Bultmann especially is quick to point out, the significance of the "mighty acts" of God for me as an individual living today is crucial. I must ascertain the meaning of these acts in the plan and program of God. C. H. Dodd notes in his volume, *History and the Gospel* (New York: Charles Scribner's Sons, 1938, pp. 67 and 68), "The meaning of what happened is of greater importance than what happened. At least it is as important for us as what happened." The revelation of mighty deeds of God without revelation of the meaning of those deeds is like a television show without sound track; it throws man helplessly back upon his own human guesses as to the divine meaning of what God is doing.

Christ's death on the cross, for example, is a fact of human history. But, wisely asks Paul Minear (*Eyes of Faith: A Study in the Biblical Point of View* [Philadelphia: Westminster Press, 1946], p. 143), "How could a bystander in Jerusalem watching one of the innumerable executions beyond the city wall detect that scene [the crucifixion] of Christ as one decisive for all history?"

The immediate contemporaries who witnessed Christ's death on the cross did not automatically interpret it as a victory for law and order. Even by Christ's own disciples it was mourned as a defeat. It could, with considerable justification, have been interpreted as an example of dying for a principle. The resurrection, likewise, could have been interpreted as God's justification of Jesus as really righteous and as wrongly condemned by the Jews.

The New Testament gospel is not the message that Christ died. Rather the gospel is the good news that Christ died for our sins and rose again for our justification. It is the event plus the meaning or significance of this event that together constitute the essential good news of the New Testament.

In spite of objections to propositional revelation, many theologians see clearly the biblical conjunction of interpretive word and act. Brunner thus writes (*Revelation and Reason,* pp. 84 and 85): "Revelation takes place through the words of God and through the acts of God. Both together equally constitute the fact of historical revelation. This speaking and this acting of God took place within Israel and nowhere else. It took place in a chain of historical events in which word and act were fused into an indissoluble unity." Later Brunner adds (*ibid.,* p. 85), ". . . God gives to His prophets the authentic interpretation of His revelation in history which without this interpretation would remain more or less an insoluble enigma."

Biblical revelation thus becomes a blend of act and interpretation; both are essential to redemptive history as recorded in Scripture. As Oscar Cullmann observes (excerpt from his new book, *Heil als Geschichte,* translated by Sidney Sowers, soon to be published by Harper and Row, this citation used by permission): "The act of interpretation based on revelation to the prophets is regarded as belonging to redemptive history itself. The mediator of revelation, in the Old Testament the prophet and in the New Testament the apostle, aligns himself, along with this his function and the revelation in which he has shared, with the redemptive history interpreted anew by him. The fact of revelation which has come to him, together with the commission to communicate it, is conceived of, therefore, as belonging to redemptive history itself. This inclusion of the saving communication in the saving events is very essential for the New Testament."

From the biblical perspective, moreover, this communicated "Word of God" has the same objective revelational status as does the act revelation. In refutation of Leonard Hodgson's attempt to limit revelation to the mighty acts of God, Vincent Taylor remarks ("Religious Certainty," *The Expository Times*, LXXII [November, 1960], pp. 49-52) : "And if for our answer we go further, and claim the aid of the Holy Spirit, we cannot rule out the greater probability that the self-same Spirit guided prophets and apostles. And so we are back again to the view that revelation may well be embodied in statements as well as in divine acts. On *a priori* grounds there is no compelling reason why revelation should be found in mighty acts of God but not in words. Indeed, words can be a better medium of communication than events which need to be explained. Moreover, the explanation of events as mighty acts of God is itself an historical judgment, no doubt valid, but nevertheless exposed to all the uncertainties of such judgments. The truth is we cannot avoid some theory of biblical inspiration if we are to find a worthy doctrine of revelation."

Certainly the Old Testament prophets understood their function to be the reception of truths revealed to them by God who also commissioned them to speak forth His truth to others. C. H. Dodd delineates the prophetic psychology (*The Bible Today* [New York: Macmillian, 1947], p. 351) : " . . . they [the biblical writers] were not philosophers constructing a speculative theory from their observation of events. What they said was 'Thus saith the Lord.' They firmly believed that God spoke to men, spoke to the inward ear, the spiritual sense. He spoke to them out of the events which they experienced. The interpretation which they offered was not invented by a process of thought. It was the meaning which they experienced in the events when their minds were open to God as well as open to the impact of outward facts. Thus the prophetic interpretation of history, and the impetus and direction which that gave to subsequent history, were alike the word of God to men."

In the foundational law of Israel, tests for a true prophet of God are laid down so that false claimants to a message from God may be discerned and obedience rendered only to those who can rightfully establish their claim to come with the truth of God (cf. especially Deuteronomy 13 and 18) .

According to the record in I Samuel 3:7, "Samuel did not yet know the Lord, neither was the word of the Lord yet revealed unto him." Then the Lord spoke, and Samuel heard the word of God spoken to him. In similar fashion God directly addresses Abraham, Moses, and others throughout the history of divine revelation. Prophets took their "burden" from the Lord and spoke forth His message, "Thus saith the

Lord" (see especially Amos 3:7, Daniel 2:29 and 30, Isaiah 22:14, and II Samuel 7:27).

In the New Testament, numerous passages reflect the same reliance upon propositional revelation of truth. Matthew 11:22 gives us revealed truth regarding God's future judgment. Unto the Jews, Paul declares, "were committed the oracles of God" (Rom. 3:2). In the third chapter of Ephesians the same apostle refers to the revealed truth that Jews and Gentiles are to be one body. In Matthew 16:17 the revealed truth is that Jesus Christ is the Son of God, and in Luke 2:26 the revelation (*chrematizo*) brings to Simeon truth as to his own destiny.

Of the New Testament examples which he cites, Walter Bauer (*A Greek-English Lexicon of the New Testament and Other Early Christian Literature,* tr. William F. Arndt and F. Wilbur Gingrich, 4th ed. [Chicago: University of Chicago Press, 1952], *in loco*) lists ten usages of *apokalupto* as referring to revelation of ideas or truth, and cites three instances where the noun form, *apokalupsis,* indicates truth as the object of revelation.

When the various Greek words referring to communication of truth are considered, such as speak, talk, warn, utter, answer, and a host of others, the New Testament references to divine revelation of truth become legion (note, for example, the excellent word studies of revelation in the New Testament to be found in Hannelis Schulte, *Der Begriff der Offenbarung im Neuen Testament* [Munich: C. Kaiser Verlag, 1949]).

According to II Peter 1:15 to 20 the apostle Peter recognizes the need of those who should follow after him for a permanent body of truth to guide the Church and to sustain its spiritual life. Bauer translates Peter's assurances to them: "We possess the prophetic truth as something altogether reliable." Then Peter adds that this complete reliability is derived from the source of this truth — the divine revelation of the Holy Spirit; for prophetic truth did not stem from merely human impulses but rather "men moved by the Holy Spirit" spoke from God.

The apostle Paul likewise defends his gospel as that which he received not by men nor through man but from God. As Cullmann points out (*loc. cit.*), the purpose of the giving of the Paraclete was to provide illumination and guidance for the apostles so that they could obtain the truths which our Lord in His earthly ministry could not yet give them. They were commissioned by Christ as His mouthpieces to speak this truth, and this word-revelation took its place alongside the mighty acts of God in Christ as part of the historical process of divine redemption.

The classic passage from the New Testament ties together divine revelation of truth and the role of the prophet or apostle. Thus in I Corinthians 2:9-13 and 16, we read:

> But as it is written, Eye hath not seen, nor ear heard, neither have entered into the heart of man, the things which God hath prepared for them that love him. But God hath revealed them unto us by his Spirit: for the Spirit searcheth all things, yea, the deep things of God.
>
> For what man knoweth the things of a man, save the spirit of man which is in him? even so the things of God knoweth no man, but the Spirit of God.
>
> Now we have received, not the spirit of the world, but the Spirit which is of God; that we might know the things that are freely given to us of God.
>
> Which things also we speak, not in the words which man's wisdom teacheth, but which the Holy Ghost teacheth; comparing spiritual things with spiritual. . . .
>
> For who hath known the mind of the Lord, that he may instruct him? But we have the mind of Christ.

The flow of Paul's logic is inescapable. God has certain plans for those who love Him. These plans are, of course, quite unknown and undiscoverable by men. Just as man can know what is in his own mind, however, so the Spirit of God knows fully the truth lying within the divine mind and out of His love and grace chooses to convey this otherwise inaccessible truth to the minds of men. The process whereby this communication of divine truth takes place is specifically labelled as revelation.

This truth-revelation "stood revealed." The verb in the Greek aorist intensifies the past and objective character of the revelation. Just as it was given to the apostle, it is in turn imparted to others in a process (inspiration) by which the Spirit of God supernaturally guides the apostle in what he says so that he may adequately record and communicate the revealed truth given to him.

The biblical view of divine revelation of truth is well summed up by James Barr ("The Interpretation of Scripture," Part II — "Revelation Through History in the Old Testament and in Modern Theology" [Inaugural address delivered at Princeton Theological Seminary in December, 1962], *Interpretation,* XVII [April 1963], 201, 202): "Direct verbal communication between God and particular men on particular occasions is, I believe, an inescapable fact of the Bible and of the Old Testament in particular. God can speak specific verbal messages, when He wills, to the men of His choice. But for this, if we follow the way in which the Old Testament represents the incidents, there would have been no call of Abraham, no Exodus, no prophecy. Direct communication from God to man has fully as much claim to be called the core of the tradition as has revelation of events in history. If we persist in saying that this direct specific communication must be subsumed under revelation of events in history, and taken as subsidiary interpretation of the latter, I shall say that we are abandoning the Bible's own presentation of the matter for another which is apologetically more comfortable."

So, too, agrees Oscar Cullmann ("The Resurrection: Event and Meaning," *Christianity Today,* IX [March 26, 1965], p. 8) : "Revelation consists in both — in the event as such and in its interpretation. . . . not only the interpretation but also the event is regarded as revelation."

According to the Bible, the meaning of the mighty acts of God, including that crowning act of all — God incarnate in Jesus Christ, is not a humanly drawn conclusion based on observation of these acts; rather, the meaning of the act is itself also a divine revelation — God's interpretation of His own divine acts. This revelatory word is given by God to man in just as objective a form as are the acts of God in history. These revelations of truth represent God's interpretations. They are God's meaning of events in history. They are God's truth for men. Truth-revelation, in fact, constitutes an enormously important segment of biblical revelation, not only accompanying act-revelation as its needed interpretation, but predicting, containing, and canonizing the story of divine act-revelation. Truth-revelation has, therefore, every whit as much right to be considered of the essence of biblical revelation as do "mighty acts." Biblical revelation is a continuous interdependent unity or act-revelation and truth-revelation.

We may summarize the biblical perspective of revelation as act and interpretation under the following headings:

1. *Revelation Is Historical*

God has revealed Himself in His mighty acts in history. The story of these divine acts may be traced from the earliest records of the Old Testament through the entire gamut of biblical history.

Of course, if history be defined as a naturalistic science based upon non-miraculous presuppositions, then the revelatory acts of God are not historical. The mighty acts of God are historical, however, in the sense that they are factual, that they actually occurred in a world of time and space and human history, and that the mind disposed to the truth can find them true on the basis of available data. They are, in short, part of the warp and woof of the human story.

By these mighty acts in behalf of His people, the God of the Bible thus distances Himself from the philosopher's god of rational theism, whose existence must be posited as a necessary and general truth. By these same acts, of course, the biblical God is to be distinguished from the god of the deists, who never could quite sustain the necessity and integrity of truly personal theism. The biblical God is active by doing something for men. In the warmth of His grace and love He participates in the human scene and demonstrates by His personal concern in behalf of those whom He loves that He is their personal God.

These mighty revelatory acts in history culminate in Jesus Christ as the God-man. In their day and in their own way prophets and apostles served their Lord as His instruments to perform mighty acts of righteousness and love. Others, too, spoke the word of God. But Jesus Christ was unique. He was, in truth, God acting and God speaking.

2. *Revelation Is Objective and Factual*

These mighty acts of God, as Karl Barth has so valiantly argued against Bultmann, are not merely illustrations of the truth nor do they represent the language of symbol drawn by prophet and apostle from the mythology of a past culture. They are — and the New Testament writers take great pains to let us know this — straightforward and factual accounts of objective events occurring in our world of space and time. These things were not "done in a corner" Paul testifies to King Agrippa (Acts 25:25). Luke addressed his literary work to Theophilus in order to convince him of the truth of the mighty acts of Christ and of His Spirit (Acts 1:3 and 4). Jesus Christ performed many miracles in His earthly ministry, so the author of the Fourth Gospel reminds us, but those which he selected for his record are included to convince us that Jesus of Nazareth really stepped into history as the promised Messiah and, therefore, man can confidently trust Him for eternal life (John 20:30 and 31).

Bultmann, who denies the objective reality of the divine-human Christ and relegates the mighty acts of God to mythologized insights into the meaning of authentic human existence, is not really *interpreting* the teaching of the New Testament; he is rather *eliminating* the teaching of the New Testament. We agree with Barth, against Bultmann, that the heart of biblical Christianity is what God did objectively in history as He from His eternity took time to become man, to die on the cross, and to rise again from the dead on the third day in order to redeem man to Himself.

3. *Act-Revelation Is Objectively Verifiable*

This divine revelation by means of events in objective history is, moreover, embedded in the stream of ordinary events of the time and space world. The mighty acts of God cannot be *completely* explained as the products of ordinary events in history; and they are not *always* capable of being fitted into any web of cause and effect relationship within the world of nature; nonetheless, they fit into the series of other events and affect the course of subsequent history. Their factuality, therefore, may be verified in essentially the same way as other facts of human history.

The empty tomb, for example, was observed by the women and apostles to be empty. The grave clothes no longer enshrouded a body. Eyes of witnesses could perceive and hands could touch the body of the resurrected Christ. The apostle Paul in I Corinthians 15 calls us to the historical trustworthiness of human witnesses to the revelatory act by which God raised Jesus Christ from the dead.

Against Barth and Bultmann and all who with them tear the mighty acts of divine revelation from the web of verifiable history, we side with Althaus, Kümmel, and in general the school of *Heilsgeschichte,* to defend the legitimate role of the historian in his endeavor to ascertain the facts of these biblical revelations. As Adolf Köberle, the Tübingen theologian, charges, Karl Barth "failed fully to engage the historical background of the New Testament, and this failure gave later scholars an opportunity to correlate the data with contrary conclusions."

In removing these mighty acts of God from the record of events that could be ascertained by the student of history, Barth found himself defenseless before Bultmann, who quietly removed these events also from the realm of the objective and actual stream of historical events. The step down from Barth's quasi-historical events, truly objective events but events which left no objective traces of their occurrence and were, therefore, not objectively verifiable, proved to be a very short step indeed. Biblical revelation through the acts of God in history are not only objective and factual occurrences, they are, at least in principle, also objectively verifiable by the historian whose presuppositions are such as to permit the possibility of a supernatural act of God.

4. *Act-Revelation Must Be Supplemented by Word-Revelation*

The mighty acts of God in history are supplemented by further divine acts by which God gives to His people His own interpretations of these mighty deeds. These revealed meanings or revealed truths do not originate from human insight into the significance of the revealed events. They are not human postulates representing the most reasonable explanation of the divine acts. Neither are they the products of subjective manner as is act-revelation. The revelation of truth is given in history the content of revealed meaning for himself as God creates it anew for him personally. In Holy Scripture, word-revelation is not, by contrast with act-revelation, an ever recurring revelation of the meaning of the past acts of God. Word-revelation is given in the same once-for-all objective manner as is act-revelation. The revelation of truth is given in history to particular men at a particular time and place. Its content is determined by what God then revealed. No repeated mystical experience, suprarational ecstasies, or existential encounters add one iota to the revealed content of truth. Biblical revelation is a blend of historically mediated, objectively given acts of God, and the truth of God. Each is the necessary supplement to the other, and both together belong to redemptive history as presented in the Bible. This may not make for a popular apologetic in the mid-twentieth century, but it *is* biblical.

Earlier we stood with representatives of the *Heilsgeschichte* school in their splendid biblically rooted emphasis upon an objective revelation of divine acts objectively verifiable upon the grounds of historical data. Unfortunately many of these scholars proceed to limit the divine disclosure to wordless acts and deeds of God and thus suspend knowledge of the meaning of these acts upon subjective constructions available only in personal response. In so doing they compromise radically their biblical position. They, too, along with Barth and Bultmann, fall into subjectivism. They fail to see that the objective act-revelation and the objective truth-revelation stand or fall together. An act cannot even be known at all except within the framework of incipient interpretations. The real meaning of an act is frequently far more important than the act itself. Certainly the glory of the biblical gospel is not merely that Christ died, but that He died *for our sins*. Only truth-revelation delivers man from the helpless uncertainty of human guesses as to the meaning of divine revelation and thus plants man's hope firmly upon the solid foundation of divine revelation of truth.

Biblical revelation, of course, not only provides man with the divine interpretation of events which are past. As in the "servant" prophecies of Isaiah, it may also take place antecedently to the historical acts whose meaning it unfolds. It may, on occasions, foretell future acts of divine judgment and blessing. Or, as Paul explicitly claims in I Corinthians 2: 7ff., biblical revelation may even convey knowledge of God's perfections and purposes quite independently of revelatory acts witnessed by the prophet or apostle of God.

Against the *Heilsgeschichte* school, therefore, and with Edwin Lewis, Oscar Cullmann, James Barr, and William Hordern, we refuse to compromise the biblical view of revelation by rejecting divine revelation of propositional truth or by restricting the knowledge of the meaning of the mighty acts of God in Christ to subjective human judgments constructed as the product of an existential experience. According to the Bible, act-revelation is supplemented and climaxed by the divine revelation of objective truth.

5. *Holy Scripture Is the Inspired Record of Revelatory Acts and Words*

The revelatory acts and revelatory words of God would be rendered of little value if they could not be ascertained by man with confidence. A fundamental weakness of most modern theology is its penchant for making revelation esoteric, which leaves the simple believer helpless to discover truth about what God has done and what is God's will. With respect to the exact nature of the acts of God he is left, all too often, at the mercy of the historian to ascertain the facts. Was Jesus Christ born of a virgin or not? Was the tomb empty or was it not? Moreover, when the question is one of meaning, he is at the mercy of the philosopher or the rational theologian to discover what is true. Do we have an authoritative word of Christ or do we not? What is the role of faith as over against sacrament in a proper relationship to God?

Deliverance from this uncertainty into which much modern theology has fallen is to be found in an authoritative Bible. The Jesus Christ of history (true history, not pseudo-history) not only presents Himself as the divine Lord and Saviour but also chooses to exercise His Lordship over His disciples through His written Word of Holy Scripture. He has set His seal upon both Old and New Testaments. The authority of Jesus Christ stands solidly and unequivocally behind the authority of the Bible. Our Lord's testimony to the complete trustworthiness and divine authority of the Old Testament is so well documented that it scarcely needs defense (see J. W. Wenham, *Our Lord's View of the Old Testament* [London: Tyndale Press, 1953]). Our Lord also, by His promises and their fulfilment, gives His authority to the New Testament. He commissioned His disciples as His witnesses to speak with His authority to the Church (John 14:16; 15:26; 16:13ff.). His promise was fulfilled in the days following Pentecost (Acts 3ff. and Heb. 2:4). The apostle Paul, accordingly, claimed to give forth divine revelation not in words that were merely his own human words, but in his words that were guided by the Spirit to enable him to speak the divine wisdom with divine authority (I Cor. 2:3).

The teaching of the apostles was not really their own; it was Christ's true teaching, which He promised them when on earth and which He provided for them by His Spirit in the founding of the Church (Eph. 2:20).[3] The biblical Christ, according to His own testimony, thus gives substantiation adequate to warrant the trust of His followers and His true disciples in the complete trustworthiness of Holy Scripture as

---

3 See Oscar Cullmann's distinction between apostolic tradition carrying the authority of Christ and ecclesiastical tradition which has only human authority ("Scripture and Tradition," *Scottish Journal of Theology*, VI, 2 [June, 1953], pp. 126f.).

the divinely appointed record of the works and words by which God seeks to reveal Himself to man.

The faithful disciples of Christ are warned not to subtract from Holy Scripture and not to add to it (Matt. 5:17-19; 23:23; Mark 7:7-13, Luke 24:25). They are not to seek a Jesus Christ of history behind the text, to seek an encounter with an unknown existential Christ, to create for themselves a "higher" ethics or to put the Bible through any sieve of a preconceived "Christ" or "law of love," or twentieth-century mythology. Rather, Jesus Christ directed His disciples to the Scriptures for "they . . . testify of me" (John 5:39), and He commanded His disciples to believe "all that the prophets have said" (Luke 24:25).

Holy Scripture is not merely an historical record of the acts of God and of Christ. It is not a repository of human guesses as to the significance of the mute acts of God. Holy Scripture, by contrast with all this, is God's gracious Word to lead man to Jesus Christ and to provide for the man in Christ an infallible and divinely trustworthy guide to the works of God and the revealed will of God by which Jesus Christ can exercise His Lordship over His obedient disciples.

6. Objective Revelation Must be Complemented by Subjective Illumination

Divine revelation of events and their meaning, set forth infallibly in the pages of Holy Scripture, must be complemented by a personal encounter with Jesus Christ in which man receives internal spiritual illumination and full assurance that the objective revelation given in act and word is truly a revelation of God. By this work of divine illumination man grasps subjectively what has already been available to him objectively. What had already been revealed of the truth about God's plans for man (I Cor. 2:10) and had been declared openly as revealed truth by Paul the apostle (I Cor. 2:13), remained unperceived by man because of the inability of the natural mind to recognize divine truth (I Cor. 2: 14). Only the Spirit of God, working upon the heart and mind of the recipient of revelation, can enable him to judge adequately and thus recognize the Word of God for what it is — so declares Paul in I Corinthians 2:14-16.

Both in the history of the Church and in Holy Scripture the work by which the Spirit of God creates certitude in the mind of the believer is referred to as the "Testimony of the Holy Spirit." Thus Calvin, speaking for Protestant theologians in general, writes (Institutes of the Christian Religion, tr. Henry Beveridge [Edinburgh: Calvin Translation Society, 1845, reprint, Wm. B. Eerdmans Publishing Co.], I, 109): "In vain were the authority of Scripture fortified by argument or supported by the consent of the Church or confirmed by any other helps if unaccompanied by an assurance higher and stronger than human judgment can give. The same Spirit, therefore, who spoke by the mouth of the prophets, must penetrate our hearts in order to convince us that they faithfully delivered the message with which they were divinely entrusted" (*Institutes*, I, 94 and 95).

In Scripture itself the Spirit's testimony is directed specifically to the believer's relationship to Jesus Christ. The repentant sinner may know with assurance that Jesus Christ is his Lord and personal Saviour as the Holy Spirit creates such assurance within him (Gal. 4:4-5, Rom. 8:14-15, and I John 4 and 5).

The direct object of this testimony is thus the gospel or the saving content of the message of Holy Scripture, rather than the inspiration or infallible authority of the entire Bible. Indirectly, however, this same witness validates also the divine trustworthiness and authority of the Bible because Christ certified its truth and enjoined His disciples to obey it as they would obey Him. The authority of Holy Scripture over the thought and life of the believer is merely an extension of the Lordship of Jesus Christ over His faithful followers. Although Calvin and other evangelicals denote the object of the *testimonium* to be Holy Scripture, they are usually careful to point out that there is an inner core which represents pre-eminently the object to which the Spirit testifies. Calvin, for example, can write: "I point to the promise of mercy as its special object" (*Institutes*, II, 130).[4]

True faith in Christ as Lord and Saviour and an obedient response to the divine authority of Holy Scripture are never merely products of historical investigation. This is not due to any lack in the validity of the data or in the adequacy of the historical grounds for justifying faith in Christ. History affords us data that can be fitted together coherently only on the supposition that the biblical record about Christ is true. Accordingly, history can produce a human conviction or opinion that Jesus Christ demonstrated divine power, that the tomb was empty, that He rose from the dead and appeared to His followers, and that He commissioned His apostles to speak for Him with authority and to write with divine trustworthiness His testimony to the revealed acts of God and to the true and right interpretation of these acts. The data of history can prepare the way for faith. They may lead to faith. Ideally they may even produce an "historical" faith in Christ and in the validity of biblical revelation.

One thing history cannot do. It cannot produce true faith in Jesus

---

4 Contrary to Otto Ritschl, I do not find a significant difference between Lutheran and Calvinistic interpretations of the witness (cf. Otto Ritschl, *Dogmengeschichte des Protestantismus* [Leipzig: J. C. Henricks, 1908], I, 179).

Christ or in His Word. By itself it cannot call forth from man the abiding conviction that the revelation of God set forth in Holy Scripture and focusing in Jesus Christ is worthy of our abiding trust. It cannot bring full commitment to the God who really did these acts in history and who really revealed these interpretations. True faith in God and His Christ is the work of the Holy Spirit as He bears His divine testimony to the Christ of Holy Scripture.

In man's personal response to the Christ whom he meets in the pages of Holy Scripture the Spirit bears testimony by creating new data, the data of personal experience, which complements and corroborates the truth of history. The Spirit illuminates the mind of the believer so that he may evaluate rightly the data of both history and experience. Finally the Spirit seals the truth upon the heart and mind of the repentant sinner, who wills to know the truth and to commit himself to Jesus Christ as His Lord and Saviour. By this "testimony" the Holy Spirit creates true faith and gives to men assurance and trust in the biblical answer to the ultimate question of human existence: "How can I know God and His will for my life?"

Such a work of the Spirit is given only to those who are committed earnestly to seeking the truth, to those who are willing to repent and render obedience to the revelation as it comes from God, and to those who humbly look to God in prayer, because it is of the grace of God that any man can rightly know the Truth.

A SELECT BIBLIOGRAPHY

1. CROSS-CURRENTS IN CONTEMPORARY THEOLOGY

G. C. Berkouwer, *The Triumph of Grace in the Theology of Karl Barth*. Grand Rapids: Wm. B. Eerdmans Publishing Co., 1956.

Gordon H. Clark, *Karl Barth's Theological Method*. Philadelphia: Presbyterian and Reformed Publishing Co., 1963.

Oscar Cullmann, *Salvation as History*. New York: Harper and Row, 1965.

Birger Gerhardsson, *Tradition and Transmission in Early Christianity*. Lund: C. W. K. Gleerup, 1964.

Leonhard Goppelt, *Jesus, Paul and Judaism,* An Introduction to New Testament Theology. New York: Thomas Nelson & Sons, 1964.

Carl F. H. Henry (ed.), *Christian Faith and Modern Theology*. New York: Channel Press, 1964.

2. THE NEW QUEST OF THE HISTORICAL JESUS

Günther Bornkamm, *Jesus von Nazareth* (1956). E. T. *Jesus of Nazareth*. London: Hodder and Stoughton, 1960.

Rudolf Bultmann, *Das Verhältnis der urchristlichen Christusbotschaft zum Historischen Jesus* (1960). E. T. in C. E. Braaten and R. A. Harrisville, *The Historical Jesus and the Kerygmatic Christ*. Nashville: Abingdon Press, 1964.

Hans Conzelmann, "Jesus Christus," in *Religion in Geschichte und Gegenwart*, III. Tübingen: J. C. B. Mohr (Paul Siebeck), 1959.

W. D. Davies, "A Quest to be resumed in NT Studies," in *New Directions in Biblical Thought*. New York: Association Press, 1960.

Gerhard Ebeling, "The Significance of the Critical Historical Method. . . ; and The Question of the Historical Jesus" in *Word and Faith*. London: SCM Press, 1963.

Ernst Fuchs, essays in *Zur Frage nach dem historischen Jesus* (1960). E. T. *Studies of the Historical Jesus*. London: SCM Press, 1964.

Joachim Jeremias, "Der gegenwartig Stand der Debatte," *Wissenschaftliche Zeitschift der E. Moritz* (1956-1957). E. T. *Expository Times,*

69 (1958), and more fully in *The Problem of the Historical Jesus*. Philadelphia: Fortress Press, 1964.

Ernst Käsemann, "Das Problem des historischen Jesus," in *Zeitschrift für Theologie und Kirche*, 51 (1954). E. T. "The Problem of the Historical Jesus" in *Essays on New Testament Themes*. London: SCM Press, 1964.

T. W. Manson, "The Life of Jesus: Some Tendencies in Present-Day Research," in Dodd *Festschrift* (1956) and in *The Background of the New Testament and Its Eschatology*, W. D. Davies and D. Daube, eds. Cambridge: Cambridge University Press, 1956.

J. M. Robinson, *A New Quest of the Historical Jesus*. London: SCM Press, 1959.

3. THE AUTHENTICITY AND AUTHORITY OF REVELATION

Oscar Cullmann, *Heil als Geschichte. Heilsgeschichtliche Existenz im Neuen Testament*. Tübingen: J. C. B. Mohr (Paul Siebeck), 1965.

Birger Gerhardsson, *Memory and Manuscript*. Oral Tradition and Written Transmission in Rabbinic Judaism and Early Christianity (Acta Seminarri Neotestamentici Upsaliensis xxii), 2nd ed. Lund: C. W. K. Gleerup, 1964.

————, *Tradition and Transmission in Early Christianity* (Coniectanea Neotestamentica xx). Lund: C. W. K. Gleerup, 1964.

Ian Henderson, *Myth in the New Testament* (*Studies in Biblical Theology, No. 7*). London: SCM Press, 1952.

J. M. Todd (ed.), *Problems of Authority*. London: The Helicon Press, 1962.

R. R. Williams, *Authority in the Apostolic Age*. London: SCM Press, 1950.

4. JESUS CHRIST, THE CENTER OF HISTORY

Oscar Cullmann, *Christus und die Zeit*. Die urchristliche Zeit- und Geschicht-sauffassung. Zürich: Evangelischer Verlag Zollikon, 1946.

————, *Heil als Geschichte*. Tübingen: J. C. B. Mohr (Paul Siebeck), 1965.

Adolf Köberle, *The Quest for Holiness*. New York: Harper and Row, 1936.

————, *Christliches Denken*. Von der Erkenntnis zur Verwirklichung. Hamburg: Furche-Verlag, 1962.

————, *Gottes Tage*. Biblische Meditation zu den hohen Festen der Christenheit. Hamburg: Furch-Verlag, 1964.

————, *Die Welt,* in der Christus leidet und siegt. Metzingen: Brunn-quell-Verlag, 1964.
Gustaf Wingren, *Die Predigt.* Göttingen: Vandenhoek and Ruprecht, 1955.
————, *Die Methodenfrage der Theologie.* Ebenda, 1957.

5. THE LAST DAYS IN THE BIBLE AND QUMRAN

Louis Berkhof, *The Kingdom of God.* Grand Rapids: Wm. B. Eerdmans Publishing Co., 1950 (out of print).
F. F. Bruce, *Second Thoughts on the Dead Sea Scrolls.* Grand Rapids: Wm. B. Eerdmans Publishing Co., 1961, rev. ed.
Theodore H. Gaster, *The Dead Sea Scriptures in English Translation.* Garden City: Doubleday Anchor, 1964, rev. ed.
George E. Ladd, *Crucial Questions about the Kingdom of God.* Grand Rapids: Wm. B. Eerdmans Publishing Co., 1952.
Charles F. Pfeiffer, *The Dead Sea Scrolls.* Grand Rapids: Baker Book House, 1962, rev. ed.

6. HISTORY AND THE GOSPEL

Paul Althaus, *The So-Called Kerygma and the Historical Jesus.* Edinburgh: Oliver and Boyd, 1959.
Hugh Anderson, *Jesus and Christian Origins.* New York: Oxford University Press, 1964.
C. H. Dodd, *History and the Gospel.* London: Nisbet, 1938.
————, *Historical Tradition in the Fourth Gospel.* Cambridge: Cambridge University Press, 1963.
F. V. Filson, *A New Testament History.* London: SCM Press, 1965.
W. G. Kümmel, *Heilsgeschehen und Geschichte.* Marburg: Elwert, 1965.
T. W. Manson, *Studies in the Gospels and Epistles.* Manchester: University Press, 1962.
H. G. Wood, *Jesus in the Twentieth Century.* London: Lutterworth Press, 1960.

7. THE TEACHING OF JESUS AND THE GOSPEL RECORDS

Rudolf Bultmann, *History of the Synoptic Traditions.* New York: Harper and Row, 1963.
Ethelbert Stauffer, *Jesus and His Story.* New York: Alfred A. Knopf, 1960.
N. B. Stonehouse, *The Witness of Luke to Christ.* Grand Rapids: Wm. B. Eerdmans Publishing Co., 1951.

————, *The Witness of Matthew and Mark to Christ.* Grand Rapids: Wm. B. Eerdmans Publishing Co., 1944.

————, *Origins of the Synoptic Gospels.* Grand Rapids: Wm. B. Eerdmans Publishing Co., 1963.

8. THE FOURTH GOSPEL AND HISTORY

C. H. Dodd, *Historical Tradition in the Fourth Gospel.* Cambridge: Cambridge University Press, 1963.

Birger Gerhardsson, *Memory and Manuscript.* Lund: W. C. K. Gleerup, 1961.

Leon Morris, *The Dead Sea Scrolls and St. John's Gospel.* Campbell Morgan Memorial Lecture, 1960.

Studia Evangelica, Relevant articles in Vol. I, 1959, Vol. II and III, 1964. Berlin: Akedemia-Verlag.

9. THE HISTORICITY OF THE RESURRECTION

Martin Kähler, *The So-Called Historical Jesus and the Historical, Biblical Christ.* Tr. and ed. by Carl Braaten. Philadelphia: Fortress Press, 1964.

A. Michael Ramsey, *The Resurrection of Christ.* Philadelphia: Westminster Press, 1946.

Merrill C. Tenney, *The Reality of the Resurrection.* New York: Harper and Row, 1963.

H. E. W. Turner, *Historicity and the Gospels.* London: A. R. Mowbray & Co., 1963.

G. D. Yarnold, *Risen Indeed.* New York: Oxford University Press, 1959.

Heinz Zahrnt, *The Historical Jesus.* Tr. from the German by J. S. Bowdan. New York: Harper and Row, 1963. See Chapter 9, "On the Third Day."

10. "ON THE THIRD DAY"

Karl Barth, *The Resurrection of the Dead.* New York: Fleming H. Revell, 1933.

————, *Die Auferstehung der Toten.* Zurich: Evangelischer Verlag, 1953.

Daniel P. Fuller, *Easter Faith and History.* Grand Rapids: Wm. B. Eerdmans Publishing Co., 1965.

James Orr, *The Resurrection of Jesus*. New York: Hodder and Stoughton, 1908.

A. M. Ramsey, *The Resurrection of Christ*. Philadelphia: Westminster Press, 1946; London: Geoffrey Bles, 1945.

Merrill C. Tenney, *The Reality of the Resurrection*. New York: Harper and Row, 1963.

11. *GEMEINDETHEOLOGIE*: THE BANE OF GOSPEL CRITICISM

W. D. Davies, *Christian Origins and Judaism*. Philadelphia: Westminster Press, 1962.

R. H. Fuller, *The Mission and Achievement of Jesus (Studies in Biblical Theology, No. 12)*. Chicago: Alec R. Allenson, 1954.

Birger Gerhardsson, *Memory and Manuscript*. Lund: C. W. K. Gleerup, 1961.

C. F. D. Moule, *The Birth of the New Testament*. New York: Harper and Row, 1962.

Stephen Neill, *The Interpretation of the New Testament 1861-1961*. London: Oxford University Press, 1964.

H. E. W. Turner, *Historicity and the Gospels*. London: A. R. Mowbray and Co., 1963.

12. FAITH AS HISTORICAL UNDERSTANDING

Oscar Cullmann, *The Christology of the New Testament*. Tr. by Shirley C. Guthrie and Charles A. M. Hall. Philadelphia: Westminster Press, 1959.

————, *Heil als Geschichte*. Tübingen: J. C. B. Mohr (Paul Siebeck), 1965.

R. H. Fuller, *The Mission and Achievement of Jesus (Studies in Biblical Theology, No. 12)*. Chicago: Alec. R. Allenson, 1954.

James P. Martin, "Beyond Bultmann, What?" in *Christianity Today*, Vol. VI, No. 4, November 24, 1961.

————, "History and Eschatology in the Lazarus Narrative John 11:1-44," in *Scottish Journal of Theology*, Vol. 17, No. 3, September, 1964.

13. FACT AND FAITH IN THE KERYGMA

Paul Althaus, *Fact and Faith in the Kerygma of Today*. Tr. by David Cairns. Philadelphia: Muhlenberg Press, 1959.

Hugh Anderson, *Jesus and Christian Origins*. London: Oxford University Press, 1964.

Carl F. H. Henry, *Frontiers in Modern Theology*. Chicago: Moody Press, 1966.

Walter Künneth, *The Theology of the Resurrection*. London: SCM Press, 1965; St. Louis: Concordia Publishing House, 1966.

J. M. Spier, *Christianity and Existentialism*. Tr. by David Hugh Freeman. Philadelphia: Presbyterian and Reformed Publishing Co., 1953.

14. BULTMANN'S HISTORIOGRAPHY

Carl L. Becker, *Detachment and the Writing of History*. Ithaca: Cornell University Press, 1958.

R. G. Collingwood, *The Idea of History*. Oxford: Clarendon Press, 1946.

Oscar Cullmann, *Christ and Time*. Philadelphia: Westminster Press, 1950.

J. H. Hexter, *Reappraisals in History*. Evanston: Northwestern University Press, 1962.

Reinhold Niebuhr, *Faith and History*. New York: Charles Scribner's Sons, 1949.

Frederick J. Teggart, *Theory and Processes in History*. Berkeley: University of California Press, 1941.

15. TOWARD A CHRISTIAN PHILOSOPHY OF HISTORY

Herbert Butterfield, *Christianity and History*. London: George Bell, 1949.

Earle E. Cairns, "Philosophy of History," in *Contemporary Evangelical Thought*, Carl F. H. Henry, ed. Great Neck: Channel Press, 1957.

Allan Leonard Farris, "The Relation of the Bible to History," in *Christian Perspectives 1960*. Toronto: Association for Reformed Scientific Studies, 1960.

Donald C. Masters, *The Christian Idea of History*. Introduction by John Warwick Montgomery. Waterloo: Waterloo Lutheran University, 1962.

John Warwick Montgomery, *The Shape of the Past: An Introduction to Philosophical Historiography* ("History in Christian Perspective," Vol. I). Ann Arbor: Edwards Brothers, 1963 (2nd printing with corrections).

C. Gregg Singer, *A Theological Interpretation of American History*. Philadelphia: Presbyterian and Reformed Publishing Co., 1964.

16. THE CHRIST-REVELATION AS ACT AND INTERPRETATION

Oscar Cullmann, *Heil als Geschichte.* Tübingen: J. C. B. Mohr (Paul Siebeck), 1965.

Daniel P. Fuller, *Easter Faith and History.* Grand Rapids: Wm. B. Eerdmans Publishing Co., 1965.

Carl F. H. Henry (ed.), *Revelation and the Bible.* Grand Rapids: Baker Book House, 1958 (Chapters three and four).

Kenneth S. Kantzer, "The Authority of the Bible," in *The Word for this Century,* Merrill C. Tenney, ed. New York: Oxford University Press, 1960.

H. D. McDonald, *Theories of Revelation.* London: George Allen and Unwin, 1963.

Bernard Ramm, *Special Revelation and the Word of God.* Grand Rapids: Wm. B. Eerdmans Publishing Co., 1961.

SUBJECT INDEX

Apocalypticism, 73ff.
Atheism, 14
Atonement, 10f.
Authority, 50ff., 57f., 218ff.

Bible, 12, 14ff., 17ff., 22, 26ff., 32ff., 36, 57, 59, 112ff., 139, 151, 161f., 210f., 240, 252ff., 261ff.

Canon, 53, 73, 111, 137, 210
Christianity, 4f., 10, 21f., 26, 39f., 129, 140, 148, 189
Concepts, 10, 12f., 19f.
Conscience, 20, 68, 208
Conservative school, 7f., 14, 16, 21, 38f.
Creed, 53, 59, 73, 107

Dead Sea Scrolls, 15, 67, 73ff., 94, 101f., 127
Decision, 13, 20f., 31, 36, 51f., 155, 207
Deism, 26
Demythologizing, 5f., 10f., 41, 49, 51, 53f., 56, 58, 217, 223
Dialectical theology, 4, 6, 8f., 20ff., 37f.
Docetism, 7, 32, 40f., 151

Early Church, 5, 16, 28ff., 32, 34f., 37, 39, 43f., 73ff., 78ff., 82f., 114ff., 130f., 136ff., 159ff., 165ff., 178ff., 187ff., 238ff.
Encounter, 7, 9f., 12f., 14, 20, 27, 218ff., 234ff., 244ff.
Enlightenment, 50
Eternity and time, 9, 20, 64ff., 230
Existential theology, 4f., 6ff., 10ff., 13ff., 20, 26, 35f., 41f., 51ff., 149f., 205ff., 216ff., 223ff., 228, 231ff.

Faith, 13, 15, 30, 68, 159ff., 189ff.; and understanding, 12, 20f., 177ff.; and history, 107, 148ff., 153ff., 173, 177ff., 187ff., 201ff., 216ff., 247ff.

Formgeschichte, 5, 16, 28f., 31ff., 42, 91ff., 114ff., 131, 136, 159ff.
Fundamentalism, 4, 9

Gemeindetheologie, 159ff.
German scholarship, 4, 8, 28
Gnosticism, 67, 130, 151
God, acts, 55, 155;
  immanence, 4;
  independence, 13;
  in-Himself, 12, 15, 18;
  initiative, 5, 9;
  judgment, 20, 178, 196;
  mercy, 230;
  objectivity, 5ff., 10ff., 13;
  presence, 211;
  reality, 10, 13, 51f.;
  reign, 30;
  speech, 55;
  subjectivity, 13;
  transcendence, 4, 9, 20, 195;
  wrath, 9, 126
Gospel message, 55f.

Heilsgeschichte, 7f., 14ff., 21, 38, 41, 58, 65ff., 177ff., 189ff., 259
Hermeneutics, 43ff., 177, 231ff., 251ff.
Historicism, 16, 26ff.
Historiography, 27, 35, 90, 215ff., 227ff.
History, 5ff., 10ff., 14ff., 20, 27ff., 35ff., 35ff., 42, 44f., 56, 63ff., 68ff., 89ff., 92ff., 98ff., 107, 112ff., 123ff., 132, 135ff., 147ff., 159ff., 201ff., 216ff., 230;
  and Interpretation, 124ff., 153, 160ff., 204ff., 216ff.;
  Historical Probability, 138ff., 148;
  Historical Skepticism, 95ff., 103, 130, 138, 147, 154, 220ff.
Humanism, 42

Idealism, 64

273

AUTHOR INDEX

275